# The Gothic Impulse in Contemporary Drama

# Theatre and Dramatic Studies, No. 63

## Oscar G. Brockett, Series Editor

Professor of Drama and Holder of the
Z. T. Scott Family Chair in Drama
The University of Texas at Austin

## Other Titles in This Series

# The Gothic Impulse in Contemporary Drama

by
MaryBeth Inverso

U·M·I Research Press

Ann Arbor / London

Produced and distributed by
UMI Research Press
an imprint of
University Microfilms Inc.
Ann Arbor, Michigan 48106


Library of Congress Cataloging in Publication Data

**Inverso, MaryBeth.**
  The Gothic impulse in contemporary drama / by
MaryBeth Inverso.
     p. cm.—(Theatre and dramatic studies ; no. 63)
     Includes bibliographical references and index.
     ISBN 0-8357-2009-8 (alk. paper)
     1. Drama—20th century—History and criticism. 2. English
drama—20th century—History and criticism. 3. Gothic revival
(Literature) 4. Experimental theater. I. Title. II. Series.
PN1861.I58    1990
809.2'045—dc20

89-20481
CIP


British Library CIP data is available.


The paper used in this publication meets the minimum requirements of
American National Standard for Information Sciences—Permanence of Paper for Printed
Library Materials, ANSI Z39.48-1984. ⊗ ™

# Contents

# Acknowledgments

"Invention," observes Mary Shelley in her 1831 preface to *Frankenstein*, "does not consist in creating out of the void. . . . The materials must, in the first place, be afforded." My materials were afforded to me by several generous and creative people. I wish first to express my gratitude to Elaine Scarry, a superb scholar and a gentle lady, whose sensitive and incisive criticism sustained and heartened me throughout. I wish also to thank Stuart Curran, who likewise read my manuscript with great care and whose uncompromising insistence on excellence taxed my powers of argumentation to their fullest. Of great value also was the commentary of Pat Day, who read early drafts of the first three chapters and whose course in Gothic Literature was one of the most enjoyable experiences of my graduate years. A special thank you is extended to Cary Mazer, who guided my first studies in Gothic Melodrama and gallantly read my work in record time.

Materials in the material sense were provided for me by the University of Pennsylvania, the Mellon Foundation, and Bentley College. Thanks to the Mellon Foundation, I was able for a full year to pursue my research unencumbered by the chores of teaching and to travel to Britain and conduct research there.

To Messrs. Barnes, Poliakoff, and Halliwell, who graciously consented to be interviewed by me, I am indebted for several hours of stimulating conversation and a wealth of behind-the-scenes information about London theatre.

I thank the Interlibrary Loan Staff of Van Pelt Library, University of Pennsylvania—they often went out of their way to track down obscure, hard-to-locate sources for me. My sincere appreciation also goes to Sister Rita Geraldine, SSJ, for all her clerical and moral support and to Diane Viveiros who managed to decode and word process my tattered, blotted, often barely legible Gothic manuscript.

Finally, my deepest thanks to Anthony Inverso, my own Simonne Evrard, who soothed me, comforted me, believed in me.

# Preface

On 26 May 1976, a group of British "Fringe" playwrights gathered by invitation for an informal discussion billed "New Gothics vs. New Realists," a discussion which had been proposed by John Calder, then editor of the theatrical periodical *Gambit*. The participants began by trying to define these two terms. Unfortunately, however, the discussion, really impromptu in genesis, had not been well planned—no agenda had been prepared, no preliminary definitions to which the participants could respond had been provided (David Halliwell, personal interview, 20 August 1985). Consequently (though such is frequently the case when attempts are made to define the term "Gothic"), exact definition eluded the definers and the discussion drifted to more immediate concerns. As one of the participants, David Halliwell, remarked at the outset of the meeting, "I don't see that these terms apply to me at all. . . . I'm not sure what 'Gothic' means in this context" (*Gambit* 1976, 5).

Even if Calder had clarified what he meant by "New Gothic," odds are that he would still have defined it in terms of Gothic "machinery" and formulaic conventions.[1] Certainly the prevailing, popular view of the Gothic is that it is long since defunct—though it can occasionally be resurrected to produce agreeable shivers or creepy fun. Considered in such a light, the label "Gothic" is obviously one not likely to be welcomed by a serious playwright. It is, therefore, hardly surprising that Halliwell and his colleagues "discarded the terms as meaningless," absolutely irrelevant to contemporary theatre (*Gambit* 1976, 5).

The popular view notwithstanding, Gothic literature has become the subject of a great deal of recent scholarly attention. It is no longer being dismissed out of hand as spectacular nonsense. The quality and the intensity of the critical debate it has instigated contravenes its previous reputation as a trifling literary curiosity.

These reevaluations of the Gothic suggest that Calder may actually have stumbled on an insightful and accurate descriptive label for a school of drama that emerged mainly in Britain in the 1960s and 1970s (although examples may be found in non-British drama of this period). As will become evident, "New Gothic" *is* in fact a most appropriate designation.

Actually, this peculiar kinship of the Gothic and the alternative theatre movement has been suggested, albeit fleetingly and indistinctly, by a few observers. Katherine Worth, for example, speaks of a "'mystery' theatre," of "strange new forms . . . concerned with the irrational and the primitive, with ecstatic or demonic states of being" (1972, 143). John Grillo, himself a Fringe playwright, refers to a theatre "that has abandoned social realism for poetic fantasy, . . . a fantasy of horror and not delight" (1973, 18). Robertson Davies in a commentary footnote in his study of the nineteenth-century stage remarks that the plays presented during the 1961–65 London theatre seasons "make demands on their audiences which are not, giving due allowance to changes in psychological fashion, unlike those made by melodrama in its Gothic and other forms" (Davies et al. 1975, 6: 214, n.1). All of these comments, though fragmentary and allusive, do assert some predilection of the contemporary stage for Gothic themes and materials.

I would contend that these claims can be supported and considerably amplified. Thus the chief aim of this study will be to demonstrate that this "New Gothic" or "NeoGothic" drama exhibits to a remarkable degree the stylistic features, themes, and structures of Gothic narrative as they have been translated into a dramatic idiom. In fact, it is *not* the eighteenth- and nineteenth-century Gothic Melodramas which gave dramatic voice to the Gothic imagination. As will gradually become apparent in chapter 1 and throughout, these Gothic Melodramas—even those which were adaptations of Gothic narrative texts—alter significantly the aesthetic orientation and moral cosmology of the Gothic. The didacticism and sentimentality of the melodrama accorded ill with the fundamental atavism and moral ambiguity of the Gothic. (This initial failure of the Gothic to embody itself on stage is implicitly recognized in the fact that the Gothic is still regarded as an almost exclusively narrative mode.)

This assumption is due for reappraisal. The models which will be offered for examination by this study do indicate that the Gothic sensibility has in the twentieth century metastasized and now locates itself primarily in the genre of drama. Several contemporary dramas which have been heretofore categorized as cerebral, sportive, even "playful" will be reassessed here. As we shall discover, the world of the New Gothic drama is decidedly unplayful, distinctly disconcerting. It is, in short, the world of the Gothic narrative fantasy.

Chapter 2 identifies specific stylistic features endemic to eighteenth- and nineteenth-century Gothic narrative prose through analysis of specific models. I demonstrate how those features operate in conjunction to form the Gothic cosmos. I then explicate the translation of these narrative conventions into their theatrical analogues. This examination serves to indicate that the Gothic Melodrama actually repudiated Gothic forms as well as content whereas the twentieth-century NeoGothic drama resurrects them with a vengeance. The chapter concludes with a consideration of the Gothic grammar of intimidation, the bespeaking of threat as it manifests itself in Gothic narrative texts and in the NeoGothic drama.

Chapter 3 takes up this notion of power and turn to the sociopolitical manifestations of the Gothic. Since this subject is a human matter, the focus here is the Gothic character and character interrelationships. I argue that character in the Gothic is largely a matter of *role*—victim or victimizer. I study the two sole political modes of the Gothic—tyranny or anarchy. I conclude that the nature of power in the Gothic is highly theatrical—a theatricality borne out by both nineteenth-century narrative and twentieth-century dramatic texts.

Chapters 4 and 5 are companion chapters in that both deal with Gothic space. Chapter 4 concerns itself with onstage space; chapter 5, in which I discuss boundary transgression, attends to offstage spaces. Chapter 4 navigates its way through the Gothic's dangerous spaces, while chapter 5 recounts the Gothic's penchant for stories of invaded spaces.

The discussion will range freely over the fields of British, Continental, and American drama, although British models predominate. The Gothic narrative texts chosen are mainly from the nineteenth-century and were selected for their representativeness of the genre. Some plays will appear in only one chapter; others appear in several different contexts. Peter Weiss's *Marat-Sade,* the most paradigmatic Gothic play ever to be produced by the modern stage, materializes in one guise or another in every chapter.

The Gothic impulse has overleaped generic and disciplinary boundaries before—it has done so again. It now inhabits the twentieth-century stage. The cultural phenomenon known as "Gothic" has at last been given a dramatic voice.

# 1

# Gothic Narration and Gothic Melodrama: Some Crucial Distinctions

"In the Gothic universe," writes Peter Thorslev, "evil and chaos are ultimate and irreducible" (Thorslev 1984, 128). This "evil" is not mere human nastiness, despite the fact that the Gothic does indeed furnish abundant instances of human vice and cruelty. As David Richter remarks, "No form of literature has been so persistent in representing evil as an exterior force" (Richter 1983, 293). This conception of a hostile universe is central to the Gothic. The Gothic cosmos is one which enforces a sense of human "creatureliness," the oppressive apprehension, as Thorslev puts it, that "outside the tiny ordered area of our experience there are fates or destinies or even consciousnesses which are inscrutable in their designs, and at best capricious or at worst actively malevolent" (Thorslev 1984, 131).

What emerges from these more recent reappraisals of the Gothic fantasy is a tacit agreement that the Gothic is, as David Punter reminds us, "neither escapist literature nor light reading" (Punter 1980, 96). The Gothic, in fact, resists any attempt to reduce it to agreeable shivers. The prologue narrative to Henry James's *The Turn of the Screw* is instructive in this context. Douglas will not tell his "charming" story to an audience predisposed to find it "delicious." By the time Douglas delivers his "final auditory," the thrill-seekers have departed. The Gothic appeals not to a vulgar, mass sensationalism, but to a deep, abiding sense of danger and of pervasive dread. It punishes both the rationalist who explains away its terrors and the spook-dabbler who insists on uncomplicated happy horror.

Yet it has been, until only recently, the fate of the Gothic to be consistently misconstrued as simpleminded entertainment, or else dismissed as a species of transparent moral allegory whose finale lays the ghost to rest and stakes the vampire. Many commentators have been deluded by the seemingly "normative" endings of so many Gothic novels into perceiving them as unsophisticated fables of good versus evil. This view is articulated by Elizabeth Napier in her 1987 study: "Many of the first Gothic romances are simply moral tales in supernatural dress" (25). Such interpretations, however, miss the mark because, as Patrick Day contends, the Gothic world is "so subversive as to outweigh any conventional warning or happy ending which might be attached to it" (Day 1985, 62). Napier relies heavily on Ann Radcliffe's novels to support her conclusions. While it is true that Radcliffe provides a semblance of resolution and closure (more so than do most Gothicists), even here her stridently happy denouements strike us as forced, tacked on. Napier's description of *The Italian* betrays her own sense that Radcliffe's assertions of restored moral and social stability ring a bit too shrill:

> [W]ith dancing and with shouting, the nuptials of Vivaldi and Ellena are celebrated in "a scene of fairy land" that leaves all memory of the Inquisition behind . . . and the reader is transported into a world in which moral values and familial relationships, once skewed, are set happily to rights (though in doing so, Radcliffe pays tribute to a moral and emotional system that lies outside her own novel). Schedoni's power may linger, but it is clearly not meant to. (Napier 1987, 146)

Perhaps Paolo's happy noises *are* meant to drown out the earlier "darker tones" of the novel, but in fact they do not—and Schedoni's power does linger. Radcliffe ultimately retreats from her own most disturbing intuitions, yet those insights remain stubbornly embedded in her text.

Radcliffe's "stable" closures are actually atypical of the genre. It was more characteristic of the form to eschew closure or to render it highly problematic. Unlike fairy tales, Gothic tales "don't come out right." They strike us as arbitrary, unsettled, uncertain. The effect of this lack, according to David Morris, is that the Gothic tale "remains an edgy, uncomfortable, disquieting text. Its conclusions always dissatisfy since they can never be more than substitutes for other unallowable, perhaps unthinkable endings" (Morris 1985, 313). The endings of *Frankenstein* and *The Turn of the Screw* are especially obvious examples of the Gothic text's disinclination to satisfy the reader's desire for explanation and resolution.

The Gothic subverts closure as part of its ongoing program of destabilization and deconstruction. This disintegrative activity is far too pervasive to serve the more limited aims of satire or didacticism.[1] Gothic literature absolutely pulverizes any sense of a morally operative universe, instead substituting a radically amoral one in which the innocent perish alongside the wicked—or instead of them. Hence the Gothic tends to be obsessive about injustice, whether meted out by a demonic god or by his minions here below. Gothic crime and punishment tend to become disjunctive events; as Judith Wilt contends, retribution is "random" and "irrational" (Wilt, 1980, 29). Translated into political terms, what the Gothic "celebrates" is riot; what it chronicles is tyranny.[2] These are the only political modes in a universe "red in tooth and claw."

Although subversion is probably the most crucial index of the Gothic, the nature of that subversion eludes exact definition. For one thing, the Gothic, while it features a great deal of manacled fist-clenching, does not imply the feasibility, or even the possibility of the redress of wrongs. It parades the indignation and bitterness of polemical literature, while simultaneously insisting that nothing can be done. As Punter puts it, "Gothic writers . . . do not 'advocate' anything at all, for Gothic fiction is almost never didactic . . . yet it points implicitly and constantly to the insupportability of the accepted alternatives" (1980, 411). Thus the Gothic position with regard to problems of power and authority is a disturbingly alogical, flagrantly self-contradictory one.

This simultaneous engagement and noninvolvement, this refusal to confront issues, has confused, even irritated many commentators. It prompts Punter to characterize Gothic literature as "a middle-class and an anti-middle-class literature" (1980, 423). It leads Napier to designate "disequilibrium" as the trademark of the Gothic, a condition wrought by the juxtaposition of "two opposed and often battling" impulses of the genre—"a tendency towards moral and structural stabilizing" and "a contrary inclination towards fragmentation, instability and moral ambivalence" (1987, 5). This desire for stability exists in the Gothic as a yearning that can never be fulfilled and one that would be highly suspect if it ever were.

Another factor that complicates our ability to understand Gothic subversion is that it always, as Jan Gordon suggests, *"pretends otherwise"* (1983, 234). It pretends to support the status quo, to uphold the standard of a conventional world view. Its modus operandi is the use of parody. In the Gothic, parody is not only a method of subversion, it is likewise a cloaking device, a way of "pretending otherwise." As Day points out, parody "subverts the original" but also "affirms it, since it is a likeness of the original" (1985, 60). In the Gothic, parody operates as both a stylistic feature and as an embodiment of Gothic ideology. This remarkable synchronization of form and theme is particularly endemic to the Gothic.

The sweeping annihilative activity of the Gothic is exerted upon physical as well as moral and political certitudes. The Gothic subverts any view of physical reality as at all knowable, analyzable. It creates a condition akin to R. D. Laing's notion of "ontological insecurity"; Gothic nature is a "Kingdom of Inorganization"—chaotic, arbitrary, hostile. The correlative to the reign of terror is a cruel cosmos that rains terror; the analogue to civic riot is the storm-swept seascape. The categories and parameters of this cosmos are not reliable; identity is not fixed, but fluid, shifting. Gordon captures this inconstancy:

> Such a fiction perpetually threatens the collapse of difference in one or more of several ways in order to create a univocality of being. . . . [D]iscrete objects . . . always threaten to coalesce and coagulate into a univocity or degenerate into some collective ruin. (1983, 224)

This endangerment of discreteness applies to both objects in space and to human personalities. Herein lie the wellsprings of the Gothic fascination with metamorphosis and doubling. Rosemary Jackson, urging a view of Gothic as a literature of the *"nonthetic,"* essentially concurs: "[A]ll that mocks or undermines a rational tradition's positive, unified propositions—all that tends towards destructuring or threatens definitions of a stable 'self' and its location within a stable culture"—this is the special province of the Gothic (1979, 109).

Not coincidentally, both Gordon and Jackson resort to a vocabulary of threat—what is implied is subtle, simultaneous erasure and preservation of boundaries: barriers are maintained in order that they may be transgressed.

This violation of frames characterizes not only Gothic representations of space, it likewise structures the reader-text relationship. The Gothic fantasy continually threatens to transform the reader's condition from one of safe voyeurism to one of perilous enthrallment. The reader is invited, lured, in a sense forced into participation, forced to share the agony of uncertainty experienced by the first-person narrator, or else, subjected to a barrage of conflicting narrative voices, forced to bear this burden alone. In fact, Gothic frame narratives dramatize this captivation of the reader by inserting into their contexts a proxy— a beguiled listener. Punter believes that this process of ensnarement, which he deems "paranoiac structure," is the hallmark of the best Gothic texts: in paranoiac fiction, he claims, "the reader is placed in a situation of ambiguity with regard to fears within the text," and so "is invited to share in the doubts and uncertainties which pervade the apparent story" (1980, 404). At the same time, the reader is simultaneously withheld from a full-fledged Gothic experience because the intervening frame narratives distance and exclude the reader from the inner content—thus what the reader is left with is merely the story of a story, the tag-end of a long sequence. This concurrent inclusion and exclusion of the reader jeopardizes boundaries though it does not eradicate them. The establishment of margins and the simultaneous violation of them is one more instance of the problematic nature of Gothic subversion.

As this admittedly brief discussion suggests, the driving force of the Gothic is the urge to make a shambles of all certitudes and verities (even though it longs for their retention) and its choicest mode for doing so is the mode of parody. Recognition of the Gothic as a radically destabilizing aesthetic form makes it possible to recognize its presence even as it mimics and appropriates other aesthetic forms.

Although contemporary scholarship has obviously learned to detect and analyze the impetus and modalities of the Gothic narrative tradition, it has yet to take more than superficial notice of the fact that the Gothic was never really an exclusively narrative genre. There is, in fact, only one full-length analysis of the Gothic on stage—Bertrand Evans's 1947 study *The Gothic Drama from*

*Walpole to Shelley*. Evans's discussion suffers from the same defect as do other early analyses of the Gothic: a sole reliance on Gothic machinery as a means of identification; not surprisingly, Evans is led to classify as "Gothic" any play which exhibited such machinery. Given the sophisticated and exhaustive explanation of the Gothic narrative tradition now available, the subject of Gothic as a *dramatic* tradition is long overdue for reevaluation. The insightful perceptions brought to bear on Gothic fiction need to be applied to the Gothic drama. However, in order to determine whether the Gothic impulse was able to survive intact once it was transferred to the stage, we need to turn our attention to the inner dynamics of the so-called "Gothic Melodrama." We shall discover that, for a variety of reasons and in a variety of ways, the deconstructive energies of the Gothic narrative were vitiated and tamed by the nineteenth-century stage.

The first Gothic novel, Walpole's *The Castle of Otranto*, saw its first stage adaptation in 1781 at Covent Garden. The adaptor, Robert Jephson, according to Willard Thorp, transformed Walpole's Gothic novel into "a romantic tragedy about a wicked Count" (1928, 477). In so doing, Jephson succeeded in enervating the crude power of Walpole's Gothic tale.[3] Any consideration as to how Jephson did so foregrounds the difficulty of mediating between the Gothic sensibility and the exigencies of eighteenth- and nineteenth-century stage presentation.

I will argue that Jephson's decision to jettison the supernatural paraphernalia of *Otranto* is in itself less significant a factor in the play's abjuration of a Gothic aesthetic than is its resolute banishment of the nonthetic. What truly de-Gothicizes the play is the manner in which the laws of causality and of character motivation, so strikingly absent in *Otranto,* are reactivated. Jephson deletes the absurdities, the craziness, the indecorousness of *Otranto,* thus rendering it coherent, plausible, even gentlemanly. No longer recognizable as a story of the labyrinthine castle and of the creatures who wander its mazes, *Otranto* is transformed into a standard-fare psychomachia.

Even one explicit comparison is sufficient to establish this thoroughgoing reorientation. In Walpole's narrative, Conrad, the young prince, is killed at the outset (squashed, to be more precise) by the giant helmet. In the novel, his death is reported; thus, in effect, Walpole has presolved a ticklish staging problem: the event need not be presented, merely narrated. Jephson avails himself of this convenience, but he goes even further. The demise Jephson contrives for the hapless Conrad is at once more dignified and more credible. Conrad (now inexplicably renamed Edward) has met his end in a hunting accident, the details of which are left deliberately vague. The point is that had Jephson wished to retain the helmet even merely as a diegetic prop, he could easily have done so. The chief significance of Walpole's helmet is that it is so inscrutable, so inexplicable. The effect of Conrad's spectacular annihilation is a kind of gruesome ridiculousness—Conrad has never been anything other than a cypher born to be smashed. Jephson's decision to scrap the helmet completely has more to do, one suspects, with a desire to shun the inexplicable, the undignified, the horrid. Perhaps Jephson worried that the unseemliness of this royal death would offend the sensibilities of the reigning censor, John Larpent. Perhaps they offended his own. In any event, this shift from sportive ghoulishness to stately gravity epitomizes the whole transition process, not only in the case of Walpole's novel, but in subsequent stage adaptations of other Gothic texts.

Ultimately the overall impact of Jephson's play is sentimental, not Gothic. Its audience was neither disquieted nor enthralled, but simply granted the indulgence of a good cry. As the dying Count himself puts it, "[A]ll are [and were] satisfied" (Jephson [1781] 1980, 57). The eulogy pronounced by Austin (*Otranto*'s Father Jerome) points skyward at a totally comprehensible, even-handed cosmos—"[E]ternal palms shall crown" the saintly Adelaide as will "heav'n in all its ways be justified" (Jephson [1781] 57). Jephson's play offers us no reason to think otherwise.

Thorp's explanation for this sentimentalization and rerationalization of the Gothic mode is not satisfactory. He speculates that, since theatre-goers of the day were "not willing to suffer a romanticized theater" (he does not explain what he means by a "romanticized theater"), "horrors [had to be] eliminated or the audience would mutiny."[4] The underlying issue here is not so much the viability of staging the ghostly per se as it is the ideological message which the staging of the macabre might transmit. This wholesale sentimentalization of the Gothic is even more self-evident in the work of another Gothic stage adaptor, James Boaden.

Thirteen years after Jephson's play made its debut, another Gothic novel was transmogrified for dramatic presentation. In this case it was Ann Radcliffe's *The Romance of the Forest,* published three years before in 1791. Unlike Jephson, Boaden *was* willing to tackle the problem of presenting an onstage Gothic ghost; in so doing, he appears at first glance to have out-Gothicized Radcliffe herself, for his ghost, unlike Radcliffe's, is never explained away as the product of an overactive imagination. What the heroine sees, the audience sees, and there is never any doubt about the matter. For Evans, this very fact makes Boaden's piece "a play more elaborately Gothic in its furnishings than any previously acted" (Evans 1947, 93). The operative term for Evans is "furnishings"—yet, as we have already noted, "furnishings" do not render a work Gothic, at least not in and of themselves. Oddly enough, it is Boaden's insistence on the actuality of his ghost which expurgates Radcliffe's paranoiac structure and substitutes "spectacle," according to Steven Cohan, "as a theatrical equivalent to the novel's use of fantasy as a basis of fear and horror" (Cohan 1980, lvi).

The drawback of staging the supernatural, though, no matter how effectively carried out, is that it actually *reduces* the audience's participation in the paranoia of the seer-character. Cohan rightly observes that such spectacles in fact "served to mask the more disturbing psychic experiences that the Gothic plots enacted" (Cohan 1980, lvi). What Cohan is suggesting is that, paradoxically, Boaden is least Gothic precisely at those moments when he appears to be most so.

Boaden's eschewal of paranoiac structure in favor of extravagant special effects represents an attitude toward Gothic adaptation that will culminate almost two centuries later in films of pyrotechnic virtuosity, such as *The Exorcist*. David Punter's discussion of filmic spectacle in and audience response to *The Exorcist* indicates that he would concur with Cohan's assessment of *Fountainville Forest*:

> *The Exorcist* is simply a sequence of special effects. . . . Let it not be said that there is much wrong with the effects themselves: they are extremely effective for the most part, and several of the images of terror which are called upon are also quite new. What is good in the best horror films . . . is their ability to use images of terror to provoke powerful tensions between different interpretations. This is a process which *The Exorcist* sets out to short-circuit. From the first moments, we are left in no doubt whatever as to the reality of the little girl's possession. The audience is reduced to a nadir of passivity. . . . This being said, *The Exorcist* is a horror film, and as such it corresponds to the most uninspired Gothic magazine fiction of the 1840s in its literal-mindedness and lack of ironic tension.

This proneness of Gothic dramatization to overexplicitness, obvious from its very inception, almost seems to foredoom any likelihood of its achieving the same degree of subtlety and sophistication as its narrative sibling. For Albert Lavalley, the stage and film history of *Frankenstein* offers overwhelming evidence that such is indeed the case:

> In the novel . . . that hideousness terrifies us because it is so indefinite. We do not really see the Monster's hideousness. . . . Each reader's imagination provides details taken from private dreads. . . . The "ghastly grin" terrifies us *because* it terrifies Victor. To represent such a scene on stage or in film is to destroy the suspension of disbelief, the cooperation of our own willing powers of fantasy and phantom-building. The novel strongly suggests that our notions of beauty are questionable, that an apparent monster may be moved by emotions like our own. The physical representation on the stage or in the film, however, obviously discourages such ambivalences. . . . [T]he stage and film must fix that outward appearance from the very start. . . . [T]he problem of makeup in dramatizing *Frankenstein* would remain an occasion for drama and spectacle and a barrier against the deeper themes of the novel.

One gets a very strong sense here that it is narrative and narrative alone which is the proper milieu for the Gothic. Yet this prejudice arises from the assumption that the dramatized Gothic has no resource other than spectacle by which to present the Gothic. As will gradually become evident, the stage does have several other resources at its disposal, and spectacle is probably (albeit arguably) its least effective one.

At the time when the vogue for Gothic adaptations was strongest, however, those resources had yet to be discovered. Given these conditions, Boaden's decision to opt for a graphic approach to staging the Gothic was warrantable. There is other, more compelling evidence, however, that virtually all adaptors were deliberately de-Gothicizing their material, quietly conferring moral clarity and Christian retribution upon the ethical chaos of the Gothic text. Even Matthew Gregory "Monk" Lewis, himself a Gothic novelist, conformed to this same pattern when he wrote for the stage.

Lewis produced a play loosely based on an episode of *The Monk* which he entitled *Raymond and Agnes,* presented in 1797 and again in 1809. The staged Bleeding Nun, unlike her narrative counterpart, represents a principle of cosmic order and benevolent protection. In the novel, on the other hand, she appears in the stead of the hero's beloved, a menacing figure, the ghost of a depraved murderess. This difference in the characterization of the Bleeding Nun is crucial. When ghosts appear as portents of disaster, as avatars of something rotten in the State, or as protectors of rightful heirs, we can be fairly sure we are not in the presence of the Gothic. In other words, as Day claims, the supernatural in the Gothic "does not represent an order or a plane of reality higher than that of physical reality. [It is] the manifestation, not of transcendent order, but of chaos and disruption" (Day 1985, 36). *The Monk*'s Bleeding Nun is a Gothic ghost; the ghost of *Raymond and Agnes* constitutes an avatar of a supernatural-ized melodrama.

This distinction is a crucial one, for the Gothic and the melodramatic, while they exhibit some striking affinities, are not interchangeable genres. In fact, as will become evident, they are deeply antithetical modes, so much so that the appellation "Gothic Melodrama" is in effect a self-contradiction. Yet, most commentators continue to conflate the two. Evans early on anticipated this difficulty in differentiating between the Gothic and the melodramatic: "The precise dividing line between Gothic drama and that later kind of melodrama which betrays no Gothic origins is difficult to fix" (Evans 1947, 173) (hence his reliance on readily discernable machinery as an index).

More recently, Louis James betrays the same generic confusion in arguing that the later, more refined melodramas (he cites Leopold Lewis's *The Bells,* 1871, as an example) were approaching a level of psychological complexity similar to that normally attained only by prose fiction. Yet, he implicitly classifies three *Gothic* novels—*Dr. Jekyll and Mr. Hyde, The Picture of Dorian Gray*, and *The Turn of the Screw*—as examples of melodrama. Once again it is implied that it is narrative alone which is the only authentic voice of the Gothic. Other commentators have attempted to predicate a qualitative distinction between the two modes, arguing, for example, as does Dale Kramer, that "Gothicism is the more aesthetically demanding form" whereas "melodrama needs only stock speeches and gestures" (1973, 57). Certainly this argument fails to provide the rigor necessary to disentangle these two seemingly hopelessly enmeshed genres.

Fortunately, Peter Brooks, in his study *The Melodramatic Imagination* provides a preliminary but very useful distinction: melodrama "tends to diverge from the Gothic in its optimism, its claim that the moral imagination can open up the angelic spheres as well as the demonic depths and can allay the threat of moral chaos" (Brooks 1976, 20). While the Gothic tends to raise demons it can neither control nor exorcise, the melodrama, choosing the mode of fantasy and wish fulfillment, conjures demons, only to quash them with a thunderbolt from a morally operative heaven. Both modes evoke chaos, but only the melodrama achieves resolution. The Gothic tumbles us into a dizzying vortex; the melodrama grants us a quick, safe glimpse of the downward spiral while simultaneously keeping us firmly anchored to the path of righteousness. In essence, "Gothic Melodrama" allows us to have our elixir and drink it too. Moreover, restabilization in melodrama is neither forced nor tacked on; it is implicit from the outset. Brooks's analysis enables us to see that the Gothic as a sensibility is capable of taking up residence in virtually any genre, even though it has been thought to haunt only the narrative.

J. R. Planché's 1820 *The Vampire,* inspired by the Polidori tale of the same name, nicely illustrates Brooks's differentiation. The action of the drama proper is pointedly preceded by an "introductory vision," a prologue in which two guardian spirits conspire to protect the heroine from the grasp of the vampire. Hence, no matter what disasters may loom over the fair Margaret's head, the audience can rest assured that "extermination waits" the vampire Ruthven. Moreover, whereas Polidori's vampire mysteriously disappears (thereby potentiating the revivification of the creature), Planché's vampire-villain is unequivocally demolished by a lightning bolt.

Melodrama's overriding drive towards stability at all costs manifests itself in political terms as well. Like the Gothic, much of melodrama is about injustice. Like the Gothic also, melodrama is neither hortatory nor polemical. Both modes treat injustice as a personal affliction. For both the Gothic and the melodramatic sensibility, injustice cannot be defined as a specific social ill.

Despite this mutual tendency to personalize injustice, however, the Gothic and the melodramatic differ substantially in their responses to injustice. If the Gothic can be said to "celebrate" riot, it is the province of melodrama to quell it. Its very championing of the political underdog short-circuited the raising of any working-class consciousness. Melodrama, if examined closely, does not, as Michael Booth contends, give evidence of "a rebellious class spirit in action" ([1969] 1980, 1:27). Rather, as Martin Meisel more convincingly argues, in "discharg[ing] the social resentments of its audience, it encouraged that audience's passivity" (1983, 297). The ill-fed, factory-exploited multitudes who flocked to the theatre of melodrama identified with persecuted virtue, and when it was vindicated, so were they. Most seductive of all, for an audience comprised largely of an oppressed class, or one that perceived itself as such, was melodrama's valorization of victimization, the alluring proposition that the oppressed can do no wrong.

The most politically conservative melodramas even went so far as to deny class oppression altogether. For example, we can readily observe the transformation from a grim recognition of "things as they are" to complete disavowal when we compare Charles Maturin's Gothic masterpiece *Melmoth the Wanderer* with its stage adaptation by Benjamin West. West's *Melmoth* (1823) replaces Maturin's unvarnished treatment of poverty with a love-in-the-cottage fantasy.

In Maturin's novel, material want assumes a vampirish quality: a young boy sells his own blood in exchange for grocery money. In the stage adaptation, the entire incident is deleted, poverty is merely so much talk, and Walberg's distress seems hyperbolic, unmotivated. In Maturin's novel, poverty is palpable; deprivation is recorded in the deterioration of bodies and houses—the "shattered wainscotting," the threadbare clothing, the "sordid meals." Absolute destitution never becomes quite real in West's adaptation. Thus, here there is a sense that nothing is wrong with "the way things are," and even if there is, it will soon right itself.

Melodrama's urge to stabilize manifests itself most legibly in a marked resistance to "ontological insecurity." One knows exactly where one stands in melodrama. As Brooks suggests, "Melodrama handles its feelings and ideas virtually as plastic entities, visual and tactile models held out for all to see and handle" (1976, 41). Melodrama is in this limited sense pure theatre. Nonetheless, it differs from the Gothic impulse, which is also markedly theatrical, in that, given its drive to demonstrate a morally decipherable universe, its semiotic signals never lied and they remained remarkably static. The costumes, gait, makeup, even hair color of the characters of melodrama functioned as reliable indexes to character. Heroines, for example, wore white as a matter of course, while for villains, black hair and mustache was *de rigueur*. Though melodrama shares the Gothic's distrust of language, it does insist that *nonverbal* signifiers be unambiguous, accurate, and unchanging. By contrast, in the Gothic universe, where metamorphosis is the rule, things are *not* what they seem. The senses are unreliable, no matter how acute; sensory data only serves to deepen ontological confusion.

Melodrama's resilient faith in the nonverbal signifier explains the difference between Gothic treatments of disarticulation and melodramatic portrayals of muteness. In the Gothic, the condition of muteness, the condition of not being able to make oneself understood or believed, represents the nadir of powerlessness. In melodrama, on the other hand, muteness "speaks"; it is surcharged with meaning, perfectly understood. In Matthew Gregory Lewis's Gothic melodrama

*The Wood Demon,* the mute child Leolyn is a facile communicator, easily understood and correctly interpreted by his "audience":

> *Una:* Now then, let us away. . . . Come and once safe within the castle—(*Leolyn expresses alarm*)—You shudder at the word. Is it *there* then, that the ruffian—(*Leolyn points to the portrait she wears around her neck*)—How, this picture?—the count? Oh! . . . Tell me—while I can still hear you—tell me for what purpose—(*Leolyn takes the dagger from the altar and points it at his own heart*)—to murder you?—and this very man in a few days should be my bridegroom!—my blood freezes. . . . (1824, 61)

Leolyn's wordlessness reverberates with meaning; in fact, his condition elicits assistance. However, in the Gothic world, for example, of Polidori's "The Vampire," incoherence signals powerlessness—Aubry's "incoherence became at last so great that he was confined to his chamber" ([1819] 1966, 281). Since Aubry cannot speak clearly, he is effectively silenced, shut up, and shut in. In the Gothic, silence is futile, though eloquence may be so as well. *Frankenstein*'s Monster is helpless before he learns the "godlike science" of language, yet he finds that its mastery purchases him no mercy.

We begin to see at this point why Gothic Melodrama was such an unstable compound. At the same time that it pillaged Gothic motifs and conventions, it repudiated the Gothic sensibility. Nowhere is this divergence more apparent than in its deployment of the sentimental. While it is true that both modes assert the primacy of feeling, the Gothic's commitment to a cosmology of cruelty dictates a complete overthrow of the sentimental. Whereas melodrama trusts completely the sentimental, regards it as a viable mode, *the* viable mode, the Gothic parodies it relentlessly.

One shibboleth of the sentimental was the innate, instinctual benevolence of parents. Melodrama ratifies this doctrine at every turn: the real father always loves his child. Melodramatic fathers may be bunglers, but they are never figures of menace. Mutual, instantaneous, and instinctive affection is the rule (even between parents and children who are virtual strangers to one another). The following father-daughter exchange from John Calcraft's *The Bride of Lamermoor* (1822) is typical:

> *Sir W:*   My child! My child!
> *Lucy:*   My dear, dear father! (*Runs and embraces him*)
> *Sir W:*   My dear, dear Lucy, are you safe? Are you well?
> *Lucy:*   I am quite well, Sir, and still more that I see you so. . . . (n.d., 11)

In the world of melodrama, filial piety is a virtue that makes sense. In fact, in Planché's *The Vampire,* Margaret's filial devotion is a material factor in her deliverance.

The Gothic father is, however, as Wilt dubs him, a "great old one"—the absolute inversion of the sentimental father (1980, 44). Maturin's "The Tale of Guzman's Family" (one of the inset tales of *Melmoth*) chronicles a metamorphosis from the benign father of the melodrama to the child-devouring Gothic father. At first, Walberg's father is presented as a child-loving Santa Claus. Imperceptibly, gradually, however, the figure mutates. As the fortunes of the family decline, the old ones remain stupidly unconscious of their children's deepening misery. As the family's food supply diminishes, the old continue to eat and eat and eat. Their daughter-in-law, with all the filial piety of the child of the melodrama, begins to forgo her own meals and those of her children so that "the aged pair" can dine on "everything that can tempt the tasteless palate of age" (Maturin [1820] 1961, 313). Even so, we are unprepared for the sudden, savage spring of the beast that was kindly old grandfather:

> [T]he old man rose from his seat, and with horrid unnatural force, tore the untasted meat from his grandchildren's lips, and swallowed it himself, while his rivelled and toothless mouth grinned at them in mockery at once infantine and malicious. (1961, 321)

Paralleling this dreadful transformation is the mutation of Walberg himself as father. At first he is full of "fond anxiety" for his children; as poverty inexorably eats away his household, he exhibits fits of temper "bordering on insanity." Finally, in his extremity, he resolves to murder his children, ostensibly to spare them further pain. Yet it is clear that Walberg has turned beast as the little one asks him, "Are you the wolf?" (Maturin [1820] 1961, 329).

Nothing of the sort, of course, occurs in West's stage version. Although this Walberg briefly considers putting his child out of its misery, the child's smile is enough to blunt his purpose. (Children, like parents, are sacrosanct in melodrama.) Furthermore, this Walberg rescues his daughter much as Lady Margaret's father had saved her from her demon-lover. Melodramatic fathers may grieve, but the possibility of derangement as an entailment of despair is never seriously entertained.

It should be readily observable by now that the underlying mechanism of the melodrama is a suppression, a muzzling of the countercultural, antisentimental voice. This tendency is exceptionally apparent in melodramas which stage a confrontation of beauty and beast—the monster and the maiden. The various stage versions of *Frankenstein* ring only the most minute changes on this unvarying arrangement. For example, in Milner's 1826 adaptation, the heroine Emmeline (the Elizabeth figure) conquers "his monstership," moving him to tears by playing a melancholy air on a small flageolet (in lieu of Radcliffean lute, one supposes). Cornered, despairing, he leaps into a volcanic crater. In a 1927 unpublished script by Peggy Webling, this basic pattern is repeated except that the monster accidentally murders the maiden. Nonetheless, she conquers from beyond the grave. The Creature is subdued by the awakening of his moral conscience. Suddenly comprehending his responsibility for the girl's death, he breaks into "a storm of uncontrollable grief" and posthaste hurls himself off a mountain crag. David Campton's 1959 *Frankenstein* dispenses with the taming of the Monster, yet insists that now more than ever the monstrous must be expelled; so the maiden must shoot it—in self-defense of course. While Campton's adaptation avoids the bathos of the Milner and Webling versions, it nevertheless sanctions as necessary the expulsion of the monstrous.[5]

In all three versions the Monster is devoiced, then destroyed. It is as if the disturbing, articulately phrased questions posed by Mary Shelley's eloquent Monster must be heard in this forum. By reducing her orator-monster to a grunting beast or a slobbering fool, the melodrama can provide a ready-made justification for his extermination.

By ignoring, or (as was more common) quelling its own subversive content, the Gothic Melodrama repeatedly signalled its unwillingness to evoke the "disturbing psychic experiences" which contemporary Gothic fiction could and did elicit. Although Gothic Melodramas continued to be produced well into the twentieth century (as Webling's and Campton's versions testify), the Gothic claptrap itself appeared less and less frequently, no doubt due to changes in public taste, but perhaps too as mute testimony to the bankruptcy of the genre. It was not so much that the Gothic had all but disappeared from the stage—it had never really taken up residence there (hence the widespread misapprehension which persists even today that Gothic is an exclusively narrative mode).

One astonishing exception, however, to this generalization, which should be noted, is Shelley's *The Cenci*, a play which does approach a genuinely Gothic vision. Its content is so subversive, its darkness so uncompromising, that it was never performed on the Romantic stage even though Shelley had written it to be played (and had even chosen the actress he wished to portray Beatrice).[6] Though the play contains no Gothic "furnishings" and no spectre prowls the corridors of the Cenci Palace, it is nonetheless a Gothic nightmare in theatrical form. In fact, Shelley's play could stand as a repudiation of Gothic Melodrama. Stuart Curran explains:

> Shelley had little respect for his contemporary theater. . . . The traditional horrors of the Romantic stage inhabited a comfortable Gothic land of fantasy far removed from the terrifying nightmare of the Pallazo Cenci and the landscape of hell. . . . The terror of *The Cenci* allows no retreat. Nor does the passion reduce to sentimentality. The heroine of Shelley's time always suffered, but she was not systematically destroyed like Beatrice. (1970, 158; 177)

Actually, the comfortableness of Gothic Melodrama, as we have seen, is endemic to melodrama, not the Gothic. Curran is quite right that *The Cenci* does not work when "mounted as melodrama" (1970, 253–55). It does not work because *The Cenci,* while it appropriates some elements of melodrama (as does Gothic), reinterprets them through the lens of the Gothic—a reversal of the process by which stage adaptors had fashioned melodramas from Gothic novels. *The Cenci* is more faithful to the spirit of the Gothic than the most blatant adaptations had ever been; it serves as a corrective to those innumerable Forest Foundlings and Castle Spectres. If we isolate a few motifs shared by the Gothic novel and the Gothic Melodrama and study their treatment in Shelley's drama, we can observe Shelley deliberately turning back to the articulation of a starkly Gothic sensibility, unalloyed by the cloying sweetness of melodrama.

We can readily perceive Shelley's repudiation of the sentimental, for example, in his portrait of horrific fatherliness. Cenci, ghoulishly toasting his own sons' deaths, is a Gothic "great old one," an utter perversion of benevolent paternity. Moreover, as in Gothic fiction, individual cruelty is but a miniaturized manifestation of an unconditionally pervasive brutality. Thus when Beatrice turns to the Pope, another "father," another "great old one," clemency is denied. Decisions in such a world have nothing to do with guilt or innocence but only to do with power. Tyranny replicates itself endlessly: as Beatrice confronts her judges in the "Hall of Justice," she finds that her Gothic father has been replaced with a whole panel of them.

It is instructive to contrast Shelley's Inquisitors with those of James Boaden's *The Secret Tribunal* (1795). There is no indication that this tribunal tortures its prisoners or errs in its judgments. Indeed it seems to operate as a force for justice. Herman's confidence in the fair-mindedness of the tribunal is entirely justified. There is never any real doubt that the guiltless Ida will be acquitted and released. In contrast, Bernardo's trust in the judging powers in *The Cenci* is pathetically misplaced. He urges Beatrice to confess with the argument that "the Pope will surely pardon . . . [a]nd all will be well" (Shelley [1886] 1970, 81). Beatrice is as guilty in the technical sense as Ida is innocent, yet in this utterly perverted world, she is in terms of a "higher truth . . . most innocent" (Shelley [1886] 1970, 78). Shelley's trial scenes reveal more affinity with the Gothic novelists' Inquisitions and persecutions than with Boaden's, despite Boaden's showcasing of Gothic trappings. As in the Gothic, in the world of *The Cenci,* mercy is impossible, innocence impotent, eloquence unavailing.

So too, as in the Gothic narrative, human cruelty in *The Cenci* merely mimics cosmic malevolence. For Beatrice, the world has become alien, incomprehensible, demonic, Other. Cenci, "[e]ven tho' dead" lives "in all that breathe" (Shelley [1886] 1970, 86). The universe itself has become a predatory great old one. Nature is relentlessly hostile with its earthquakes, famine, frost, "wind-walking Pestilence" (Shelley [1886] 1970, 87).

*The Cenci* is probably the most Gothic play of the nineteenth century. But there is another drama that is worth some discussion in this context. Although not like *The Cenci*, a Gothic drama, Joanna Baillie's *Orra* (1811) is a play *about* the Gothic. One of Baillie's so-called "Plays of the Passions," *Orra* is a psychological study of fear and of the nature of enthrallment. While it itself makes no pretense at enthralling its own audience, it does grapple with the implications of Gothic enthrallment in a way that the more overtly spooky Gothic Melodramas did not.

Initially, *Orra* bears a faint resemblance to *The Castle of Otranto*. Orra, the heroine, is slated to be married off to her guardian's foppish son. No slavishly obedient Walpolean daughter, though, Orra spiritedly rejects him. In order to force her compliance, Orra is packed off to a reputedly haunted castle.

Orra is terrified at this prospect by reason of the ghostly lore she has heard concerning this castle, lore to which she seems strangely addicted. In this fashion the telling of ghost stories and the related dynamics of audience enthrallment become thematic concerns of the play. Orra suffers the affliction of *Northanger Abbey*'s Catherine Morland—an insatiable appetite for tales of terror:

> *Or.*   And let me cow'ring stand, and be my
> touch
> The valley's ice: there is a pleasure in it.
> .................................................
> Yea, when the cold blood shoots through
> every vein:
> When every hair's-pit on my shrunken skin
> A knotted knoll becomes, and to mine eyes
> Rush stranger tears, there is a joy in fear.
> (*Catching Hold of Catherina*)
> Tell it, Catherina. . . . (Baillie 1812, 3:29)

Unlike Austen's Catherine, though, Orra's hunger for horrific sensation is satiated to the point that, by the end of the play, she is quite mad, having been terrified into insanity. Both her lover and her enemies deploy psychological terror tactics for their own ends. Rather than obtaining her acquiescence, they succeed only in driving her over the brink.

The essential question posed by the play, it seems, is whether Orra is punished in classic Gothic fashion for spook-dabbling, or whether she is punished for taking the Gothic *too* seriously, in the sense that her predilection for ghost stories is what makes her susceptible in the first place to the machinations of the villain. One suspects the latter, for Orra, though she proclaims the "pleasure" of terror, does not seem to be enjoying agreeable shivers. She takes the Gothic quite seriously. Another reason to favor this reading is that *Orra* was one of a series of plays Baillie wrote "to delineate [and implicitly rebuke] the stronger passions of the mind." Thus it seems more likely that Baillie is portraying Orra's overindulgence in fear as a kind of emotional flaw.

Plea for moderation that it might be, the play does, nonetheless, pay a backhanded tribute to the power of the Gothic—it suggests that, with or without ghosts, one can be frightened out of one's wits. That in itself is a sobering reflection. All of this is by way of saying that *Orra* does not appear to belong to the genre of the mock Gothic, despite the interesting parallels it offers to *Northanger Abbey*. If, as Paul Lewis contends, the mock Gothic "uses humorous irony and exaggeration to repudiate its encounter with the unknown and feared," surely *Orra* does not belong to the canon (1981, 316). Even though Orra is absurdly hypersensitive, the consequences of that hypersensitivity are not lightly to be dismissed. The world of *Orra* is not one in which, as Lewis remarks of the mock Gothic, "nightmares are nonsense, terror a thing of the imagination" (1981, 318).

In any event, neither *Orra* nor *The Cenci* had any impact on the course of the Gothic drama through the nineteenth century. *The Cenci* was not performed until 1886 and *Orra* remained a closet drama. Both were essentially prophetic aberrations; meanwhile the woodsmen's huts proliferated.

As the Romantic era gave way to the Victorian, melodrama of the Gothic variety, as well as the increasingly popular domestic type, grew decidedly more and more pictorial. Drastic improvements in stagecraft permitted the creation of elaborate visual, even painterly effects. As one commentator puts it, "The Victorian arch had become a gigantic picture frame which the melodrama filled with gigantic pictures" (Smith 1973, 26). The effect of this pictorial bias was an even more definite abduration of paranoiac structure and an increase in the psychic distancing between audience and stage.

In other words, the proscenium picture-frame style of staging allowed the audience to occupy and retain the position of voyeur, safe in the knowledge that its position was impregnable. This is not to say that the nineteenth-century playgoer did not emotionally participate in the onstage event. We get some sense of the emotional impact of the melodramatic performance on the spectator from this account of Charlotte Cushman portraying Bianca in an 1847 production of Henry Hart Milman's *Fazio:*

> The words are commonplace enough, but the tone, the look, the action, as she clutched at the great tumbling masses of hair as if about to tear them up by the roots, were awe-inspiring! . . . A mist rose before my eyes; a thrill, half-pleasure, half-pain, passed through the spinal column; a lump arose in my throat; and I sat shivering and shuddering till the fatal bell, which heralded the death of Fazio, sounded the death-knell of his hapless wife, and she, collapsing, fell an inert and helpless thing, dead ere she reached the earth. (Coleman 1904, 1:294)

Although this spectator is participating vicariously through his identification with the character (and through his response to the magnetic force of the performer's personality), he himself is in no sense put at risk. The pleasure, the "thrill," is contingent upon an unwavering belief in his own security. Ann Ubersfeld sums up the pleasure of this kind of spectatorship:

> Theatre shows everything the spectator fears. . . . All this is shown, but after it has been tamed, put at a distance, veiled by a kind of negation. . . . Violent death, extermination, blind tyranny, torture, the situations of victim and of executioner are all summoned up and kept at a distance, and this "mithradatizing" is one of the powerful roots of tragic pleasure. What one sees is the Other who suffers, and there is pleasure in the fact that it is someone else; but there is pleasure also in the fact that it is not true. . . . [T]he pleasure of seeing human relations in their most conflictive and passionate forms, while one is feeling quite protected oneself (protected but concerned) and knows full well that no real blood will be shed—this is the pleasure at the centre of bourgeois theatre, but also, in the broadest sense, at the centre of all theatre. (1982, 135–36)

As will gradually become evident, this description, while it accurately delineates the psychic distancing provided by most theatrical forms, does not take into consideration those recent forms, such as the NeoGothic drama, which render more problematic—and dangerous—the audience-stage interrelationship.

Even though the melodrama readily furnished ocular extravaganzas and portraits of passion (such as Cushman's Bianca), it took care not to offend the sensibilities of its audience. The most violent, horrific, gruesome "pictures" of Gothic fiction never materialized on the melodramatic stage. Furthermore, even if such scenes had been staged, the melodrama's strict observance of the proscenium border would have ensured that the Gothic spectacle remained nothing more than a thrilling picture confined within its frame. Thus the Romantic Gothic Melodramas and the Victorian Gothic Melodramas (of which there were only a comparative few) served up eye-dazzling pyrotechnics which allowed the audience to spook-dabble as much as it pleased, in no danger whatsoever of being swept up into the vortex of the Gothic spectacle.

One way these points of difference between the Gothic mode and the melodramatic can be understood is to differentiate the degree of power that each grants to its audience. Melodrama is so accommodating as to accept the audience's utter tyranny. Throughout the century it catered unabashedly to the tastes and demands of its patrons. Moreover, as we have already determined, the staging practices of the melodramatic stage permitted the spectator to remain safely ensconced behind the proscenium barrier. The Gothic mode, on the other hand, is totally unaccommodating: its modus operandi with regards to the spectacle-audience relationship is enthrallment—the deliberate assertion of power over a captive audience. Unlike melodrama, the Gothic toys with audience expectations and desires. Thus an authentic Gothic drama would imperil audience voyeurism, or at least jeopardize the inviolability of the spectator.

*Melmoth the Wanderer*'s mob execution scene offers a paradigm of this conversion of the watcher from detached voyeur to spellbound thrall. Moncada describes the scene of butchery, himself watching the horrifying spectacle, and the whole mesmerizing process by which the boundary between self and spectacle collapses:

> It is a fact, Sir, that while witnessing this horrible execution, I felt all the effects vaguely ascribed to fascination. I shuddered at the first movement of the crowd. . . . I shrieked involuntarily when the first decisive movements began among them. . . . I echoed the wild shouts of the multitude with a kind of savage instinct. . . . Then I echoed the screams of the thing that seemed no longer to live, but still could scream. . . . My resistance was so purely mechanical that without the least consciousness of my own danger . . . I remained uttering shout for shout and scream for scream—offering worlds in imagination to be able to remove from the window, yet feeling as if every shriek I uttered was as a nail that fastened me to it—dropping my eyelids and feeling as if a hand held them open, or cut them away—forcing me to gaze on all that passed below like Regulus, with his lids cut off, compelled to gaze . . . till sense and sight and sound failed me, and I fell . . . mimicking in my horrid trance, the shouts of the multitude. . . . I actually for a moment believed myself the object of their cruelty. The drama of terror has the irresistible power of converting its audience into its victims. (Maturin [1820] 1961, 196–97)

One can readily see that Moncada's experience of spectatorship is quite different from that of the spectator of Cushman's performance. We detect no trace of "the pleasure of the spectator." The experience here is one of unmitigated pain, horror, and helplessness. So completely is Moncada drawn into the scene he witnesses that he is transformed into an unwilling participant. His own performance in fact endangers his own safety—it draws the officers of the Inquisition to his door.

In practice very few plays of the late-eighteenth and nineteenth centuries were willing to assert this sort of raw power. In its allegiance to melodrama and to all that that allegiance entailed, the stage of this era was in effect precluding the emergence of an authentic Gothic drama. Various reasons for this state of affairs may be and have been proffered. Meisel, for instance, concedes that the nineteenth-century stage was under pressure to produce melodrama in a way that the era's fiction was not: "Outside the drama, the compulsion toward metaphysical reassurance was not as great" (1983, 200).

One wonders why this should be so, why, after all, the British theatre was subject to censorship for over two hundred years while other varieties of discourse remained comparatively unfettered. Implicit in this interdict was the recognition of a power deemed potent, unpredictable in its effects. Notwithstanding its reputation as the embodiment of the rehearsed and the repeated, the theatre is, as Marie-Hélène Huet argues, "rupture and discontinuity" and so can never be "entirely foreseeable" (1982, 108–109). Indeed, it is the unpredictability of the live performance that is in large measure the source of its power. Narrative in the final analysis is fixed, hence in a sense predictable. Not surprisingly, banned plays could be printed though they could not be performed. Richard Findlater, acknowledging that the theatre has always been "singled out for special anxieties," suggests that this anxiety stems from the fact that "a live actor . . . is a disturbingly free element" (1967, 208). This "disturbingly free element" can, with the slightest gesture, the subtlest intonation, reinvent a text. Melodrama's "relative rigidity, its unswerving adherence to set formulae represents, along with censorship itself, a gesture of containment, not just of seditious or indecorous subject matter, but of the explosive energies of the stage itself" (1983, 200).

It is tempting to argue that the decline of melodrama augured the rise of a NeoGothic drama, but the facts do not support this argument. Instead, the reaction to melodrama came in the form of a commitment to realism. The interval between the demise of melodrama and the emergence of a NeoGothic drama was dominated by what one commentator has dubbed "the realists' reign of terror" (Rosenberg [1964] 1965, 242). This preeminence of realism (and of the hortatory Shavian and Brechtian models which followed) did not, however, rule out the florescence of various antirealist movements which persisted alongside, or perhaps beneath, as Gothic narrative itself had always done, the mainstream form. One can detect shards of the Gothic randomly scattered among these antirealist forms, forms which constitute, according to George Kernodle, a "theatre of disruption" (1967, 291–326). It was from these fragments that Antonin Artaud would eventually assemble a startling collage—*The Theater and Its Double*—his program for a theatre that can aptly be described as NeoGothic.

We can find, for example, in Jarry's *Ubu* cycle the moral anarchy of the Gothic, albeit displaced into farcical violence. In the various manifestations of Expressionism, both early and late, we can discern some of the patterns and motifs of Gothic fantasy. Here, for instance, is August Strindberg describing the structure of his *A Dream Play:* "Time and space do not exist. . . . The personalities split, take on duality, multiply, vanish and disperse and are brought into a focus" ([1902] 1970, 2:171). Wedekind's nightmarish forays into the taboo territories of sex and violence and his obsession with the mechanics and consequences of repression hark back to the likes of *The Monk*.[7] Especially in the realm of scenic design, we can observe the Expressionist formulation of a Gothic landscape—anthropomorphic, hostile, distorted: walls slant crazily, perspective is amiss, coloration is garish and unnatural. The Expressionistic setting of O'Neill's *The Emperor Jones* (1920) presents a prototypic Gothic landscape; Jones's experience of the predatory forest is remarkably akin to that of the Gothic victim snared in the toils of the labyrinth.

In a small way, the 1920s Parisian Grand Guignol Theatre represents yet another piece of the collage. The Grand Guignol can trace its lineage back to Boaden's staged ghost and can locate its progeny in the likes of *The Texas Chainsaw Massacre*. It was a theatre of the graphic and explicit. Unlike the Expressionist Theatre, the Grand Guignol remained, in decor and plot, resolutely naturalistic. It sought to assert the horrific amid the reassuringly banal, a pattern that many Victorian Gothic fantasies had already adopted. Nonetheless, beyond this superficial similarity, the Grand Guignol had little else in common with the Gothic, for it blithely sidestepped the most troubling and subversive aspects of the Gothic. It catered to an audience that wished to be titillated but did not care to be profoundly disturbed. These spook-dabblers, as one historian of the Grand Guignol points out, "knew where they were going, knew what they were going to be offered and what they were supposed to experience."[8] Thus, the Grand Guignol's orientation to horror was not, in the final sense, Gothic.

The penultimate snippet of the collage was supplied by Surrealism, the movement with which Artaud himself had most clearly been associated. While Surrealism, like the Gothic, embraced the antirational and fulminated against all manner of structures—political, social, aesthetic—it, unlike the Gothic, entertained hopes for social and personal transformation. Thus most Surrealistic texts were, in sharp contrast to the Gothic, extremely hopeful. The Surrealist artwork was perceived as an alchemical instrument that would split mind-forged manacles and thus liberate and eventually transform the world.

These notions resurface in Artaud's text (1938) as metaphors of surgery, alchemy, and "redeeming" plague. When Artaud speaks of theatre in these terms, he is speaking as a Surrealist. When, however, he tells us that life and theatre are "a cruelty," when he insists that "the sky can still fall on our heads," when he claims that "evil is the permanent law," Artaud gives voice to the Gothic mind. In Artaud's manifesto we can discern the crucial element of the Gothic that had been missing in all of these other antirealist forms—a deep, abiding sense of the theatre itself as a place of exceptional danger. If the theatre, as Artaud contends, "obeys all the exigencies of life," while life itself is "always someone's death," then we are, in the theatre, subject to, at the mercy of secret, unpredictable, menacing forces. Therefore, when Artaud calls for a "dangerous" theatre, he is not being metaphorical; he is in deadly earnest. Cruelty for Artaud, as it is for the Gothic consciousness, is not the Grand Guignol, not "bloodshed," not "martyred flesh," but simply the way things are—an inhuman, brutal fact. There runs throughout Artaud's prose an overwhelming sense of this hostile, chaotic cosmos, and he brings to bear again and again a Gothic vocabulary of vortices, whirlwinds, engulfments, and convulsive gestures that seem as if they were lifted from the pages of *Melmoth* or Poe.

Artaud is the first to assert a theatrical aesthetic of enthrallment as opposed to an aesthetic of detached voyeurism. His spectators, "like the snake charmer's subjects," are to be mesmerized, bewitched by the theatrical event—"compelled to gaze," like Maturin's Moncada. The pleasure of fascination is to give way to the impotence of enthrallment as audience and victim become one. This is the "drama of terror" to which Maturin alludes and which Artaud envisions.

Nor is the danger and terror confined to the spectator. The Artaudean actor is just as much at risk; he or she too is subject to "exigencies." The smashing of the barrier between actor and spectator makes the performers more vulnerable than when the proscenium barrier afforded some protection. The potential metamorphosis of passive audience into Gothic horde is a turn of events that Artuad does not foresee (here he seems to be thinking as a Surrealist), but one which is made more likely by his removal of the whole code of theatrical conventions that accompanies proscenium staging. Yet Artaud seems oblivious to the fact that the whole process he envisages could just as easily backfire, that the audience may resort to violence in order to resist enthrallment, or that violence itself may be the outcome of that enthrallment. The spectacle, Artaud forgets, is no more predictable than the rest of life. The Artaudean stage is an even more Gothic place than Artaud himself realizes. Artaud is of the devil's party without knowing it.

It is not whether Artaud consciously invokes the Gothic (though surely he was drawn to it, as his translation into French of *The Monk* and his own production of *The Cenci* attest), or whether he ever consistently applies the tenets of a Gothic ideology to the special conditions of the stage. In fact, his demand for "precise" and "immediately readable symbols," his call for a one-to-one, unwavering correspondence between visual sign and internal reality, his insistence on a "label[ing]" and "catalog[ing]" of facial expressions—all these smack of the melodramatic mode rather than the Gothic. What matters ultimately is that Artaud, like the Gothic, sanctions the "unleash[ing] of the monstrous" (Gordon 1983, 211).

In his own day Artaud's theories were dismissed as arrant nonsense (and his incarceration in a mental asylum further damaged his credibility). However, in 1958, when *The Theater and Its Double* was translated into English, it quickly achieved wide currency in theatrical circles. Artaud's apocalyptic language seemed to speak to and for an era of political and social turmoil. Likewise, Artaud's demand for audience involvement seemed to address the goals of the alternative theatre movement, which sought to bring theatre to the People. And it powerfully appealed to a theatre which chose or was forced to situate itself in tight, intimate (sometimes uncomfortably so) quarters. In the context of a movement that performed in what Catherine Itzin calls "non-theatre places" and for "non-theatre audiences" (1980, xiv), Artaud's substitution of the visceral and concrete for the verbal and abstract seemed ready-made for immediate adoption. Quite simply, its time had come.

Along with the other idols which were being smashed was the unauthentic, pale imitation of the Gothic which the traditional stage had been serving up for the delectation of voyeurs. The production note appended to Howard Brenton's *Christie in Love* (1969) might well serve as an epitaph to the old-style Gothic Melodrama:

> Christie's first appearance is in the Dracula tradition. Happy horror, creeps and treats. He rises
> from the grave luridly, in a frightening mask. It looks as if a juicy evening's underway, all
> laughs, nice shivers, easy ohs and ahs. But that's smashed up.

Brenton, with his contempt for "juicy" Gothic, ought to remind us of *The Turn of the Screw*'s Douglas, whose "charming" story turns out to be anything but "delicious."

The NeoGothic play does "unleash the monstrous" both on stage and in unexpected offstage spaces. The audience which expects "creeps and treats" will instead find itself dis-eased, threatened by the Gothic spectacle which is no longer safely caged by the proscenium frame. Like King Kong, an avatar of the Gothic world displayed for the thrill of gawking spectators, the NeoGothic play bursts its shackles, "smashes up" its audience's expectations, subverts its desires—in short, cuts loose. We may now move on to consider how this unleashing occurs and what happens when it does.

# 2

# Multiple Acts of Narration

"The form and thematics of Gothic fiction," writes Jan Gordon, "are remarkably synchronous" (1983, 234). If, as Elizabeth Napier claims, Gothic prose fiction "exhibits . . . procedures of fragmentation and disjunction" (1987, 7), it is because the Gothic is *about* fragmentation and disjunction. The tattered, blotted, weather-beaten, partially illegible, vestigial manuscript over which the intrigued and troubled young John Melmoth pores is the Gothic text incarnate.

As we have already concluded in a preliminary sort of way, the *idée fixe* of the Gothic mode is the undermining of all precepts, dogmas, formulas, whether aesthetic, ethical, empirical, or metaphysical. The more positivistic and reassuring tenets are precisely those to which the Gothic is most drawn. As noted earlier, sentimentality was a particularly frequent target of the Gothic's deconstructive energies.

As we have also discovered, the Gothic mind mimics the mannerisms of its prey, all the better to discredit and dismantle. That is to say, the Gothic is a supremely parodic mode, ranging freely and eclectically over the vast panorama of human art and culture: all literary forms are so much grist for the Gothic mill. Thus Robert LeTellier is enabled to generate a bemusingly long list of supposed "sources" of the Gothic:

> [m]edieval romance, Italian Renaissance painting and literature, Elizabethan tragedy, the great seventeenth and eighteenth-century poets, French and English eighteenth-century novels of sentiment as well as English and German legends, ballads, folktales . . . Tasso, Shakespeare, Milton, Richardson, Prevost, Ossian, Percy, Goethe and Schiller. (1980, 4)

Despite the impression one gets here of exhaustiveness, LeTellier's list is nonetheless incomplete. For example, one has only to recall *Vathek* and the tradition of the Oriental tale to realize that yet another "source" must be added. Indeed, later Gothics parodied the realistic novel and even, in time, went on to parody earlier versions of themselves. (Surely *The Turn of the Screw* is, among other things, a reworking of the Radcliffean model and of *Jane Eyre*.)[1]

Most casual readers of Gothic literature properly intuit the Gothic's parodic relationship to the realist mode. Most such readers, however, are content to lump the Gothic together with other varieties of fantasy discourse. Admittedly, the relationship of the Gothic to the genres of romance or allegory, for example, is more problematic. It is not, however, unintelligible. Day offers some much needed clarification:

> In a romance or allegory, . . . narrative form implies a pattern of order or meaning that has significance in the world outside it. . . . The writers of Gothic though, make no claims upon the real world in their works. . . . It [the Gothic fantasy] is made up of other versions of the world, versions that the Gothic reveals as incomplete and inadequate. (1985, 42–43)

The conclusion to be drawn here is that the Gothic parodies the techniques and conventions of nonmimetic narrative forms as well as those of more realistic modes. And, as Day points out, the Gothic text "always subverts the conventional expectations the reader brings to such genres" (1985, 45). Later Gothics go on to parody and subvert the conventions of earlier forms—thus, in Poe's "Masque of the Red Death," the lifted mask discloses not the expected grinning "Gothic" skull, but rather a faceless void.

This parasitism, this dependence on existent models, is not accompanied by a willingness to invent an alternative structure. This refusal, which Stanley Solomon detects in *Vathek,* is more or less present in every Gothic text: *Vathek* "deflates not only the assumed values of the book but also any possible countervalues implicit in the rejection of the given norms" (1971, 115). Not all commentators espouse this view. Napier, for example, regards the Gothic impulse as "essentially conservative."[2] The problem with this interpretation is that it ignores the wholesale dismantling operations which the Gothic texts performed on these models. One can instead argue that, if the Gothic writers consistently failed to provide viable alternative systems and instead pursued a pattern of breakdown and dismemberment, it was because the deconstructive act itself seemed to them to be a more authentic representation of human experience. We do not have to conclude that the Gothic writer was incapable of invention; we can just as easily infer that such a "failure" was deliberate. Even in the somewhat atypical case of Ann Radcliffe, one can argue that her implausible, sentimental endings originate in her own inability to believe in them herself.

We can begin to understand that almost all of the formal characteristics typical of Gothic prose—interpolated narrative, unreliable narrators, circular as opposed to linear plot movement, problematic closure—are variant expressions of the Gothic's determination to break down order, to subvert normal expectations. These are also the formal structural devices by which the Gothic advertises and maintains its discontinuous relationship to reality.

Thus the Gothic's predilection for obtuse or hysterical first-person narrators, for example, may be apprehended as a means of interdicting certainty. In

Gothic literature, the inadequacy of the account is foregrounded. The Gothic narrator remains unable to render an account that is not in some way confused, distorted, slanted, or thoroughly unverifiable.

In non-Gothic multiple-account fictions, the addition of alternative views may corroborate the initial account or perhaps expose it as a fraud. In Gothic literature, the unsatisfactoriness of a given account seems to provoke the other accounts into being,[3] and the accumulation of multiple accounts fails to provide clarity; indeed it exacerbates confusion because the several accounts fail to combine themselves into a cohesive whole. The tales do not illuminate one another (though they may comment on one another); frequently they function as enemy brothers, rival texts. The end result is that more questions are raised while the original ones are left unsettled. Each narrative itself sustains several variant readings, so that as more narratives are added, the number of possible interpretations proliferate in geometric progression. As Day explains, the Gothic "subverts the possibility, not simply of an objective reality, but of any common perception at all" (1985, 48). Hence we are directed to focus our attention not so much on the event itself, whose very existence is, by this point, questionable, but on the manner in which the human perceiving consciousness converts experience into story.

Beth Newman articulates this useful distinction between the use of multiple point of view in Gothic narrative and its use in other narrative forms: other forms, she notes, "offer us multiple narrators in order to provide multiple points of view, each of which expresses the unique psychology of the character who tells a given story" (1986, 143). Gothic writers, however, she contends, "are less concerned with the motivations in individual psychology for the telling of a given story than with general tendencies in the nature of narrative itself." As a consequence, in Gothic fiction our attention is deflected away from character analysis and toward the phenomenology of the narrative act.

Haunted by the insistent clamor of so many discordant voices, the reader feels driven to seek meaning in the ordering and placement of each narrative within the text. In some Gothic narratives, the tales are simply juxtaposed and the reader is invited to establish connections between the stories and to discover the rationale of their sequencing. For readers of *Dracula* this activity proves relatively satisfying, yet for the reader of a text such as Hogg's *The Private Memoirs and Confessions of a Justified Sinner,* which is more thoroughgoing in its Gothicism, the process yields nothing but frustration.

Encapsulation, an alternative arrangement which relies on the use of frame narratives—that is, the story-within-the-story structure—is more typical of the Gothic. In fact, this "Chinese-box" composition, though utilized by other narrative forms, is so frequently pressed into service by the Gothic writer that it may be said to be its most readily identifiable structural feature. A number of reasons have been proffered as to why this arrangement was so popular with Gothic authors. The inset-tale pattern subverts linear and chronological sequence; it captures to some degree the fragmentation and disarray associated with extreme subjective states such as dream, hallucination, madness; it implies a kind of magnetized core; it reminds us that the world we have entered is a purely aesthetic one. The Gothic tale seems less preoccupied with "what happens" per se than with how it gets itself told and how it is received. This intense self-referentiality of the Gothic is achieved to a great extent through the strategy of encapsulation. Thus the Gothic is, as Day remarks, "a display of story-telling" (1985, 47), as well as a pensive meditation on the phenomenology of story-making and story-transmission.

This transmission is enacted over and over in Gothic fantasy as its narrator-readers decipher all manner of decaying manuscripts and as its rapt listeners are spellbound by a teller who burns to divulge some ghastly tale. Gothic fantasy dramatizes to an unusual extent the interactive relationship of performing story-teller and audience-listener. This preoccupation appears, albeit in undeveloped form, as early as Radcliffe's *The Italian,* whose framing preface provides an enveloping context in which the lurid story of Schedoni will unfold: "[C]annot you relate it now?" pleads the fascinated English tourist ([1797] 1968, 3). A century later Henry James invokes the same framing device: a bevy of houseguests will beg to hear the "charming" story of a governess and her ghosts. In *Melmoth* especially, as Mark Hennelly notes, "[A]ll the many acts of reading, narrating and performing before an audience create a *Doppelgänger* relationship between Maturin's own readers and the fictional audiences who are first terrified and taught" (1981, 666).

The Gothic fantasy also, through its manipulation of the frame-narrative device, sets forth some useful distinctions between the roles of reader-audience and listener-audience. For example, it urges us to consider the impact of the storyteller's appearance and voice and thus to compare the experience of hearing a story with the very different experience of reading one. The Gothic fantasy, in dramatizing the storyteller in the act of storytelling, raises to prominence the related issue of performance, normally more a theatrical concern than a literary one. Oddly enough, Gothic fantasy seems to suggest that the activity of listening and seeing—acting as an audience—is fraught with more danger than the activity of reading. Newman's comments on the reader-audiences of *Frankenstein* render this distinction apparent:

> Mrs. Saville . . . is kept safely outside the scheme of the novel precisely because she is *reading,* because what she confronts is the written word. The novel's logic suggests that Walton, by offering her a transcription of the stories he hears, exposes her merely to a simulacrum, a representation of a monstrous story. . . . Mrs. Saville can read the story without any danger to herself. It may, as Walton fears, make her blood "congeal with horror," but it poses her no real threat. Like Medusa's head in Perseus's mirror, what she reads is only an image of monstrosity; it therefore loses its power, its danger. The frames thus mark [this] . . .

exclusion of Mrs. Saville—and the reader as well—from the horror of the narratives they contain.

Implicit here is a recognition that the physically present listener stands in much greater danger of enthrallment than a safely distanced reader counterpart. Thus what the Gothic novel itself implies is that it is the drama, not the novel, which is the more effective vehicle for representation of the Gothic.

Yet, as we have already discovered, the earliest theatrical adaptations of Gothic tales failed to exploit this inherent potentiality. *Melmoth*'s Stanton alludes to this failure, delivering a withering condemnation of the happy-horror mentality of the Gothic Melodrama and its clamorous audiences: "In the galleries were the happy souls who waited for . . . the ghost . . . in her dripping shroud." Pandering to "happy souls" who demanded uncomplicated excitement and agreeable shivers is what the Gothic Melodrama did best. Maturin, it would seem, like Shelley, had little patience with such sham-horror mongering. In Gothic narrative, on the other hand, audiences are shocked into receptivity, punished for their deafness, or else, in the case of the thrill-seeking variety, removed from earshot. In every instance the Gothic insists that the story to be told is startling, somber, and worthy of its audience's deepest concentration. This meta-Gothic commentary which the Gothic renders on itself is brought about through the strategic deployment of the encapsulation structure.

Napier contends that this intense self-regardedness of the Gothic is due to the fact that "[i]t does not entirely trust itself as genre" (1987, 67). This manic self-fixation, however, should be attributed to the Gothic's parodic impulses—having demolished all other systems, the Gothic is left with nothing but itself to look at. Thus its endings do not gesture, even vaguely, toward some alternative system. Instead, the Gothic ending points backwards, explicitly or implicitly, to its point of origin—which in turn propels the reader forward toward a most unfinal finale. Gothic plots, with their disconcerting predilection for looping back on themselves, are so many closed circuits. Plot in the Gothic accomplishes little or nothing in the way of purposeful activity; Gothic plots have more to do with stasis, impotence and encryptment. Plot of the conventional sort, that moves "from point a to point b, either physically or psychically," as Day puts it, is replaced in the Gothic with a trembling, a running in place, or a frenzied running in circles. Acceleration does nothing to alter the direction. Many Gothics seem in retrospect to resemble so many relay races which finish up where they started.

These structural features—encapsulation, circularity, pointedly unreliable narration, problematic closure, pervasive parody—and the thematics they embodied ran deeply counter to the fundamental orientation of the nineteenth-century stage, a stage which Geoffrey Wall has aptly characterized as "a lavish ethical-sentimental picture book" (1984, 19). Paralleling the stage's persistent sentimentalization of Gothic content was its refusal to seek theatrical equivalents for these stylistic features.

Granted, this would have been no easy task even under more felicitous circumstances. Those early stage adaptors were attempting to graft a genre absorbed with its own literariness onto a genre which evinced little interest in such matters. A second complicating factor, one which plagues all would-be adaptors of narrative source material, is the unavoidable collision of two temporally alien modes of discourse. As theatre semiotician Keir Elam notes, whereas narrative is "oriented towards an explicit *there* and *then,* towards an imaginary 'elsewhere' set in the past, . . . dramatic worlds are presented as hypothetically actual constructs . . . seen in progress here and now" (1980, 110). This temporal discrepancy is exacerbated in the case of Gothic adaptation because Gothic narrative is so often rendered as retrospective. In other words, by the time "the thing"—the precipitating event—gets "taken down," it has already receded into an unreclaimable past. This tendency of Gothic narrative makes it doubly resistant to stage adaptation.

In the face of these considerable obstacles, the early adaptors opted for an easy "solution"—they consistently selected a small, episodic portion of the parent narrative, refurbished this snippet as a self-sufficient entity, and scrapped the rest of the text. The effect was one of "concentration," as Meisel suggests, as opposed to the sprawling, rambling effect of the Gothic novel (1983, 263). There was no attempt to represent, for example, the frame-structure of Gothic fiction. One tale would be dramatized (usually the one with the most sentimental interest—stories of young lovers and of parent-child reunions were popular); the rest would be discarded. In this manner the whole problem of incongruent temporal relationships posed by the enframing narrative could be sidestepped. Similarly, by ignoring the pressure of competing narratives, the issue of verification (a central preoccupation of the Gothic novel) could likewise be disregarded.

Benjamin West's adaptation of *Melmoth* illustrates the consequences of this failure to discover and deploy theatrical formulations of the Gothic narrative's structural features. As already indicated, West's play was a dramatization of one of the inset tales of *Melmoth*—"The Tale of Guzman's Family." Whereas Maturin's version concludes uneasily, hesitantly, West's terminates with resounding finality. Maturin presents an enframing context for the tale; West presents it as a discrete entity. The ramifications of this shift are extensive. In the source narrative, Melmoth's role is that of a storyteller, and the tale is offered as a veiled warning: Melmoth recounts the story of Guzman's family to a particularly obtuse listener who remains incapable of seeing that the story has anything to do with himself. Aliaga fails to hear the threat posed to his child, a threat encoded within Melmoth's apparently irrelevant digression. His deafness serves to align him with the insensate old ones of the Guzman story. As in the

story, the child pays; Aliaga's unfitness as an audience eventuates in dire consequences. West, however, declines Maturin's invitation to dramatize the interactive dynamics of storyteller and listener. His audience has no reason to consider
the implications of inattentive audition. In this case, the play really does have
nothing to do with them. Audienceship, which in *Melmoth* is fraught with
danger, is simply not an issue in West's adaptation. *Melmoth,* although much
preoccupied with problems of narration, does, surprisingly, have a great deal
to say as well about the nature of theatrical activity. Yet West, because he has
eliminated the frame structure of his source, remains mute on the subject,
instead diverting his audience's attention to the villainous machinations of his
nefarious Melmoth.

The same policy of avoidance was pursued even in the adaptation of Gothic
texts that relied on the simpler strategy of juxtaposition rather than encapsulation. Hamilton Deane, in revamping *Dracula* for the stage, followed the practices of his predecessors, streamlining and compressing his unwieldy source.
In so doing he jettisoned substantial portions of the novel. He deleted, for
example, the contents of the Harker journal, that section of the novel which
recounts Jonathan's terrifying experience in Dracula's castle.

Instead, predictably, Deane concentrated on the theme of the imperilled
maiden and on the inevitable but suspenseful demise of the demonic villain. The
loss of the Harker narrative is crucial, for it functions as a kind of prologue to
and a point of reference for all subsequent events. Even more critical, however,
is the consequent exclusion of a scene of storytelling and audition. While
*Dracula*, even more than *Melmoth*, consistently proclaims its textuality, it too
ruminates on the roles of performer and of audience. Like Señor Aliaga, Harker
is told a tale that seems to have no direct bearing on himself. Yet it is, like
Melmoth's story of Walberg, a cryptic threat, which he, like Aliaga, fails to
decipher.

Dracula's chronicle of feudal conquest is more than just a bedtime story
for his guest. Although there is no direct evidence that the tale is consciously
intended to frighten Harker, the story's savagery and the teller's unfeigned relish
in its gruesome details betrays a latent, barely withheld ferocity. Harker describes the performance: "He grew excited as he spoke . . . grasping anything
on which he laid his hands as though he would crush it by main strength" (Stoker
[1897] 1965, 39). For a brief instant, Dracula is not dissembling. His story
possesses him, tells itself. It is a performance that could not, should not be
misread. Yet it is. Ignoring all visual and aural evidence to the contrary, Harker
accepts for truth the duplicitous disclaimer: "The warlike days are over. Blood
is too precious a thing in these days of dishonorable peace; and the glories of
the great race are as a tale that is told" ([1897] 1965, 39). Harker, his name
notwithstanding, hears the text, but the subtext completely escapes him.

To dismiss the story as "a tale that is told" is the classic blunder of the

Gothic listener. For Harker, the account is "most fascinating"—interesting, thrilling, but certainly not frightening—while the teller is merely quaint. In the midst of this very "writerly" text is a highly charged theatrical moment in which a sinister teller performs a deadly tale before an unsuspecting, endangered audience. Such a scene needs no adaptation to be suitable for the stage. Yet these are precisely the scenes which Deane's *Dracula* and the Gothic Melodrama never undertook to portray. Instead it titillated its audiences with lurid lighting and trick bats.

In essence then, the model which the stage adapters needed to consult was the model of theatrical activity which the Gothic texts themselves were able to furnish. Certainly no stage adaptation could present a verbatim transcription of its source text. (After all, the most "faithful" stage adaptation one could imagine of a text such as *Frankenstein* would be the tossing on stage of a packet of letters for the audience to read.) While it is quite true that the stage can not legitimately represent the literariness of the Gothic text, it is quite capable of representing other aspects of the Gothic—and not exclusively thematic ones, either.

The synchronousness of Gothic form and thematics demonstrated by Gothic narrative texts suggest that any portrayal of Gothic thematic concerns by the stage would demand the implementation of at least some Gothic structural features. As we have already seen, much of the thematic content of the Gothic is generated by the concerted interaction of these stylistic elements. Thus, for example, if the source Gothic narrative employs the frame-narrative structure, the would-be Gothic dramatist needs to apply its theatrical analogue—the play-within-the-play arrangement. (There is no need to invent it—the form was common in Renaissance drama.) If the parent-narrative offers multiple accounts of the same event, the dramatic adaptation must follow suit by providing multiple, variant presentations of the same scene. If the procreant text parodies readily identifiable prose models, the stage adaptation is obliged to parody dramatic ones. Not to do so is to disturb this synchronousness which is such an indispensable attribute of the Gothic mode. Thus, in ignoring the structural imperatives of the Gothic, the Gothic melodramatists were in fact disregarding its animating spirit.

Given the nineteenth-century stage's passion for reproductive fidelity whatever the content of any given play (even if fairyland, it was to be a convincing fairyland), it is small wonder that the adaptors discarded a structure which emphasized its own artificiality. While the nineteenth-century Gothic narrative was flatly denying that it was itself any sort of an analogue to reality, the nineteenth-century stage was strenuously engaged in making itself over into just that. The "realization"—the enactment and animation of a painted canvas—emblematized this self-imposed mission. Given the context of the staging practices and dramatic aesthetics of the day, the failure of the Gothic melodramatists to invoke Gothic structural features makes perfect sense. Furthermore, given its proclivity for protecting and pleasing its audiences, it is again not surprising that the Gothic Melodrama did not actualize the performance model embodied in Gothic fiction, a model which stressed the danger inherent in theatrical activity.

The novel *Dracula* itself demonstrates the tension between these two conflicting impulses. There is, on the one hand, the melodramatic impulse made manifest in the novel's tableau scenes, scenes which are visually unambiguous—Mina's bloodstained nightgown speaks for itself. The Gothic impulse, on the other hand, is represented by the interposition of the narrative voices who for so long misread these scenes, who try, in David Seed's words, "to avoid recognizing their disturbing implications" (1965, 66). Like Dracula's recitation, which Harker mishears, these picture scenes are likewise misread. The inability or unwillingness to recognize danger in the narrated story or in the spectacle always, in the Gothic, augurs dire consequences. *Dracula* at such moments presents the collision of the melodramatic and the Gothic modes—the skewed interpretation of a semiotically unambiguous vision.

As long as the stage continued to embrace the structure of the melodrama with its linearity, its insistence on resolution and closure, its disinterest in metatheatrical commentary, the Gothic mode could not survive the transition to the stage. Likewise, as long as the stage persisted in its commitment to "realization," the Gothic would remain confined to the pages of narrative text.

Even when the melodrama was abandoned, the subsequent popularity of realism, as we have already discovered, once again precluded the emergence of a Gothic drama. Besides the fortuitous influences which have already been cited—the Expressionist movement, the manifestoes of Artaud—the rediscovery in the 1960s of the techniques of metatheatrical performance abetted a new willingness to experiment with form. The quality of self-referentiality, which had for so long been absent from the stage and which is a crucial stylistic feature of the Gothic mode, was becoming evident in the plays being produced by the alternative theatre movement. Peter Ansorge remarks that, while metatheatre was "not . . . a discovery of the fringe," the "language of the fringe . . . abound[ed] in theatrical metaphors" (1975, 73). The stage was renouncing its allegiance to realization, insisting instead on the derealized and the theatrical. This shift, while it did not in itself produce a Gothic drama, did, however, create an environment that was much more hospitable to its inception.

Gradually, unconsciously, the avant-garde playwrights were beginning to tread the trail which the Gothic novelists had, in a sense, already blazed. Harold Pinter, for example, discovers, as we shall see, a theatrical analogue to the narrative's unreliable narrator; Tom Stoppard, in the wake of Pirandello, creates the encapsulation effect by means of the play-within-the-play structure.

As will become evident, the NeoGothic drama exhibits the structural strategies of Gothic narrative transformed into theatrical equivalents. As in Gothic fiction, thematics and form remain highly "synchronous." Moreover, as is also typical of Gothic fiction, the various structural devices are themselves tightly enmeshed. However, for the purposes of examination and in the interest of sharper clarity, each structural feature will be attended to separately, with the exception of encapsulation and self-referentiality, which seem to demand discussion as a single unit. Each formal feature will be studied as it appears in a specific Gothic text and as it reappears in a selected NeoGothic play. (This is not to claim, however, that the feature under discussion is the only Gothic structural element in any given play: most of the plays discussed contain a number of such Gothic stylistic features.) The final portion of this segment of the chapter will be devoted to a more extensive investigation of the structure of Peter Weiss's *Marat-Sade,* a play which contains so many Gothic structural features as to seem almost paradigmatic. It affords a useful recapitulation of the whole discussion and, more significantly, it demonstrates conclusively that the Gothic does indeed haunt the Postmodernist stage.

The foregrounding of narrative unverifiability is a useful feature with which to begin because it broaches in a straightforward way the Gothic formulation of the problem of narrator reliability. Pinter's *The Caretaker* is well suited to this discussion, for its inset monologues are not theatrical soliloquies, but instead stories which function much as first-person narratives do in Gothic fiction. A comparison between this play and Henry James's *The Turn of the Screw,* though they seem an unlikely match, yields some uncanny parallels.

Both, to begin with, have inspired a giddying assortment of responses. As one commentator has remarked wryly of *The Turn of the Screw,* "The literary criticism has itself grown to horrifying dimensions" (Siebers 1983, 560). James's caretaker has been labelled a sexually repressed spinster, a victimized clairvoyant, a psychopathic killer, a lovelorn maiden, a brave and resourceful heroine; her charges have been variously characterized as demonic, naughty, terrified, innocent, victimized. Even the apparently prosaic Mrs. Grose undergoes a strange sea change depending on the predisposition of her interpreter. There is even some basis in this trap of a text to argue that none of the characters of the governess's account exist—that they are all figments of Douglas's creative imagination, or even that he himself is a fictional creation of the prologue narrator's imagination. While the readings elicited by Pinter's play are not quite so numerous, they are still so extraordinarily diverse as to give one pause: Aston is a Christ-figure, an artist, a maniac, a victim, a wreck, a fool; Mich is brotherly, vicious, materialistic, sadistic, sensitive, insane. Even Davies, who hardly seems inscrutable, becomes an enigmatic figure—cunning, stupid, selfish, helpless, victimized, neurotic.

The ultimate source of these wildly diverse readings can be located in the phenomenon of storytelling. In the case of *The Turn of the Screw,* all of the characters are the creatures and creations of a master storyteller. Siebers elaborates this point:

> The frame places in doubt the superficial difference between characters by undermining its authority. If the reader wishes to impose a difference on either the governess or the children, he must do so on his own authority. (1983, 569)

Even if we arbitrarily accept the governess as "real," we must still take into account that *she* is telling a story—her interpretation (of indeterminate reliability) of what may or may not have been a real experience. When we turn to Pinter's play, we believe ourselves to be on firmer ground because we are not asked to make the same sorts of distinctions that James seems to demand of us. In other words, we are not distanced and displaced from the core event by any intervening structure. Why then is it that we cannot precisely decide what is happening in *The Caretaker*?

The mystery can be traced back to the onstage storytelling event. These inset narratives do not adhere to dramatic conventions, but rather to narrative ones, specifically the conventions of Gothic narrative. Hence they do not reveal the "true self" of the teller, and they are not any more reliable, true, or untrue than the character's interpersonal dialogue. Guido Almansi, though he uses the term "monologue," makes the same point:

> On the traditional stage, characters use dialogue for their underhanded strategy, but reveal their true selves in monologues. This is not true of Pinter's plays, where both dialogue and monologue follow a foolproof technique of deviance. You can trust his characters neither when they are talking to others nor when they are talking to themselves. (1981, 80)

He summarizes thus: Pinter's characters "are not just occasionally unreliable; they are untrustworthy by definition. . . . The Pinter hero lies as he breathes: consistently and uncompromisingly" (1981, 82–83). He goes on to suggest that the contradictory interpretations that Pinter's work usually evokes is due to the fact that "[h]onorable critics ponderously assess or discuss the declarations of the Pinter character as if they were reliable" (1981, 82). Almansi's reasoning, while it goes a long way toward explaining the diversity of opinion regarding the Pinter narrator, is nonetheless too pat. To decide that Mick or Aston or Davies always lies is just as arbitrary as deciding that their dialogue is duplicitous but that the stories are always "true." How then are we to "hear" Aston's story? The best clue as to how to respond has been given to us by Pinter himself: "The thing that people have always missed is that it isn't necessary to conclude that everything Aston says about his experiences in the mental hospital is true" (Bensky [1966] 1967, 105). We are not advised to dismiss Aston's tale as a lie or even a fiction; rather, we are gently reminded that the boundary is impossible to fix. This interdiction of certainty, even the certainty of disbelief—even, in the extreme instance, the certainty of uncertainty, is characteristic of the Gothic. It does not honor such wishes as those of Stoppard's Guildenstern, who "like[s] to know where [he] is, [and] even if [he doesn't] know where [he] is, [he] like[s] to know *that*" (95).

Thus we have no means of verifying Aston's story. Even a perceptive commentator such as A. R. Braunmuller, who recognizes that Aston's "meditative memory-discourse may be largely a retrospective fiction," is, despite this insight, misled into assuming that Aston perceives his story as a finished, polished explanation of his condition: the story "represents his satisfying conception of his origins and his present state" (1981, 162). Actually, Aston's story has the sound of a work-in-progress, the details of which he is still tinkering with, much as he fiddles with sockets and toasters. This rough-draft status provides yet another explanation for the abrupt self-contradictions in the narrative—"I used to have kind of hallucinations. They weren't hallucinations" (54–55). We could, on the other hand, accept the "explanation" Aston himself offers: "I couldn't . . . get . . . my thoughts . . . together" (57). (The ellipses, rendered as brief pauses by the actor, parallels the semantic meaning. Aston may be having trouble just trying to get his sentence "together.") Still another way of hearing Aston's story is to hear it as the noises made by a mind turning itself about, trying to get its bearings—backtracking, making false starts, reversing directions. In any event, no matter which way we hear the story, there is no reason to be certain that Aston perceives or presents his story as a justification for his "present state"—which itself is open to conjecture. What the story simply provides is, in classic Gothic fashion, a sequence of facts, or information presented as fact. Nor have we any means of sorting out which portions of the story are Aston's and which are cribbed from some other source. The descriptive phrase " a man of distinction" could well be someone else's expression which Aston has plagiarized because he likes the sound of it. Certainly the approbatory description jars with the starkly crude "[w]e're going to do something to your brain." If Aston is less than sane ("shell-shocked" is the epithet often applied to him), his narrative becomes that much more suspect. Whatever its defects may be, however, Aston's recital of this bizarre, pathetic story rings so painfully true that the offstage audience is charmed into believing every word. Not surprisingly, Aston is hardly ever vilified by commentators.

In contrast, James's novella (*the* textbook for narrator unreliability) occasionally appears to offer some means of verifying its narrator's story. It does so by seeming to provide two renditions of one event—one "direct," the other "retrospective." A useful illustration in this context is the apparition of the ghost of Miss Jessell in the schoolroom. In the first, the "direct" rendition, Miss Jessell remains silent; in the second version (the governess's subsequent conversation with Mrs. Grose), the governess supplies lines for Miss Jessell. This discrepancy would seem to indicate that the governess is embroidering the "facts" of her experience and/or that she is manipulating Mrs. Grose. But this commonsensical conclusion collapses under the weight of the realization that *both* accounts are filtered through the same consciousness. We have no way of making contact with the event itself, no authority to credit or discredit either version. The ontological status of Aston's narrative is analogous because here too the event is locked away from us in the past (if indeed it ever transpired at all). Thus the effect of both novel and stage piece is the creation of a sense of gaps which we are invited, even lured, to close. "The most important part of conversation," as Ronald Schleiffer astutely surmises, "are James's ubiquitous dashes— . . . the hushes," what is left out (1980, 310). He might just as well be describing the Pinter pause.

The Pinter example admirably illustrates the confusion generated by a single first-person account. When other accounts are added, the disorienting effect is compounded. The use of multiple accounts was, for this reason, much favored by Gothic writers. In Gothic narrative, of course, the tension is established between narrative a and narrative b (and c and d, etc.). This multiple-account technique is well suited to a foregrounding of the acts of perception and recall as distressingly problematic. However, in Pinter's drama, as we have discovered, the tension is instead established between narrative (past event reconstituted into unverifiable story) and performance (the story as rhetorical speech-event transpiring in the present moment of the stage). Thus Pinter is able to theatricalize what is ordinarily an exclusively narrative device.

The dramatization of multiple points of view, however, is fraught with more difficulty than that which attends the dramatization of a single account. One limited solution is the specialized form of theatre known as "Readers Theatre," wherein the text *is* the action and in which the mode of oral, bardic story-telling is the dominant, if not the exclusive, mode. In Readers Theatre, the manuscript is often physically present on stage as are other literary props such as lecterns and stools. Often too the program is billed as a reading or readings, rather than as a play. As Jerry Pickering notes regarding adaptation by Readers Theater, "In the area of the novel, the Gothic works like *Dracula* or *Frankenstein* have been particularly successful" (1973, 23). One can see why this would be so. If, however, one demands a full-scale adaptation of the multiple-account Gothic text, a different strategy must be invented.

This strategy entails a shift from the presentation of multiple narratives to the presentation of multiple performances—not performances of narrative (as in *The Caretaker*) but performance of events. David Halliwell's *K. D. Dufford* affords an example of multiple performances of a single event—the same event is played and replayed, but with slight variations (indicative of a new view or interpretation of the event) each time. This strategy undermines the dramatic convention which holds that performance is more reliable than reportage (the theatrical version of the adage that seeing is believing, that eyewitnessing is privileged). Like Gothic multiple narration, this technique subverts belief in a knowable, objective reality more radically than does the use of the solitary first-person account. In order to observe the technique put into practice, we now turn to Halliwell's play and to James Hogg's *The Private Memoirs and Confessions of a Justified Sinner,* a multiple-account Gothic narrative.

The structure of Hogg's novel has been the main focus of critical investigation and with good reason. The text is a forceful and elaborate specimen of multiple-account narration. If a central project of the Gothic is the undermining of conventional conceptions about objective reality and human identity, *The Confessions* accomplishes this task brilliantly, for its commentators cannot reach a consensus even about a matter as simple as the number of its narrators and narratives. The terrifying insinuation of the novel is that the private viewpoint is all one has, that the notion of a balanced, accurate, "objective" view is merely a cherished figment of the collective imagination.

*The Confessions* mocks the progressivist impetus of a novel such as *Dracula,* whose process roundly affirms the translation of experience into what Wall terms "the soothing fixity of text" (1984, 16). In *Dracula* too, as Wall suggests, "the circulation of what is written" is valorizing: the text becomes a "gift" to be shared (1984, 16). In Hogg's deeper-dyed Gothic fantasy, the making public, the gesture of "circulation," is highly ambiguous, and it neither valorizes nor soothes; rather it promotes anxiety. In *Dracula* the opening up of the book of private experiences—Harker's journal—is rendered as an act of communal sharing; in contrast, the opening of the Sinner's pamphlet and its "laying before the public" is imaged as a ghoulishly prurient invasion of privacy, strangely akin to the rifling of the grave and its contents. Furthermore the breaking of the seal on Jonathan's diary signals an imminent restoration of clarity and coherence. The unscrolling of Robert's diary, on the other hand, serves only to augment bewilderment. Even the "Editor" eventually surrenders to the unfathomableness of his text: "With regard to the work itself, I dare not venture a judgment, for I do not understand it."

Hogg, in accordance with the Gothic principle that multiple stories enhance ambiguity, refuses to grant authority to any one of his tellers. In the Gothic, multiple view conveys nothing more than the essential unknowability of matter and personality. The Editor's supposedly more privileged, more reliable account is disclosed as simply one among others—equally incoherent, equally incomplete, equally perplexing.

This refusal to grant authority even to a recognizably public voice is freighted with all sorts of unsettling ramifications. It implies, for instance, that official versions of reality—the outsider's accounts which one encounters in a public text such as a newspaper for example—are no more to be credited than the diary of a certified lunatic. In this sense, Hogg's novel may be said to speak even more powerfully to an age of mass media than to its own. This same distrust of the official voice of public discourse emerges in a play which strikingly mimics Hogg's juxtaposed multiple narrations—David Halliwell's *K. D. Dufford Hears K. D. Dufford Ask K. D. Dufford How K. D. Dufford'll Make K. D. Dufford*. The play is, as its title suggests, a combination echo chamber and hall-of-mirrors. In *Dufford* multiple viewpoint becomes both strategy and subject. It concerns one K. D. Dufford, a hapless, pathetic "good-for-nowt" who plans and executes the murder of an eight-year-old girl, hoping thereby to "make" some record of his existence. At least that is one version of Dufford's "story," for the play provides approximately six "readings"—interpretations rendered by way of performance—of Dufford and his crime.

At first glance, *Dufford*'s structure seems to bear a closer resemblance to *Dracula*'s structure in that the various segments of the Dufford story repeatedly interrupt one another and overlap. In fact, the play draws on the scrapbook format as well: *Dufford* imitates and updates *Dracula*'s assemblage of various types of public and private texts (its telegrams, letters, news clippings, shipping bills, etc.) The private text is represented by the scenes themselves. Public discourse is inserted into the between-scene interludes. Slide projections, for example, of newspaper cuttings reporting Dufford's crime are projected onto an onstage screen during these between-scene interludes. During one of the interludes, a printed poster advertising a play by one "Claude Phillips" entitled "Nineteen Nineteen Shirley Street" appears on stage. The exhibition of these artifacts of public discourse are accompanied by a recording of a ludicrously sentimental, simpleminded pop ballad which bathetically speculates on the riddle of Dufford's motivation. Neither Phillip's play nor its author exists even though the poster itself is palpably real. The audience recognizes that the play's title is an allusion to Dufford's address. "Nineteen Nineteen Shirley Street" does, however, materialize during the course of *Dufford* as a play-within-the-play. Likewise, over the course of several scene breaks, footage from Dufford's home movie of the child's murder is shown. To further complicate matters, the audience is offered two distinct filmic versions of the event.

Unlike *Dracula*, though, *Dufford*'s various strands remain uncollated. Instead, as in Hogg's text, the various versions are simply juxtaposed. (Even the play-within-the-play is not integrated into the rest of the play, but remains a discrete presentation, yet another variant of the Dufford story.) Again, unlike *Dracula*, the various strands do not represent pieces of a puzzle, which, once assembled, will reveal the "true story."

*Dufford* translates narrative multiple viewpoint into multiple performance. Moreover, the multiple reenactments of the same event represent not the interpretations or fantasies of various narrators (as in multiple-account narrative), but rather are so many parodic reinterpretations of the event, each according to a specific theatrical style. Thus, for example, in the farcical version, Dufford is a clown, Janet is "a spoilt, willful, sour-faced child," and the murder is clumsily accidental—Dufford is so inept that he botches everything. In the operatic version, Dufford is apotheosized into a passionate hero whose only crime is a mercy-killing committed out of a pure and holy love for the girl's mother. In the melodramatic version, Dufford is "serpentine," "cool," "ruthless"; he is attired, appropriately, in a black raincoat; his victim dies spectacularly, horribly. To some extent the audience is pre-cued as to which version is being presented by changes in lighting and by Dufford's ubiquitous but ever-changing raincoat—"medium blue," "short blue," "short, smart, neat black raincoat." The Dufford-actor of "Nineteen Nineteen Shirley Street" sports a "very distinctive," specially designed raincoat. Such blatant glamorization urges us to recognize the essential fictionality of so-called docudrama.

In this matter of cuing, the reader of Halliwell's play has the advantage over his or her audience-counterpart because Halliwell's stage directions do indicate which of the versions is to be taken as the authoritative one—one of the versions conforms to the style of conventional, realistic theatre. This positing of a reliable version by means of the stage directives does, of course, run counter to the Gothic impulse to distort and confuse. Thus a strict Gothic reading of the play would be better served by their disregard. The theatre audience's selection of the "correct" version, however, is a more difficult task despite the semiotic cues. In either case, nonetheless, the play's structure remains resolutely Gothic.

It is not the concussive act at the core of *Dufford* that renders it Gothic (although violence so often figures in the Gothic cosmos), but rather its structure. *Dufford* manifests a Gothic glee in the confusion and anxiety engendered by multiple tellers and tales, and then goes it one better by demonstrating how the audiovisual gadgetry of the twentieth century fosters even greater distortion, how the implementation of mass media actually intensifies confusion among the global villagers. In this respect, Halliwell is much closer to Hogg than he is to Stoker. Whereas Stoker extols the mechanics of information transmission (Mina uses a typewriter and a dictaphone; telegrams are exchanged), Hogg and Halliwell regard the process with a wary eye. In Stoker's text, the monster is laid to rest, silenced, presumably by the clacking of a typewriter; in Hogg's text, a printer's devil of a devil invades the printing press. Both Hogg and Halliwell explicate the distortion that multiplies geometrically through public dissemination of stories that are, ultimately, unknowable and certainly unrepeatable. The telling and retelling of the tale renders it that much stranger and more sinister than ever. Halliwell adds the latest complication of the age-old problem of misconstruction—the new, appalling power of the media to generate its own stories, which in turn generate even more stories. Simon Gray, in reviewing *Dufford,* notes the self-perpetuating, circular nature of the process:

Halliwell's murderer . . . manages to construct from newspaper items and all the other jargons of "daily life" a grotesquely persuasive alternative reality—a reality which can only be entered through an act of violence which itself becomes the stuff of public sensation (through the newspapers, etc.) and thus will feed thousands of other private fantasies. (1969, 440)

The ending of the play gestures toward an endless recycling. A new potential Dufford, wearing the specially designed "Dufford Raincoat"—a fashion no doubt inspired by the "feature film" based on the Phillips play, itself based on the proceedings of the Dufford case, based on Dufford himself, who, because he is such a nonentity, must construct himself from his media texts, which are unreliable accounts of questionable events, and so on *ad infinitum*—arrives at Dufford's old hangout, the public library, to pick up his girlfriend. A sequel is being planned, suggests Halliwell, another spinoff of a spinoff. Just as origins are occluded, so too are endings. It is this aspect of the play, its working out of the implications of Gothic structure in theatrical terms, not its violence or its villain-hero (whether "monster" or "very ordinary, rather pale young man") that secures its inclusion in the NeoGothic canon.

Peter Ansorge, in his *Disrupting the Spectacle,* faults Halliwell's use of multiple viewpoint, contending that it betokens a want of originality:

The loss of a sense of authorial omniscience, the emergence of an unreliable narrator who is at sea in a conflicting wash of different "points of view" has been a feature of the modern novel ever since James wrote *The Sacred Fount.* (1975, 73)

Actually, the Gothic novelists had been experimenting with multiviewpoint long before James, but the point which needs to be addressed is that multiviewpoint on stage has rarely been attempted. Although *K. D. Dufford* retreats from a full exploitation of its own Gothic potential, it is nonetheless noteworthy as evidence that Gothic multiple-account narrative can be translated into theatrical terms.

What Hogg (and to a lesser extent Halliwell) pose by exhibiting the "formative power of viewpoint" is, in Kiely's words, "an unstated challenge to the conventional roles of spectator and player" (1972, 217) or to reader and text. This disruption is emblematized in Hogg's text by the tennis match into which Robert insinuates himself. Kiely discusses the effect of this intrusion:

[H]e [Robert] attempts to redefine the "game" in mid-play, to transform himself from witness to major participant, . . . [thus] forc[ing] the other participants, quite against their will, to *watch* him, and in doing so, to become confused about their previous roles. (1972, 217–18)

Hogg mines the chaos that lurks beneath what seems the most ordered of human events, an unambiguous athletic contest. It is only once removed from a theatrical formulation of this new configuration of performer and audience. If one can imagine a theatrical version of Hogg's bizarre tennis match, one is quite close to the theatre of Tom Stoppard. It is precisely this confusion about the role of participant-performer as opposed to that of spectator-audience that Stoppard exploits with results that are "funny"—humorous, yet alien, strange, and disturbing.

This "redefin[ing] of the game in mid-play" is the *modus operandi* of *Rosencrantz and Guildenstern Are Dead* and *The Real Inspector Hound*.[4] Unlike Pinter or Halliwell, Stoppard evinces little interest in the unreliable narrator or in multiviewpoint drama, preferring to experiment instead with encapsulation and parody. The transformation of the enfolded tale into a dramatic trope—the enfolded play—enables Stoppard to dramatize the dynamics of performer and spectator and the effects that occur when that interactive relationship is "redefined." Thus *Rosencrantz and Guildenstern* as well as *Hound* become "displays" not of storytelling, as in Gothic narrative, but of play-making and play-going. As we shall soon discover, it little matters which side of the footlights one occupies. The "drama of terror" makes victims of its audience. It is no accident that the interpolated play in both *Hound* and *Rosencrantz and Guildenstern* is a "mousetrap."

It seems at first that there could be no prose correlative to a play such as *Rosencrantz and Guildenstern:* whereas its inset play is (as in *Hamlet*) a dumb show, in Gothic fiction the interpolated matter is almost always a linguistic artifact—a thing of words. In other words, Gothic encapsulated accounts are almost never embodied in mime or tableau. However, Stoppard's Tragedians present a pantomime, a *tableau vivant*—a moving (in both the kinetic and psychological senses) "picture" of the Hamlet story. There is, though, one Gothic text which does represent encapsulated material not in story form but rather as a silent, moving portrait which mimes the history of the sitter: Oscar Wilde's *The Picture of Dorian Gray*. The inset dumb show furnishes in both cases a pretext for the author's ruminations on the dynamic of spectator and spectacle, the spectacle in both instances likewise happening to be an artistic construct. The position occupied by the mute but restless picture in relation to its framing environment is, in both Wilde's and Stoppard's texts, dead center. "The Murder of Gonzago," the inset play (which occurs in act 2), is completely surrounded by its frame play *Rosencrantz and Guildenstern*. Wilde appropriately structures his novel in painterly rather than theatrical terms, but here also the centering of the picture is clear.

This spatial positioning reifies the thematic centrality of the inset mime. That is to say, the framing structure's indexical properties confer power and heightened significance on its core content. Both silent "movies" are surcharged with a power and a meaning which defies verbalization. In both cases, the spectator, confronted with this silent double, dimly intuits its significance but remains unable to decode its meaning. The bloated, scarred fact of his painted doppelgänger "speaks" to Dorian, but the exact purport of that ghastly face eludes him.

Ros and Guil accost their unspeaking doubles but, though troubled by their reflections, mental and literal, they remain, like old Aliaga, incapable of perceiving that the show has anything to do with them:

> *Ros:*  I know you, don't I? I never forget a face—(*he looks into the SPY'S face*) . . . not that I know you, that is. For a moment I thought—no, I don't know you. Yes, I'm afraid you're quite wrong. You must have mistaken me for someone else. (82)

Unlike the melodramatic mute, who is always and immediately understood, the Gothic tableau is consistently misread or else dismissed. This failure to decipher the semiotically coded message appears to bring down upon the head of the obtuse spectator the wrath of some sadistic schoolmaster-god.

This effect is accomplished by virtue of the fact that the interpolated material simultaneously embodies and masks a threat. To misread the message is to miss the warning. The pages of Gothic fiction teem with creatures who turn blind eyes and deaf ears to all manner of veiled and garbled threats. The implication seems to be that serious attention, like the rosary beads draped around the neck of the vampire's victim, will somehow avert disaster.

However, if we scrutinize this notion in the context of Wilde's novel and Stoppard's play, the efficacy of heedful observation becomes patently questionable, for we discover that to pay close attention in the Gothic is to become enthralled, so bewitched that the threat barely contained by the story or the spectacle ceases to matter—even if it were to be understood. This is the phenomenon which *Melmoth*'s Moncada describes; it is the phenomenon that defines the relationship of Dorian and his demon Other. There is no such thing as safe voyeurism in the Gothic; spectatorship is a most dangerous condition. Even if the spectator decides to "do" something to ward off the catastrophe prefigured by the spectacle, there is little evidence to conclude that such a gesture would make any difference. As Day suggests, in the world of the Gothic fantasy, "Those who act, whatever their intent, destroy themselves" (1985, 45). Thus when Dorian stabs his leering replica, the consequences rebound on him; when Guildenstern "stabs" the Player, his would-be victim gets up and walks away. Thus, although failure to read the subtextual warning seems to warrant punishment, a successful reading is no safeguard either.

Day argues that the only means of survival in the Gothic cosmos is a kind of alert passivity. He contends that "those who are passive, who refuse to be drawn into the illusion of action can be saved" (1985, 45). Stoppard, however, seems to suggest otherwise. *Rosencrantz and Guildenstern* is less about doing anything than it is about "keeping back," resisting the spectacle, playing the voyeur. This strategy completely misfires. "I think we'd be well advised to leave well alone" (110), opines Guildenstern, who hopes vainly that by not acting, by leaving Claudius's letter untouched, he'll survive. However, neither acting nor not-acting makes any difference; noninterference is about as effective as a retractable-bladed knife. In the Gothic *theatrum mundi,* there is no special providence in the fall of sparrows or in the entrapment of mice. Stoppard's play is one which, as Thomas Whitaker remarks, "might bring a glint to the ghostly eye of Oscar Wilde" (1977, 15).

While *Rosencrantz and Guildenstern* demonstrates the uselessness of non-participation as a defensive maneuver, *The Real Inspector Hound* dramatizes the process of enthrallment. Unlike Ros and Guil, who orbit outside the magnetic field of their inset play, Moon and Birdboot are dragged willy-nilly right into the core. By allowing Moon and Birdboot to penetrate the encapsulated play, Stoppard is able to theatricalize Gothic enthrallment. Moon and Birdboot become one with the spectacle they confront whether they will or not. In *Hound* the parasite play resembles a magnetized core whose lodestar pull neither can resist. Jim Hunter acknowledges this "monstrous power" of *Hound*'s encapsulated play: "[I]ts tentacles clutch Birdboot and Moon bodily from their seats and drag them to its maw" (1982, 171). Thus while *Melmoth*'s Moncada fuses psychologically with the spectacle he observes, Moon and Birdboot are literally caught up in it, their coalescence embodied, enacted.

This merger is all the more unexpected since the inset play seems so laughably feeble, nothing but a ludicrous compendium of stage murder-mystery clichés. Furthermore, we expect that Moon and Birdboot, as critics and thus by definition figures of impartial detachment, will remain outside the parameters of the play they observe. As long as the two play worlds remain separate, *Hound* is nothing more than a clever send-up of the stage whodunit juxtaposed with a gently parodic treatment of the pretensions of play reviewers. Until the point of collision, the parodic mode operates in the ways we normally expect of parody. For example, the inset play pokes good-natured fun at the stage thriller's penchant for contrived coincidence—Mrs. Drudge inevitably switches on the radio just at the precise moment that the police message regarding the escaped lunatic is announced.

When the two plays interpenetrate, however, the parody is no longer limited to a specific genre or class of people but becomes much more pervasive and serious. Although the consolidation of the two play worlds seems sudden, we have in a sense been prepared for it: presumably wise to the ways of stage thrillers, neither Moon nor Birdboot is able to construct a reading that explains the chain of facts with which they are presented. Every interpretation they offer is immediately demolished. Their repeated failure as detective-critics—the failure to figure out what is going on and who is doing what—suggests more than simple ineptitude on their part. The play they are reviewing, though it appears to adhere to the rules of its genre, is not cooperating. The puny analytical powers of Moon and Birdboot are no match for the forces of chaos and anarchy.

Once Birdboot and Moon have been drawn in to the force-field of the play, they are fair game. What should have been a highly controllable world—the well-made, well-rehearsed world of the stage whodunit—is instead revealed as a bizarre netherworld where what is supposed to be comfortingly fake is now dangerously real. A stage prop can fire "real" bullets which in turn kill the "real" Birdboot and the "real" Moon. The convention of the stage as the realm of the derealized is thus stood on its head: what is being parodied here is theatricality itself. The elaborately contrived, blatantly conventional, stagy world of the stage thriller is transformed into an ontological wilderness in which the protean "real" Inspector Hound is murderer and detective, hero, critic, and clown. As in the Gothic fantasy, the effect is an erosion of certainty. Nearing his end, Moon, like the hysterical Gothic narrator, is only "almost sure" he's not mad.

As the triumphant Puckeridge-Hound-Magnus-Albert stands over the inert bodies of his vanquished rivals, we seem to have arrived at that "startling dénouement" which Birdboot had confidently predicted. But in fact, we are more puzzled than ever, for we have no way of determining the causal interrelationship between the two plays. How, for example, did Puckeridge worm his way into the inset play? What ever became of the first Inspector Hound-actor? How did the Higgs corpse end up on stage? Even as the offstage audience chuckles at the adroit manipulation of the thriller formula, it is also being forced to perform mental cartwheels, continually correcting its perspective in a vain effort to follow what's going on. The overall effect is that the audience is induced to look backwards, to review again and again the chain of events, searching for clues to solve riddles which remain resistant to solution. As in the Gothic narrative, "forward movement" is revealed as nothing but "endless repetition" (Morris 1985, 307).

This looping backwards is even more apparent in *Rosencrantz and Guildenstern,* a play in which origins and endings remain pointedly occluded. Like the Gothic manuscript itself, the ontic situation of Ros and Guil is that of the foundling; their past is inaccessible to them. They "want to go home," but they cannot remember even so little as how to spell the words "wife" or "home." Their story of a summons shouted in the dawn, of a fist pounding on a shutter is no more verifiable than that of any Gothic taleteller. It is simply their explanation—memory or fabrication, we have no way of knowing—for their mysterious, displaced condition. Whenever they attempt to envision a past for themselves, they experience linguistic dysfunction, and their sentences, like those of Aston, shatter into so many hopelessly scattered fragments.

In their longing for patrimony and assimilation, they resemble no one so closely as Victor's forlorn, disassociated Monster, who fondly imagines that, by mastering the word for "home," he will find one. Just as the Monster earnestly scans the faces of his cottagers, hanging on their words, Ros and Guil, like two cryptographers, puzzle over the speeches of the *Hamlet* cast, searching for the clue that will "hie" them home.

Just as the mystery of origin is preserved, likewise too is the mystery of ending. Creatures of the "middle" that they are, originless, they cannot imagine an "ending" for themselves, anymore than they could "remember" a beginning: "I try to picture us arriving," agonizes Ros, "but my mind remains a blank" (107–8). Rosencrantz and Guildenstern simply disappear with the blackout of a spotlight—"Now you see [them], now you—." Their finales are theatrical and Gothic, for they simply vanish, like the Monster, "lost in darkness." Even death is not absolutely final in the Gothic cosmos; sometimes it is implicitly preludic—"an entrance somewhere else." That is why the Gothic dead are "unquiet sleepers." In the Gothic, as David Morris suggests, death is not the natural, logical "terminus of a long or short journey" (1985, 308). It "interrupts"; it "intrudes" (1985, 308). It *has* all happened before, as Guildenstern suspects, and it will happen again. "Next time" they won't "know better." They will repeat their coin-spinning, their wandering, their anxious questions. All will be, as Judith Wilt characterizes Gothic movement, "helpless repetition" (1980, 61). In the Gothic universe, no one ever knows better next time. "Do you call that an ending?" scoffs the Player and the reader or spectator who wants "a good story with a beginning, middle and end" (Stoppard 1967, 80). "That," however, is the only ending that the Gothic will vouchsafe.

Thus far we have separately examined specific Gothic stylistic features as each has been translated by its theatrical medium. Though no one NeoGothic drama includes all of these features (any more than any one Gothic narrative text contains every feature), Peter Weiss's *Marat-Sade,* in synthesizing so many of them, is prototypical in its fidelity to Gothic narrative patterns. As Otto Reinert remarks of *Marat-Sade,* "Not much that is of importance can be said about such a play in the traditional vocabulary of dramatic criticism" (1970, 923). The adoption of a Gothic vocabulary, however, enables one to say a good deal.

Circularity is an obsessive motif in the play; in fact, in *Marat-Sade* circularity is thematized, for it is two contending definitions of "revolution" (politicized circularity) which lie at the heart of the Marat-Sade debate. Actually Marat and Sade are reenacting a real seventeenth-century debate which Ronald Paulson summarizes as a conflict "between the strictly astronomical sense of repetition, a full circle, and the sense of a single revolution as an overthrow, a half-circle, a disruption, and so an irreversible change" (1983, 50). Sade, espousing the former meaning, therefore perceives revolution as a "vicious circle," whereas Marat, endorsing the latter sense, defines revolution as sweeping change, a turning inside out, a "seeing with fresh eyes" (27).

It is Sade's meaning which seems to carry the day in *Marat-Sade,* for the play is replete with images of sometimes frantic, sometimes mechanical rotation. The most terrible of these is the ceaseless winching up and dropping of the guillotine, which in turn is propelled by the constant unscrolling of the execution list to which "more names are added at the bottom . . . as the names are crossed off the top" (88). In stark contrast to this mechanized rotation is the mad spinning, the running in circles, of the madhouse inmates.

In structural terms one could argue too that the apparent movement of the play as a whole is circular. There is no attempt to provide any semblance of a linear narrative plot—it is after all, a foregone conclusion that the Marat-figure is to be "assassinated." Sade imposes his cyclic vision of history on his play by means of the "interruptus," a scene which skillfully undercuts any sense of history as forward progress. "Marching on" is exposed as an illusion, an historian's conceit. The "interruptus," though positioned near the end of the play, is not its final word. The last moments of the "epilogue" are incontestably Gothic.

The abrupt closing of the curtain on a play that is or may still be in progress theatricalizes the Gothic tradition of arbitrary closure. As with the Tragedians' show, which is never allowed to finish (as the Player informs Ros and Guil, things were "getting quite interesting when they decide[d] to stop it" [115]), we are cut off, prevented from knowing, denied the comfort of closure. In effect, there is no way of determining which definition of revolution is being presented. In other words, we cannot ascertain whether what we are witnessing is a revolt succeeding or a riot being squelched. In terms of the astronomical metaphor, we wonder whether we are in the presence of a renegade comet, or whether gravitational pull is about to restore the orbit. Weiss ends his play, as Gothic writers figuratively do, by literally pulling the curtain. What may be forming behind the curtain is an entirely new play, a genuine happening; on the other hand, the cast is perhaps being coerced into a repeat performance of the play they have just finished performing. Coulmier's panic suggests that a sweeping change is taking place, yet at the same time, the brutal suppression of the Patients by the Nurses hints that, when the dust settles, "everything" will be "just the same." In any case, it is the arbitrariness of the drawing of the curtain that is underscored.

Frenzied movement fills up most of the time and space of the play, but at odd moments, all activity ceases and a hush falls as the actors freeze in tableau. Framed by all the spinnings and gyrations is a still point, a magnetized core—the "realization" of David's serene, idealized portrait of a corpse. For Meisel, "No modern play . . . has made such a powerful and original use of pictorial realization as Peter Weiss's *Marat-Sade*" (1983, 437). This "powerful and original use" is, as will become evident, Sade's Gothic parody of the classic restraint of David's painting. This parodic relationship is disclosed by a comparative "reading" of painting and play.

Notably, in both versions, the human body is established as having a

Figure 1.  Jacques-Louis David, *Marat assassiné*
(*Musées royaux des Beaux-Arts de Belgique, Brussels, by permission*)

relationship of mutual exclusivity with written text. Simonne apprehends that writing is the opposite of "taking care" of the body, that writing will literally be the death of Marat. Marat's words—like Simonne's, put into his mouth by Sade—similarly equate writing with sickness and slavery. He always composes, he admits, "in a fever," and the task of preparing a manuscript on "the chains of slavery" is imaged as a delirious, delirium-producing "vicious cycle" of self-enslavement:

> I sat for three months
> twenty-one hours a day
> collecting material dreaming of material
> paper piling high parchment crackling
> until I sank into the swamps of overwork. (83)

We are irresistibly reminded of Victor Frankenstein, that "pale student of unhallowed arts," laboring compulsively, collecting *his* materials, losing track of time, his loved ones, his own body. Any author of texts knows this agony, this enthrallment, this enslavement of the body to the word. Against this subjugation, Sade asserts the claims of the body, making the body into the only meaningful text: "What are all your pamphlets and speeches/compared with her . . . there's nothing else beyond the body" (90–91). Words kill the body, insists Sade as his singers conflate Marat's text with a torrent of human blood: "Your words have turned into a flood/which covers all France with her people's blood" (85).

David's painting, however, bespeaks a different "story," a different relationship between body and text. The dead right hand flacidly grasps a quill pen; the left holds Corday's death-dealing letter. The pages of his own work, his call to "awaken" the slumbering proletariat giant, lie beneath the same arm. The body has itself become a text, inscribed upon by the assassin's penknife, which lies on the floor in the foreground. The authoress of the letter and wound is absent. The body is unbloody and relaxed, the wound small and clean, the face serene. Marat, "The People's Friend," is finally at peace. It is not his writing that has killed Marat, not his cause, not even the absent Corday. What the painting calmly registers is the fact of Marat's mortality and, with great subtlety, it demonstrates yet another subtext: Marat's assassinated body speaks volumes through David's portrait, preaches more persuasively and cogently than any of his pamphlets. Marat's body, apotheosized into *objet d'art*, becomes a new kind of call to arms. The whole purpose of rendering Marat as free of pain, at peace, is to raise him above the turmoil, the "fever" of bodily existence and to enshrine him in the still, calm eternal realm of art. In David's painting Marat has transcended his role as "The People's Friend" to take on new one—glorious martyr, patron saint of the Revolution. From this lofty position, he inspires The People as he never could when he merely "scribbled." David's point is precisely the opposite of Sade's—bodies do not matter ultimately. The cause outlives the man or woman, just as art outlives the human. That art might thereby become inhuman, monstrous, would not occur to such a saint-maker. David eulogizes; Sade persecutes. It is not so much Marat that Sade despises as it is David's representation of him.

That is why Sade's whole play mercilessly converges on this pictorial realization. Sade's play is intended to be a corrective version, a re-realization of David's falsely idealized portrait. By having the Marat-actor awkwardly clamber out of his tub after his "murder," Sade renders Marat (who so convincingly plays dead in the painting) undignified, wet, and ridiculous. This piece of stage business insinuates that David's version is a stylization, mere fiction. Sade's play undermines the authority of the "official" version of the Marat story (as Gothic literature undermines the official version of histories) by hinting that David's idealization is no more true than the unflattering portraits rendered by Marat's "Schoolmaster," his "parents," or "Voltaire." Sade's parody of the David portrait is thoroughly Gothic—it dismantles its source yet at the same time refuses to provide any clear alternative.

Public past—history—Weiss's play seems to suggest, is just as ambiguous, as unknowable as the private past of a Pinter character. The writing of history is coterminous with fiction-making. "In the confusion," as Weiss himself admits, "no one" is "very exact."[5] Weiss points out in his own commentary on the play that Marat was depicted by the "bourgeois historians of the nineteenth century" as "revolting" and "bloodthirsty" (108). He fails to mention, however, how the French theatres of 1793–99, as Marie-Hélène Huet puts it, "took charge of the event," producing four plays devoted to Marat (three of which were staged) and three to Corday (1972, 73). Huet demonstrates that these stage adaptations were no more "faithful" to their "original" than the staged Gothics had been to *their* authorizing texts. For example, *Charlotte Corday, the Modern Judith* (1797) arranges for its Corday a melodramatic last-minute escape from the guillotine, after which she "marries her rescuer, a royalist officer" (Huet 1982, 84). Despite the obvious artifice of these blatantly absurd representations of historical event, the point remains that it is probably impossible to assess how accurately any play or artistic representation portrays its historical subject when that subject is itself unverifiable, enigmatic. How are we to "take" Sade's caricature of Marat when historians to this day have yet to determine whether Marat's skin disease was an indirect consequence of persecution (Marat was forced to hide in damp cellars), or whether it was a psychosomatic disorder, an insanity manifesting itself in his body? With respect to the historical Marat, we find ourselves occupying almost the same position as we did with respect to Robert Wringham, in that all that we know of Marat's early years is what he himself chooses to tell us in his *Journal de la Révolution*. If, as Leslie Miller points out, Weiss's Sade and his Marat are "dubious reconstructions" (1971, 47), the fact is that, as far as the Gothic is concerned, *all* representations are inherently "dubious."

That the play's commentators cannot come to terms with Weiss's Marat and his Sade, that they cannot decide which is the moral victor, is very much the point. For the Gothic mind, the past is a blank, a vacuum, which "histories," dubious reconstructions all, rush in to fill. Weiss's play, his own espousal of Marxism notwithstanding, undermines all party lines, and, like the Gothic narrative text, disallows any authoritative alternative vision. *Marat-Sade* is less a revision of either Marat or Sade than it is a powerful demonstration of the enigma of personality and historical event.

Thus Weiss's drama theatricalizes the Gothic narrative's circularity, its arbitrary closure and its parodic impulses. Through its seemingly endless revisions of the Marat-Corday story represented in song, mime, storytelling events, and dramatic reenactment, it implicitly invokes multiviewpoint as well, so much so that Peter Brook, who brought it to the London stage, deems it "a hall of mirrors," a "corridor of echoes."[6] As will soon become apparent, *Marat-Sade*'s deployment of encapsulation and its intense self-referentiality are equally in the Gothic tradition.

Weiss's handling of the play-within-the-play structure is quite unlike that of Stoppard. Whereas *Hound*'s inner play swallows up its frame play, *Marat-Sade*'s inside play seems constantly in danger of being engulfed by its frame play. Although the inside play occupies most of the "space" of the play's text, it is constantly under attack, continually fending off incursions which emanate from its frame. In fact, the two plays coalesce so frequently that "[w]e cannot," as one commentator observes, "always be sure which play we are witnessing" (Roberts 1975, 130). Since the Herald implies that Sade has foreseen the outbursts and composed "some extra lines in case the need arose" (31), we can never clearly determine at any given moment whether we are watching an unscripted outburst, a true "happening," or the enactment of a text that has preempted the spontaneous. Thus the audience, even though it is witnessing these play-events firsthand, would, like the eyewitnesses in Hogg's *Confessions,* be unable to provide an authoritative account of what it has seen. In Weiss's play the relationship between frame and interpolated play is even more muddled and mysterious than in the Stoppard pieces.

Another distinction between Stoppard's use of encapsulation and that of Weiss is Weiss's addition of yet another frame: the real offstage audience, which is sporadically addressed as if it were a theatre-party of early nineteenth-century Parisians, discovers in the final, frantic moments of the play that it too "belongs" to *Marat-Sade*. For most of the play, this outermost frame is not violated, that is to say, the onstage play does not spill over into it, nor is it pulled into the onstage play world. Instead, until the last few moments, Coulmier and his family function as surrogates for this offstage audience. In fact, through Coulmier's frequent objections, instructions, and comments, the offstage audience has been attempting to remold Sade's play, to impose censorship upon it.

However, near the end of the play, after Sade's play is presumably over, the "other" play, the alien drama of the inmates, threatens to pour out into the auditorium, to overleap its boundaries, to penetrate its outermost frame:

> The column of PATIENTS begins to march forward. SISTERS and NURSES try to restrain it. Several times the column advances four paces and takes three paces back. The music and marching rhythm grow in power. . . . The column advances still further, stamping some paces forward and some back . . . COULMIER's family flee, screaming and shouting . . . the shouting grows. The column reaches the front. . . . Suddenly the whole stage is fighting . . . Coulmier incites the NURSES to extreme violence. PATIENTS are struck down. The HERALD is now in front of the orchestra. . . . In desperation COULMIER gives the signal to close the curtain. (100–102)

Coulmier's is a "desperate" gesture of containment, for the play is ready to jump out of its picture frame, just as framed portraits in the Gothic often do. The structure and effect can be likened to Lockwood's dream in *Wuthering Heights*. Annoyed, like Coulmier, Lockwood stretches out his hand to silence the "teasing sound," but encounters instead a hand which has poked through the broken windowpane, a hand which grips his own, "almost maddening [him] with fear" (Brontë [1850] 1972, 30). Irritated by these sounds which disturb his insensate tranquility, Coulmier tries to make the noises stop: "That's enough/If you use any more of these passages/we agreed to cut/I will stop your play" (78). His efforts prove futile, though, because the mad anarchy of the Charenton cast is not to be stopped by injunctions, borders, or frames. Picture frames, window frames, proscenium frames pose no barrier to a ghost or a madman. Terror is Lockwood's response and terror, as he admits, makes us "cruel." The terror and bloodshed of Lockwood's dream finds it stage analogue as Coulmier's henchmen brutally beat the Patients, attempting to force them back—away from the cordon they have come so precariously close to crossing. It is only by clinging desperately to what seems to be a feebler and feebler convention— namely, that theatre is only make-believe—that the offstage audience refrains from joining the panic-stricken flight of Mme and Mlle Coulmier. This climactic moment reproduces in theatrical terms the convulsive anarchy of Gothic storm and riot. The drawn curtain is as arbitrary and unconvincing as the ending of a dream.

Thus as *Marat-Sade* appears to be in its death throes, its margins are collapsing and the play, like some too long enchained beast, is gathering itself to spring. As it threatens to burst its shackles, to run amok, it threatens to smash not only the proscenium windowpane, but the entire theatre itself. *Marat-Sade* is, as its own language proclaims, drama as "mad animal": it escapes "through *all* the walls."[7]

The preceding discussion of Gothic stylistic features as embodied in both Gothic narrative and Gothic dramatic discourse suggests that their overall effect is a thorough subversion of ontological certitudes. In Gothic texts, nothing is as it seems. Over and over the Gothic violates our sense of epistemological proprieties, repeatedly it undermines any sense of objective reality.

This subversion, as disorienting as it may be, does not, however, constitute a direct threat to the self per se. Yet, as Gothic readers know very well, the Gothic does trade very heavily in personalized menace; this more direct species of threat is not the result of these larger structural features we have already examined, but rather is encoded in the language of the Gothic power-wielder. In order to discover the nature of this linguistic terrorism, we need now to attend to the Gothic's rhetoric of intimidation.

If we look to early Gothic narrative for instances of successful verbal coercion, we discover a curious absence. The early Gothic villain most often imposed his will through either brute force or political clout. Manfred of Otranto is not, as Paul Lewis amusingly puts it, a "smooth talker" (1981, 315), but then of course he does not have to be. Even polished, fluent speakers such as Ambrosio of *The Monk* fail to work their will by words:

> By a few simple words she [Antonia] frequently overthrew the whole bulk of his sophistical arguments. . . . On such occasions . . . he overwhelmed her with a torrent of philosophical paradox, to which, not understanding them, it was impossible to reply. ([1796] 1952, 256)

Ambrosio can silence Antonia with his rhetoric, but he cannot bend her to his will. He cannot coerce her with "sophistical arguments"; only the physical power of his body will do. The passage which describes Antonia's rape is insistently physical and brutally violent. His "prey" is wounded, bruised, stifled. Afterward, the only way to "enforce her silence," when push has indeed come to shove, is with a knife thrust. Drowning in her own blood, Antonia still gets the last word while Ambrosio must flee for his life. This state of affairs, however, does not persist. In Hogg's *Confessions* and Maturin's *Melmoth,* we are presented with a new species of persecutor—the smooth-tongued, sophistical tormenter. Gil-Martin, a "smooth-talker," succeeds where Ambrosio had failed. Though Wrigham himself is a master of biblical cant, he "sinks dumb" before his companion's superior rhetoric. Ian Campbell is quite right in asserting that "Wringham openly admits to being conquered by language" (1980, 26). "All reasoning" with Gil-Martin "is to no purpose." Equally helpless, albeit for different reasons, is *Melmoth*'s Immalee. At first, like Antonia before her, she resists the Wanderer's casuistry:

> Her playful and desultory answers,—her restless eccentricity of imagination,—her keen and piercing, though ill-poised intellectual weapons,—and above all her instinctive and unfailing *tact* in matters of right and wrong, formed altogether an array that discomfited and baffled the tempter more than if he had been compelled to encounter half the *wranglers* of the European academies of that day. ([1820] 1961, 219)

But it is already clear that it is Immalee's own hunger for communication that is to be her undoing and that her attachment to Melmoth is founded on talk: "I shall never love my roses and peacocks if you do not return, for they cannot speak to me as you do, nor can I give them one thought, but you can give me many" ([1820] 1961, 219). Jan Gordon traces Immalee's destruction to language itself:

> It is language that ultimately transforms the tropical island paradise into that dungeon of imprisoned language, the Inquisition. [In] Maturin's novel . . . language has come to be associated with reduction, and ultimately with death itself. (1983, 229–30)

From *Melmoth* onward, Gothic narrative increasingly asserts a terrible synonymy of villainy and language as coercive instrument. Even Dracula, a being whom one would expect would have little care for the niceties of diction, acknowledges its mastery as essential to his successful takeover of England (Gordon 1983, 230). As Gordon points out, "The count pleads with Jonathan to allow him access to the language" (1983, 230).

Concurrently, the language of the Gothic victim, no matter how moving, remains useless as a mechanism of defense. Language in the Gothic is operative only as an offensive tactic. (Even then it requires the reinforcing presence of brute force.) Eloquence unbacked by bodily power is unavailing. *Frankenstein*'s Justine Moritz confesses a lie because she realizes that the verbal threats of her interrogators are undergirded by real political power: "[H]e threatened and menaced," she tells Elizabeth, "until I almost began to think I was the monster he said I was" ([1831] 1968, 350). Though Justine speaks in her own defense and though Elizabeth's appeal is "heart-rending," eloquence alone is useless.

On the other hand, the Gothic repeatedly affirms the terrible superiority of physical force. Shelley's Monster masters the art of rhetoric only to discover that his huge, powerful body has already spoken a threat which no words can negate. In *Wuthering Heights* Heathcliff physically detains young Cathy, "arresting her by the arm," so that body and language forces as he recounts the subjugation of Linton:

I brought him down one evening . . . and just set him in a chair, and never touched him afterwards. . . . [W]e had the room to ourselves. In two hours I called Joseph to carry him up again; and since then, my presence is as potent on his nerves as a ghost; and I fancy he sees me often, though I am not near. Hareton says he wakes and shrieks in the night by the hour together. (Brontë [1850] 1972, 227)

What Cathy is supposed to infer is clear; so potent is Heathcliff's power that even his silence can wither, can madden. The bruising grip on the arm is the "proof" which he offers.

This pattern of language's alliance with power is reproduced in the NeoGothic drama. We can perceive, for example, Pinter's power-wielders as brilliant, if cruel, masters of linguistic coercion; yet it is well to remember that their power does not derive solely from linguistic skill, that there is behind this skill the power of the body to inflict pain or arouse desire—a smashed pair of eyeglasses, an old man, his arm pinned behind him, wrestled to the floor. Mick may be an inventive linguistic strategist, but his power over Davies is based on his superior physical strength and Davies's perception of him as propertied, hence economically powerful. Having made this distinction, we may now examine the various linguistic devices these victimizers deploy against their victims. In Pinter's *The Caretaker* and *The Homecoming* and in Peter Handke's *Kaspar*, we can observe the working out in theatrical terms of the Gothic formulation of language and power.

Threat couched in narration functions in Pinter's drama much as it does in *Dracula* or *Wuthering Heights*. Physical violence toward the victim-listener is deflected (at least partially) into story, what Braunmuller terms "memory violence" (1981, 158). Lenny's stories in *The Homecoming*, tales which exhibit a common theme of violence directed against women, are designed to disturb Ruth. When she willfully misreads one of them by focusing on a minor detail, he emphasizes the status of the story as fiction:

> *Ruth:*    How did you know she was diseased?
> *Lenny:*   How did I know?
>        *[Pause]*
>        I decided she was. (31)

It would seem that Lenny ought to be providing verification; yet he pointedly refuses to do so. He thereby underscores the story's fictionality, attempting to impress on Ruth his capacity for the wanton and the arbitrary, letting her know in no uncertain terms that he need prove nothing. But Ruth will "take" him because his eloquence is not backed by real power; she intuits that Lenny is all talk.

Mick's narratives in *The Caretaker* are less overtly menacing; nonetheless, they are structured so as to unbalance, disorient, and confuse the addressee. Like Gothic tales, Mick's narratives supply a chain of facts, but the connections provided do not logically sequence or link the pieces of information. The result is bedazzling chaos. His "my uncle's brother" and "the Shoreditch bloke" stories are virtuoso displays of alogical linkage. The fact that Mick is able to impel Davies into collaborating on a story (even though Davies is not very good at it) is a measure of Mick's control over him. The moment represents a battle of narrative wills in which Davies is dispossessed of his story, his history; the Sidcup papers, which, like all Gothic manuscripts, hold forth the elusive promise of the revelation of origin and identity, no longer serve as a repository of meaning.

Mick's stories also exhibit yet another tactic of linguistic aggression—abrupt shifts of linguistic register, especially to registers inappropriate to the addressee. Mick's facility with disparate modes of discourse helps to establish him as a formidable enemy, though this facility is not the sole source of his power.

Placed side by side, *The Caretaker* and *The Homecoming* comprise a Gothic diptych—on the one side, language furnishes a cutting edge for the tormentor; on the other, it becomes the elegant but unavailing shield of the tormented. *The Homecoming,* which transpires in a bleak, martial landscape of "no-holds-barred," recapitulates the Gothic lesson that, in extremity, only the body has power. Ruth, "model for the body," is, like Weiss's Sade, its spokesman: "My lips move . . . perhaps that fact is more significant than the words which come through them."[8] Lenny, every bit as agile a talker-storyteller as Mick, is no match for the power of the body; eloquence surrenders to the force of a blow or the intensity of a kiss. The "right touch" is touch—a shove, a twist, or a caress. Dracula may pay tribute to the strategic significance of language acquisition, but it is the mesmeric force of his physical presence that renders his victim compliant. If, in the Gothic, as David Punter warns us, "health, strength and moral well-being will not at all serve to get one by" (1980, 400), eloquence is just as paltry a defense.

In Peter Handke's *Kaspar,* this bipartite structure is resolved into a unified entity. *Kaspar* embodies both formulations of the power-language equation; it retraces the path from *The Caretaker* to *The Homecoming,* offering a representation of Gothic power and Gothic language akin to that of Mary Shelley's but in terms that are resolutely theatrical. It is no accident that Kaspar looks like "Frankenstein's Monster" or "King Kong."

Handke theatricalizes Gothic power and Gothic powerlessness by transmuting a Gothic convention—the disembodied voice—into a theatrical one—the Prompter's voice. In the same fashion, the Gothic's tormented hearer is transformed into the onstage actor. As indicated earlier, in the Gothic cosmos the brute force of the body outweighs eloquence of voice. In *Kaspar,* however, embodiment does not refer to this physical power; instead embodiment refers to Kaspar's condition of being literally on the spot, "on" in the theatrical sense. Thus his condition of embodiment is one of vulnerability. The Prompters, in contrast, as keepers of the drama's voice, the script, are the power-wielders. Handke accentuates their disembodied inhumanness by insisting that their voices should sound mechanical, as if they were being relayed through a technical medium such as a microphone. In *Kaspar* language and voice is the prerogative of power; voicelessness is the emblem of the powerless.

Now begins a process of "instruction" that oddly parallels but also inverts the educative process of Mary Shelley's hideous learner. Kaspar's initial state is similar to that of a toddler—he is clumsy, barely able to walk, and his vocabulary is limited to a single, all-purpose sentence. This sentence, as June Schlueuter points out, "is adequate to encompass all the aspects of his world" (1980, 28). Whereas Victor's Monster yearns to master the "godlike science," Kaspar evinces no such desire—his single sentence, though abstract and almost meaningless, serves all his needs. Thus the Shelleyan Monster, driven by his frantic desire to learn to speak, takes charge of his own education. He spies on his tutors, learning by assiduous observation a lesson he has freely chosen to learn. His experience of language mastery is thus an exuberant one (albeit shortlived). Kaspar's learning experience, in contrast, is unmitigatedly unpleasant and absolutely unfree. It is he who is the watched one. Not by observation but through coercion and drill he learns his lesson. In this respect, the *Kaspar* model is decidedly the more Gothic in tone and spirit: to learn is to suffer. To master one's language is merely to learn how to express one's powerlessness.

The first phase of Kaspar's lesson is deconstructive: Kaspar is gradually deprived, dispossessed of his little text. In Pinter's drama, the reduction to silence signals the nadir of helplessness. Handke, however, dramatizes the successive, even more sinister, phase of the power-language game—the imposition of the conqueror's language. The slavish aping of the Master's language testifies to a more abject powerlessness than bewildered or sullen silence.

The next phase of the process is, therefore, reconstructive. Kaspar will be "needled" into speech. In English at least, the verb "needle" is freighted with meanings that are metalinguistic, domestic, yet peculiarly violent. The Prompter's juxtapositioning of good housekeeping hints with various formulations of the doctrine that language makes order is not accidental. As Linda Hill suggests, "Language is associated with housekeeping since both maintain order" (1977, 305). The underlying support of this order, however, is violence: needles mend clothing (and even human bodies), yet they can just as easily be adopted as instruments of torture. This subtle undermining of the domestic sphere, its metamorphosis into a monstrous perversion, is an instance of Gothic parody, and, as we shall see, a recurrent motif of the Gothic fantasy. "Needling," normally defined as a fairly innocuous form of teasing, begins to acquire disturbing nuances. Gradually the interchangeability of the domestic and the brutal becomes a running motif in the Prompter's speeches. The implication is that violence is a necessary prerequisite to the establishment of order. The Prompters insinuate what Coulmier could never bring himself to say—namely, that order is based on torture. This interconnectedness of stability and persecution is tantamount to a threat: Kaspar must be brought to order at all costs.

By the second act the threats have become more overt: "While giving a beating/one is/never as calm as while beating a rug" (117). It is by now all too clear which meaning of "needling" is being referred to:

> two sticks in the nostrils being wriggled
> about
> or something of that order
> only more pointed
> introduced into the ears
> without much ado
> to needle someone
> and bring him around. (117)

The form in which these threats are delivered is, unlike the threat-narratives of Pinter characters, intentionally antinarrational. The Prompters explicitly ban narrative because it is a discourse of particularization. Officialdom prefers the staccato acoustic pattern of the slogan-proverb—"Everyone must . . . No one should." This shorthand language of anonymity and uniformity is the antithesis of Gothic discourse with its intensely personal tone and tortuous length. The Prompters correctly intuit that stories chronicle trouble and that "abnormal" people and objects generate stories. Abnormality and trouble are to be banished—the deviant is demonic.

Thus Kaspar's recitation of a story constitutes a species of rebellion. Even more defiant is its intensely personal content, its tone of barely controlled hysteria. Kaspar has, despite his teachers, learned to storify. He will discover, however, like Victor's Creature, that this acquisition will not earn him a sympathetic hearing. In Gothic literature language can express only victimization; it cannot check it.

Kaspar's tale is not, therefore, greeted with an attentive audition. It is mocked, nearly drowned out, by a counter-recitation of "infernal noises" produced by a chorus of Kaspar-doppelgängers. Kaspar's mastery of the "godlike science," demonstrated by his story, is effectively upstaged by antilanguage, sheer noise. Commentators find this event perplexing: while some readers perceive the Prompters' silence at the end as a token of Kaspar's victory, others are disturbed by this noisemaking, perceiving it as a new species of persecution. Opinion is divided as to whether the doubles are attacking Kaspar or assisting him in his rebellion. Either way, the conclusion to be drawn is that, in the end, as Swinburne puts it, "it is not well." Impassioned stories are not only bootless as defensive strategies, they "drown," as Weiss's Sade would insist, "in the total indifference of Nature" (24). If the Kaspar clones are assisting Kaspar, that assistance is taking the form of a mad, "infernal" free-for-all. Kaspar, classic Gothic victim, is caught in the classic double bind—on the one side the repressive tyranny of order, on the other, the "infernal noise" of chaos and mad anarchy. In the Gothic there is no middle ground.

# 3

# Leads and Extras: Tyrants and Mobs

"The familiar Gothic space," writes Judith Wilt, "[is] inhabited only by victims and tyrants" (1980, 54). On the Gothic stage, as in the Gothic narrative, these are the only two roles available. No other modes exist. Dwellers of Gothic kingdoms are either power-wielders or helpless prey; thus, to lose or escape one role is to assume the other. Deposed Gothic tyrants, when they fall, plunge into a condition of utter, annihilating helplessness, just as victims who manage to seize power immediately invest themselves with, to invoke Caleb Williams's anguished metaphor, "the gore-dripping robes of authority." Despotism or the anarchy of mob rule—only extremes will do in the Gothic.

This perpetual falling into and out of roles, this never-ending mutual exchange of roles, is a cyclic process which the Gothic tirelessly documents. Wilt describes this cyclic role exchange as an "intolerable switchability" of outer forms and inner moods (Wilt 1980, 44–45). This intolerable switchability manifests itself in role instability, the slipperiness of Gothic power. Role instability is the political delineation of Gothic shape-shifting and metamorphosis.

Most often, the role of Gothic tyrant is filled by a solo performer. With the exception of this lead player, all Gothic players are "extras," bit-role players, "creatures," as Dracula grandiosely proclaims, "to do [his] bidding" (Stoker [1897] 1965, 312). Gothic power is lonely and jealous; it refuses to delegate itself. That Gothic tyrants are themselves truly free is debatable; that they demand total submission from their subjects, however, is axiomatic. The means of such subjugation is a terrorism which may be covert or overt. This interconnectedness of power and terror is, as David Morse ruefully notes, "not accidental but fundamental" (1982, 14).

Though most commentators dwell with mesmerized fascination on the Gothic antihero as cruel sadist, Wilt more perceptively points to his identity as an embattled creature frantically struggling to maintain his grip on a world that constantly threatens to wriggle out of his control:

> In the eyes of his victims . . . the Gothic antihero seems to be the irresistible force, the master
> of plot, sweeping obstacles out of his way in the mad dash for power. . . . And the dilation of
> his power, the solidifying of his consequence, is a struggle to hold ground, to stay in place in
> a cosmos that moves. The brilliant transfixing eye of the Gothic antihero is only secondarily
> a machine to destroy enemies; essentially it is attempting to pin the world in place. . . . The
> lesson is that eat power, eat people, dilate your powers as you may, you cannot grow big
> enough to avoid being rolled away around the curve. (1980, 41)

Gothic power is absolute but fleeting. The Gothic antihero intuits this precari-
ousness—"in the midst of his power," as Wilt suggests, "he doubts" (1980,
31). Even the most ferocious Gothic tyrants are strangely vulnerable. The vampire is, as Wilt remarks with macabre wit, "fettered by those dozens of rules . . .
that make an undead's life scarcely worth living" (1980, 89). In *Dracula* the
undead Master plays servant to Harker, making up his bed, setting his table,
serving up excellent meals. This early, albeit temporary, role exchange presages
the transformation to hunted victim which Dracula must eventually undergo.
All Gothic victimizers are themselves incipient victims.

For these reasons, the Gothic tyrant is constantly engaged in rendering a
bravura performance of autocracy so that none of his subjects will suspect how
easily he may be deposed. Gothic power is paradoxically real, yet based on the
force of theatrical illusion. From Manfred of Otranto to Count Dracula of
Transylvania, the Gothic antihero is a beleaguered aristocrat whose power is
enormous yet ever endangered—a star performer whose display of swagger and
bluster must be so stunning that no one dare upstage him. The ability to cow the
multitudes is the ability to put on a good show, as Northrop Frye observes: "The
special function of the aristocracy has always included the art of putting on a
show, of dramatizing a way of life" (1967, 126). Gothic literature accentuates
the theatrical basis and expression of power.

This crowd mastery, whether achieved through personal magnetism or
through intimidation, is a prerequisite for the role of Gothic antihero. Dracula's
boasts and threats are indeed "stagey," as Nina Auerbach characterizes them
(1981, 290), yet they linger, so that, despite the fact that Dracula is "offstage"
for most of the novel, his presence asserts itself even in his absence. Perhaps
the most overtly theatrical of Gothic crowd-mesmerizers is *The Monk*'s Ambrosio, whose sermons are the talk of Madrid. Robert Kiely foregrounds the
theatricality of Ambrosio's talent for spellbinding:

> Lewis makes it clear that Ambrosio's hold over his audience is not one of rational persuasion
> but primarily a result of his "style" of speaking, his "distinct and deep" voice from which "the
> thunder seemed to roll," or which could swell into a "melody transporting those who heard it.
> (1972, 109)

More insidious than Ambrosio, and equally artful a performer, is the Father
Superior of Moncada's monastery in *Melmoth*. Moncada at first does not per-

ceive that the man's "parade of feeling were all alike theatrical, and substituting for real interest and sincerity" (Maturin [1820] 1961, 62). Later, after Moncada has realized that he is being duped by a skillful performance, he adopts the role of uncooperative audience. In response the Superior drops the guise of kindly father: "He passed in a moment, with the facility of an actor, to a rigid and breathless sternness. . . . He dropt the dramatist and was the monk in a moment" (63). What poor Moncada fails to descry is that the monk is the actor still. Despite his awareness of the duplicity being practiced upon him, Moncada is still overwhelmed by the plausibility of the performance—"the energy and eloquence of his prayers, dragged me along with him. . . . He had reserved this display for the last, and he had judged well. I never heard anything so like inspiration . . . I began to doubt my own motives" (64).

The Gothic insistence on the theatrical dimension of political power is conceded even by a novel which appears to repudiate the theatrical in its very subtitle—William Godwin's *Caleb Williams* or "Things as They Are." Yet, as Gavin Edwards points out, "[T]he despotism which the novel describes is constituted by [the] ability, whether in courtroom or assembly room, to cut an impressive figure and to give a persuasive account" (1981, 139). Edwards's analysis confirms the presence of Machiavellian role-playing in *Caleb Williams*. If the tyrant can convince the subjugated class that it is indeed powerless, it will remain unaware of its own dormant powers, and it may even learn to internalize its own subjugation. Despite the fragility of the tyrant's power, as long as the victims are overawed by the vitality—the stage presence—of the tyrant, they remain docile spear-carriers; the inevitable exchange of roles can be deferred for at least awhile.

*Caleb Williams* offers a sustained exploration of the fundamentally theatrical nature of Gothic power. Viewed in this light, Falkland begins to emerge as a first-rate actor. Marilyn Butler's discussion portrays Falkland as a figure in need of unmasking:

> Falkland exercises a powerful spell over everyone in the world of the novel, as a hero, a "beneficent divinity," a human being of special value. Unfortunately he has also exercised it over most critics, who continue to write of Falkland's greatness and attractiveness as though these were objectively established and other than obliquely reflected in the unreliable narrations of Collins and of Caleb. (1982, 248)

If Falkland has interpreted the role of Gothic antihero a bit differently than have his colleagues, he has done so with brilliant effect. After all, the sentimental despot was a late eighteenth-century formulation of the absolute ruler. Butler argues that Falkland is actually "more dangerous" than an overt bully like Tyrrel. For Butler, Falkland provides a disquieting instance of the power which can be asserted by a shrewd, talented performer.

Caleb, in contrast, is an actor forever in revolt, a player who comes to loathe the role in which he had initially cast himself—obedient, loyal servant. All of the disguises which he subsequently adopts—Jew, Irishman, beggar—are avatars of estrangement, nonassimilation, the anathematized. The chain of events which ensues following his refusal to play the servant justifies in Caleb's mind a vision of himself as an arch-Victim, The Persecuted One, whose life has been, as he himself claims, "a theatre of calamity."[1] Caleb comes to discover, however, that such roles are not all they are cracked up to be. Playing the victim is a miserable, unromantic business.

Oddly enough, it is Caleb's unsatisfying encounters with his fellow bit-players, entranced plebeians all, which turn out to be the bleakest moments in the novel. He pleads, for example, with the unswervingly devoted Collins for a hearing. The response he receives is that of a man who has been half-awakened and who does not care to have his repose further disturbed. His fellow servant Thomas is even less willing to lend any credence to Caleb's story: "Mr. Falkland contrive? He is the best friend you have" (286). Even the gentle Laura "readily embraces Falkland's slanders about Caleb" (1984, 161), as Michael DePorte observes, despite the fact that she herself has never witnessed any of Falkland's impressive performances. Falkland's presence, like Dracula's, is asserted even in his absence.

The only applause which Caleb receives from his own class is for a role he claims never to have played—"Kit Williams," latter-day Robin Hood, lovable rascal. Gay Clifford concludes that the peasantry's "construct[ion of] a folk-hero on the basis of an unsentimental stoicism towards the class-system is relatively innocent" (1977, 607). However, I would counter that such stoicism is, in the context of the novel, a profoundly distressing phenomenon. The rabble stolidly refuses to be roused. Working-class energy, resistance to "things as they are," is wasted, deflected into storytelling—as ineffective, in terms of fomenting revolution, as the "pygmy spite of a chambermaid." The casual conversation overheard by Caleb in a local tavern epitomizes this passive acceptance of its role by the common folk: "Some folks must be hanged to keep the wheels of our state folk a-going" (236). One is irresistibly reminded of big wheels and "little men" and of the guillotine that has been set "a-going."

The published ending of *Caleb* is a study of an aborted revolution, a stillborn revolt. At the very moment Caleb is to have his day in court, to hold the stage as he recounts his story, he succumbs to pity for the "image of grief" which Falkland represents; in so doing, he finally accepts the role he has repudiated for so long—faithful slave, trusty servant. Jacqueline Miller presents Caleb's consternation and remorse as an act of self-betrayal: "Caleb finally can only portray himself as that character which Falkland has constructed" (1978, 379). Kelvin Everest explains Caleb's sense of defeat as stemming from a subconscious recognition that, in winning his case, "he has had to accept entirely his enemy's premise that truth is commensurate with public credence" (Edwards and Everest 1981, 138). He argues that in *Caleb,* "The truth is always effectively a matter of rhetoric that works on its audience with the desired effect" (1981, 135). That is to say, truth is merely a convincing performance— good theatre.

In contrast, the unpublished ending wherein Caleb is vanquished, jailed, and rendered insane paradoxically confers on him the halo of martyrdom. Caleb, conquered rebel, is an ennobled version of Kit Williams. Thus the unpublished ending grants him a lofty dignity which the published version resolutely with- holds. The published ending reduces Caleb, much as Sade in Weiss's play reduces Marat, to a figure of ridicule, a fool. D. G. Dumas argues that "this ending which gives us a triumphant Falkland, secure in position and reputation, and an insane, broken Caleb runs little risk of undermining the political doctrine beneath the story's surface" (1966, 593). Such an ending, however, assumes that Godwin's certainty about the eventual amelioration of "things as they are" was unwavering. While both endings indicate a despair with regard to human perfectibility and humane governance, the published ending registers an even more profound conviction that the Gothic power structure of victim and victim- izer will never be dismantled.

Furthermore, the published ending is not only more despairing, it is also more theatrical. Caleb had come to "accuse" but remains to "applaud." The theatrical language is insistent. It signals Caleb's imminent surrender to the role of stage servant, a role which demands deferential silence or approbatory grunts.

Dumas is quite right to describe this final confrontation as a *coup de théâtre,* but the scene does not, as he claims, "sacrific[e] thematic logic to dramatic immediacy" (1966, 594), for "dramatic immediacy" *is* a thematic concern in *Caleb Williams.* Caleb's "applause" suggests that he has come at last to interiorize his own subjugation, to lick, like a good dog, the hand that feeds and whips. From now on, he will retell only Falkland's story.[2] His own story has become the master's story. Caleb's posture of self-abasement allows him to take his place in the community of Gothic stage servants—a chorus whose function is to lionize the lead player.

Falkland's collapse too is very much in keeping with Gothic representations of tyranny. Falkland does not fall because Caleb has deposed him, but simply because the strain of keeping up appearances has taken its inevitable toll; the role of tyrant is much too taxing to perform indefinitely. Falkland belongs to a gallery of Gothic tyrants, all of whom are more or less in the penultimate stages of crackup. Wilt's simile conveys the Gothic antihero's insecure hold on his world: "Getting and keeping life on these terms is more like climbing a ladder that is itself constantly descending" (1980, 88).

Read Gothically, Godwin's novel eloquently pleads the cause of the inno- cent victim, yet simultaneously acknowledges that injustice inevitably dictates "the way things are," and that "things" refers not simply to humanly engendered injustice, but to a cosmos that is, to invoke once more Punter's description, "actively hostile." Kenneth Graham would second Punter's assessment: the "necessity" to which inhabitants of *Caleb Williams* are subject "is a Gothic necessity characterized as mysterious, inexorable and malignant" (1980, 52). The social repression which Caleb and the other victims of *Caleb* experience is simply a miniaturized, human imitation of cosmic injustice, red in tooth and claw. The *coupe de théâtre*, the performance of tyranny, is merely a dark act of complicity.[3]

If Godwin's novel dramatized only one configuration of the Gothic power-structure, subsequent Gothics went on to depict the full cycle—the 360-degree spin of revolution. The memorable mob scenes of *The Monk, Melmoth,* and even Hogg's *Confessions* enact the terrible awakening of the "swinish multitude," the transformation from subservient spear-carrier to screaming spear-thrower. The other configuration of the Gothic power structure is the brief spasm of mob rule, a violent release of anarchic energies. Wilt would concur: "[A]s a social impulse it is not revolution that the Gothic celebrates, not even reform, but riot" (1980, 46).

Not all commentators would agree, however, that the mood is celebratory. Many have ascribed the Gothic riot to a politically reactionary, conservative bent in the Gothic writer. Montague Summers, for instance, declares that "the great Gothic novelists abhorred and denounced political revolution" (1964, 399). Ronald Paulson in his *Representations of Revolution* defines the Gothic as "the form adopted by those who were either against or merely intrigued by the Revolution or by problems of freedom and compulsion" (1983, 227). For Paulson, the label "Gothic" writer subsumes not just the reactionary, but also the "merely intrigued," the uncommitted dilettante. Punter, however, detects intense engagement manifested as deeply troubled uncertainty:

> Capitalism has specific taboos: the family, the claims of the individual, the power of the repressive apparatus of Church and State. These are the areas where to probe too deeply would be to risk tearing the social fabric, and these are precisely the areas in which Gothic fiction locates itself, and where it tortures itself and its readers by refusing to let dead dogs lie. . . . In the late eighteenth century, Gothic writers started to ask questions of this kind. . . . They asked them in a very diffident way—at least until Maturin—and often, having asked them, they hastily apologized and produced normative endings to their books. Nonetheless, the questions *were* asked and Gothic is still the arena for related questions.

For Punter, the late eighteenth- and early nineteenth-century Gothic writers were not "merely intrigued" by the events playing themselves out across the Channel. Indeed there is in many of these writers, as Kiely observes of Maturin, "a genuine distaste for authoritarian political systems, especially as they are linked with religious tyranny." Kiely goes on to cite the passage in which Melmoth bitterly excoriates dictators as beings who suck the lifeblood of their people, who "drain by taxation, whatever wealth their vices have left to the rich, and whatever means of subsistence their want has left to the poor."

Nonetheless, despite its hatred of authoritarianism, the Gothic rage against prisons was always counterpoised by a horror of mob rule. The Gothic writer was acutely aware of the problematic nature of revolution, its seamy underside. Thus what Lee Sterrenburg discerns in Shelley's *Frankenstein* is true of Gothic literature in general: "*Frankenstein* goes beyond the radical and conservative traditions it appropriates. Though relying on images drawn from these traditions, Mary Shelley writes a novel that is, in many ways, a subversion of all ideology" (1979, 144). Punter would endorse this position. Most Gothic writers, he claims, "do not advocate anything at all" (1980, 411).

On the one hand, the Gothic documents the trauma of powerlessness and the self-corrosive nature of tyranny; on the other hand, its skepticism about the inherent decency of the repressed class compels it to portray the rule of the many as merely another formulation of tyranny and persecution. And in the Gothic there really is no middle ground. The transition from lone despotism to mob rule is instantaneous; the time of mob rule itself is but an interstitial moment. The rest of Gothic time belongs to the tyrant.

One distinction which might be noted between the tyrant and the mob is that when the tyrant is deposed and flung into the role of victim, he is usually utterly demolished—"decreated" as Wilt styles it—whereas the Gothic crowd, sated by its rampage of arson, looting, window-smashing and murder, most often simply disperses. Thus Ambrosio perishes in what more than one reader has been quick to recognize as a spectacular parody of Creation:

> Headlong fell the monk . . . the sharp precipice of a rock received him; and he rolled from precipice to precipe, till, bruised and mangled, he rested on the river's banks. Myriads of insects . . . drank the blood which trickled from Ambrosio's wounds. . . . The eagles of the rock tore his flesh piecemeal, and dug out his eyeballs. . . . Six miserable days did the villain languish. On the seventh, a violent storm arose. . . . The rain fell in torrents . . . the waves . . . reached the spot where Ambrosio lay, and when they abated, carried with them into the river the corse of the despairing monk. (M. G. Lewis [1796] 1952, 420)

"Finis" indeed. Similarly gruesome instances of tyrant dismemberment occur intermittently in the Gothic; one has only to recall with a shudder the "sanguine and discolored mud" that was once a human being, trampled to death by the "thousand feet" of Maturin's homicidal mob. In contrast, as already indicated, the decreation of the mob, its lapse back into its customary role of victim, is imaged quite differently: "The crowd, saturated with cruelty and blood . . ." departed (196).

Mob rule in the Gothic has little to do with political causes and everything to do with mindless violence. The Gothic insists on a demythologization of The People. Paulson's description of *The Monk*'s mob is applicable to all Gothic mobs:

> Lewis portrays the rioting mob as bloodthirsty, completely out of control, animal-like in its ferocity. The Convent of St. Clare represents corruption, superstition and repression but its overthrowers, no more admirable than the tyrants, are capable of the same atrocities or worse. (1983, 219)

Such bestial mindlessness is not accorded the extravagant ceremonies of de-creation which attend the exits of the great old ones. The Gothic crowd simply disperses, as suddenly as it had collected, and its members return to the tedium of common life, the impetus for the outbreak and the outbreak itself quickly forgotten.

There is something of the automaton in Gothic crowds, something of the insensate violence of the zombie. Gothic writers were not alone, however, in imaging the collective beast in Gothic terms. In fact, as Lee Sterrenburg observes, anti-Jacobin literature frequently invoked the demon and monster "to depict the revolutionary crowd" (1979, 153). In the conservative literature of the day, revolution was represented as a kind of invasion of the body-snatchers conducted on a colossal scale. Burke, according to Sterrenburg, "develops an externalized Gothic melodrama in his *Reflections on the Revolution in France*" (154). He cites Burke's association of grave-robbing with the revolutionists' purblind, hell-bent fanaticism:

> They [the French Revolutionists] have so determined hatred to all privileged orders, that they deny even to the departed the sad immunities of the grave. . . . They unplant the dead for bullets to assassinate the living. . . . [N]o persons were ever known to history . . . to rob the sepulchre, and by their sorceries to call up the prophetic dead, with any other event, than the prediction of their own disaster.[4]

Once jolted into life, the proletariat monster inevitably embarks on a killer's rampage. As for the "sorcerers" who had called it forth—philosophers and radicals, "People's Friends" such as Marat—they are to be numbered among its choicest victims.

Of course, Gothic fantasy itself was never so didactic or explicit as these political tracts, nor did it overtly enshrine and eulogize the ruling class (as Burke certainly had). Rather, the Gothic called into question these melodramatic polarities which utopians and conservatives alike had sought to maintain. The adoption of Gothic imagery and language by anti-Jacobin pamphleteers has no doubt misled many commentators (such as Paulson and Summers, as we have already seen) into classifying the Gothic impulse as politically conservative, when in fact it remained totally uncommitted to any ideology.

This ambivalence is nowhere more evident than in *Frankenstein,* despite the fact that mob scenes never quite materialize. Sterrenburg explains this curious absence by suggesting that while Shelley "retains the monster metaphor [of Revolution-era political literature] . . . [she] purges it virtually of all reference to collective movements" (1979, 157). Sterrenburg thus concludes that "Shelley's world-view was less political than Godwin's or Burke's" (157). While it is true that "collective movements" do not figure in *Frankenstein,* the novel can, nonetheless, be apprehended as a significant parable of Gothic politics. It does not represent a depoliticization of the "monster tradition," nor is Shelley's view "less political." The confrontation of master and servant is never strictly an in-house domestic matter. Political and psychological interpretations need not be antithetical; they are actually quite complementary. *Frankenstein* wrestles with the same disturbing political and psychological questions that haunt *Caleb Williams.* The role of unruly servant is reexplored and expanded: the full-scale revolt that remains nascent in *Caleb* is realized in Shelley's novel.

Contravening reader expectation the Monster's language, his "lines," are incongruent with his role. Yet he desperately seeks what Caleb flees—security, a well-defined position in the master's household, a cozy nook beside the domestic hearth. Separation galls him. His salutations to Victor bespeak subservience—"my natural lord and king," "my creator." Even when Caleb assumes this groveling posture, his homage is based on Falkland's presumable moral superiority rather than on his caste: "Mr. Falkland is of a noble nature . . . a man worthy of affection and kindness" (323). Throughout, Falkland is his "patron," not "lord and king." Despite his own humble prostrations, however, the monster does enact the revolution that Caleb can only talk about. The form of this revolution is, of course, relentlessly Gothic, a "celebration" of decreation and riot.

Although it is clear that the monster turns to carnage only after a series of rejections and injustice, he does play out in many respects the role usually assigned in Gothic fiction to the mob. The association of Victor's Monster with a rebellious lower class in Elizabeth Gaskell's *Mary Barton* (1848) should not be regarded as mere happenstance. Sterrenburg cites several sources which indicate that the image of the Monster seemed a ready-made symbol of a restive, latently powerful and much to be feared working class (1979, 166). Gaskell's passage is particularly evocative:

> The actions of the uneducated seem to be typified in those of Frankenstein, that monster of many human qualities, ungifted with a soul, a knowledge of the difference between good and evil. The people rise up to life; they imitate us, they terrify us, and we become their enemies. (1958, 162)

In the context of the novel the destruction of the DeLacey cottage is less a deliberate political gesture than an instinctual venting of mob fury. The terms in which the deed is rendered emphasize passion, not didactic intent:

> When I reflected that they had spurned and deserted me, my anger returned, a rage of anger. . . . I lighted the dry branch of a tree and danced with fury around the deserted cottage . . . with a loud scream I fired the straw . . . and the cottage was quickly enveloped by the flames. (Mary Shelley [1831] 1968, 426)

What is invoked here is that other "dance of fury," the carmagnole that "celebrated" the swift descent of the guillotine.

Later on, in a last-ditch attempt to make contact with the master race, which is for him the whole of humanity, he seizes a child, reasoning with Rousseau-like naiveté that it would be too young to have learned "prejudice." Then he detects in the piping voice that "load[s] [him] with epithets" the voice of insolent, smug superiority: "Let me go, or I will tell my papa. . . . My papa is a syndic—he is M. Frankenstein—he will punish you. You dare not keep me" (410). Although the monster consciously responds only to the fact of the child's relationship to his enemy, he responds as well on a subliminal level to ruling-class contempt. Had Shelley not been alive to the political implications of this confrontation, she would have portrayed the child merely as a frightened innocent who cries for his papa.

Thus Baby Frankenstein becomes the first victim of what evolves into a campaign of terrorism, a one-"man" guerilla war which the monster conducts against his unbenevolent despot. That other "vile wretch" Caleb Williams had looked around in the 1790s and found himself too very much the odd man out. The loneliness of rebellion in *Frankenstein,* as in *Caleb Williams,* has less to do with the political temper of either of their respective eras than with the Gothic sense that rebellion on a mass-scale is extremely rare, and that, if and when it occurs, it manifests itself only in the transient melee of mob riot. Revolution in the astronomical sense, revolution as the founding of a new social order, is acidly debunked by the Gothic.

The founding of a new order is impossible partly because the masses perceive revolution only in terms of the satisfaction of immediate needs, the attainment of creature comforts. Causes in the abstract have no meaning for them. Though the constituents for revolt are present on board Walton's ship, mutiny does not transpire because the crew's demand—retreat to a snug harbor and a "warm fireside"—is met. In their desire to turn the ship homeward, they resemble those traditional Gothic servants, yearning "for the end of turmoil," not for them the extremities of what Walton deems "lofty design" and "heroism" (488). Thus Victor's soul-stirring performance completely misses its mark; the silence with which it is greeted is not the silence of stunned tribute. It is the silence of noncomprehension: "They looked at one another and were unable to reply," Walton tells us and then speculates that the men must have been too "moved" to do so (488). But the true state of affairs is revealed by the applause that greets the shifting of the ice pack that reopens the passageway home.

It is not so much that the ruled class is vicious as that it is unaware, uninvolved, except peripherally, in the significant doings of its "betters." There is a belief in Shelley's Gothic classic and in the Victorian Gothics that followed that common life, ordinary labor, somehow dulls the faculties, deadens the capacity to experience extremely. For the Gothic sensibility, the ability to feel deeply, to be absolutely penetrated by terror, is a kind of psychic superiority. In fact, hypersensitivity becomes an index of aristocracy. The Gothic frequently renders the working class as stolid and spook-proof, and that stolidity translates into a fundamental numbskullery. These sorts of distinctions make for some fairly brutal moments in Gothic narrative, as this passage from *The Monk* attests:

> We were obliged to pass by the barn, where the robbers were slaughtering our domestics. The door was open; we distinguished the shrieks of the dying, and imprecations of the murders. What I felt at that moment language is unable to describe. (134)

Wilt characterizes this passage as an instance of Lewis in one of his more risible moments, but the implications of the passage are much too disturbing to be passed off so lightly. One wonders whether the narrator's queasiness results from an affront to his aristocratic sensibilities or from a genuinely empathetic human response. One can not escape the sense that the narrator would just as soon have taken another route and so avoided altogether such an unpleasant spectacle.

In any event, the Gothic writers would not abide sentimental depiction of the working class. As Joyce Carol Oates remarks of the working class of *Dorian Gray,* they are "never anything but lower. They appear, in fact, to belong to a level of consciousness distinctly different from that of their elegant masters" (1980, 426). In the Gothic world, there are, as she puts it, simply "two kinds of human beings, two species" (426).

Rosemary Jackson, in discussing Dickens as a Gothic writer, believes that this convention of lower-class "otherness" was firmly entrenched by the 1830s:

> *Oliver Twist, The Old Curiosity Shop, Dombey and Son* employ a Gothic rhetoric to tell of parts of society held to be horrific to bourgeois security. . . . [T]he poor, the working class, the "refuse" of metropolitan society are represented through a Gothic convention as horrific, melodramatic, "demonic," "other." . . . Depiction of social and sexual "otherness" as demonic, as devilish and evil, increased during the years which followed the outbreaks of European revolution in 1848. From then onwards, as Marx graphically imaged it in the opening of the *Communist Manifesto,* "a spectre [was] haunting Europe." . . . A devil was no longer even equivocally a superhuman: it was a working-class revolutionary. (1981, 130–31)

We should, therefore, not be surprised that in *Dracula* the lower class serves as the unwitting ally of the vampire. Its commonsensical prosaism is obliquely ridiculed, sometimes even sharply undercut. There is, for example, Mr. Thomas Bilder, the zoo-keeper who is, according to his cheery wife, "like an old wolf 'isself," but who is actually a staid, placid workman, the sort of person who cannot imagine why his wolves "began a-'owling . . . as soon as the moon was hup" (Stoker [1897] 1965, 146). Even more oblivious is the mortician who prepares Lucy's body for burial: "She makes a very beautiful corpse, sir. It's not too much to say that she will do credit to our establishment" (170). The portrait of the common folk is unvaryingly unflattering: grimy palms must be greased to acquire information, glasses of grog offered so as to unloose working-class tongues.

This cupidity and imperceptiveness is consistently rendered as one of the obstacles which the little band of self-styled crusaders must overcome in their holy war against the unholy undead. In essence, the lower class functions as Dracula's unwitting stooge. Thus *Dracula* presents the rather unusual configuration of feudal aristocracy and peasantry allied against a beleaguered middle class, although the inclusion of Lord Godalming in the band tends to offset Dracula's status as feudal aristocrat and thus throws the weight of censure more strongly against the dimwitted underlings. Aristocracy, it is hinted, may join forces with the bourgeoisie, but the servant class is to be firmly excluded.

The notion that the loyalty, or at least the submission, of the unwashed masses can be bought was not, of course, Stoker's invention. The tradition of lower-class avarice can, for example, be traced back to Beckford's *Vathek* (1786), in which the rage of the populace is promptly cooled by a shower of money. The crowd's lamentations over its slain children and its curses upon the murdering Caliph are effectively silenced:

> The Princess, who possessed the most consummate skill in the art of persuasion . . . began to harangue them with all the address of which she was mistress; whilst Bababalouk showered money from both hands amongst the crowd, who by these united means were soon appeased. (176)

Eloquence aids power, but it is money that does the real talking, at least among the poor; in fact, money seems to be the only vernacular the Gothic mob needs.

Thus a vulgar but abiding interest in material pleasures, especially in food and drink, becomes a staple defining characteristic of the Gothic underdog. In the midst of howlings and hauntings, he is mainly concerned about his dinner. This perception of the working class as cloddish, coarsely healthy, has a long history which predates Gothic fiction, but it does seem especially pronounced, almost formulaic, to Gothic representations of lowlife. Fear in the Gothic servant is indicative of a want of courage; fear in the Gothic aristocrat is "transmuted," as Frederick Garber observes of *The Italian,* into "an apprehension of the sublime" (ix). Janet Todd notices this master-servant dichotomy in *The Italian:* Paolo's "down-to-earthiness . . . contrasts with his master's romantic sensitivity. While his master is mind, Paolo can be body" (1982, 33). One can detect echoes of the tradition even in the late, very sophisticated Gothic of *The Turn of the Screw.* The governess, herself steeped in the conventions of Gothic fiction, describes Mrs. Grose as one who, though made "the receptacle of evil things," is nonetheless inextricably tethered to the prosaic domain of the kitchen: "[H]ad I wished to mix a witch's brew, she would have held out a large, clean saucepan" (46). This tradition goes a long way toward explaining the difference between the aristocratic Catherine Linton, who stages a hunger strike, and the hearty Nelly Dean, stirrer of porridge, roaster of meats, pourer of tea.[5]

What emerges throughout most Gothic representations of the lower orders is a pervasive sense that the common herd is by definition brutish, insensitive, and grasping. At best they are childishly, even doggishly, simpleminded and devoted.

There are, however, a few instances in Gothic literature which present plebeian torpor not as innate, but rather as a by-product of (sometimes as a defensive strategy against) deprivation. Maturin, for example, documents one family's gradual lapse into inertia under the onslaught of economic want: "There is a withering monotony in the diary of misery. . . . That evening the family sat in profound and stupefied silence" (319). Maturin points out with a grimness born perhaps of his own personal hardships in Ireland that aristocratic sensibility is the product of economic security. He is unique among Gothic writers in taking into account "the thousand petty causes that operate on human agency with a force, if not far more powerful, far more effective than the grand internal motive which makes so grand a figure in romance, and so rare and trivial a one in common life" (285). If the poor seem impervious both to beauty and the dilation of terror, perhaps it is because they are too tired, numbed, and chilled to feel much of anything. Although it might be objected that Maturin's victims here—Wallberg and his family—are not of peasant stock, the point remains: the daily grind of poverty is capable of making automatons of us all. "The real tragedy of the poor," quips the flippant Lord Henry of *Dorian Gray,* "is that they can afford nothing but self-denial. Beautiful sins, like beautiful things, are the privilege of the rich" (90).

Thus it seems possible to argue that the Gothic proletariat's stolidity may in some cases be assumed, its impassivity a mask donned for the purpose of survival. The disconcerting intuition that the docile servant may be playing out a role does occasionally crop up in Gothic fiction. Dorian Gray, for example, begins to fear that his valet knows more about him than the man's "mask of servility" would indicate: "It was a horrible thing to have a spy in one's house. He had heard of rich men who had been blackmailed all their lives by some servant" (138). Dorian begins to read duplicity into that expressionless mask: "There was something sly about him, and he had thoughtful, treacherous eyes" (134). Undue intelligence in a servant is deemed threatening—simple, mindless devotion is what is required. Wilde, a century later, echoes what Godwin already knew—that servants could be actors too, that the mien of servitude could very well be studied, that hostility and rage might smolder beneath the placid exterior.

The aristocratic fear of being exposed or ruined by the servant can be traced as far back as *Otranto,* in which the legitimate "Alfonso the Good" is poisoned and his crown usurped by Ricardo, his chamberlain, who we later discover is also Manfred's grandfather. Thus Manfred, great Gothic old one, is the scion of a butler. The rightful heir Theodore, who turns out to be no peasant at all, is curiously the less complicated, more pragmatic figure. Walpole's servants are indeed the stock-in-trade Gothic servants—goggling buffoons or chattering scatterbrains—but the juxtaposition of the insipid aristocratic Theodore and the tormented plebeian-born Manfred in some measure calls into question Gothic clichés about lower-class insensibility. In this limited sense, *Otranto* is more subversive politically than *Dracula.*

The clever servant as blackmailer or usurper, however, is not common in Gothic literature, and if he does appear, he is exploited mostly for his potential as a source of terror. That is to say, the political underpinnings are not explored in any substantive way. The usurping servant is best understood as a variation on the theme of helpless victim and all-powerful oppressor. Most often in Gothic literature, the lower class is depicted as too simpleminded, too greedy to practice such duplicity. Rarely are the lower orders idealized or sentimentalized. *The Italian*'s Paolo is an oddity in the annals of Gothic servitude.

The sentimentalization of servitude and poverty, the valorization of the humble, is instead the domain, politically, of melodrama. The incompatibility of the Gothic and the melodramatic portraiture of the working class is strikingly evident when one compares *Caleb Williams* with its stage adaptation by George Colman the Younger, *The Iron Chest* (1796).

In his advertisement to the play Colman denies any political intent on his own part and even denies perceiving any political content in his source: "I have cautiously avoided all tendency to that which, vulgarly (and wrongly in many instances) is termed Politicks; with which, many have told me, *Caleb Williams* teems" (xxi). Colman's sentiments on this score, whatever their sincerity, were perfectly in keeping with the practical realities of theatrical production during this era: the system of theatrical censorship passed into law in 1737 had been, as Richard Findlater concludes, "designed to keep politics off the stage" (1967, 35). Thus, under the circumstances, Colman's remarks are hardly surprising. If we take Colman at his word—that "the Stage has no business with Politicks," we expect *The Iron Chest* to be devoid of political content. Such, however, is not the case. *The Iron Chest,* in fact, markets a brand of ultra-conservative politics, perhaps indicating that its author apprehended the subversive political content of his source text as keenly as did its many contemporary reviewers. Close examination of the play indicates that the obliviousness suggested by Colman's preface was a pose.

In his introduction to a recent edition of Colman's play, Peter Tasch notes that Colman, "to insure that no one would think inequities still existed in Britain, . . . set the story in Charles I's reign" (1981, xxxiii). Such a precaution, however, was probably unnecessary since inequities in this play are not rendered as galling or onerous: masters are benevolent, the poor are decent and grateful, servitude is an honor. A poor man's distress over the prospect of his son's becoming a household servant would be unthinkable in the world of *The Iron Chest.* Lower-class misery is never quite real in this world—the poor are represented as actually happier than their elegant masters. The insistent urge of the melodrama to sentimentalize poverty demands that poverty be portrayed as somehow intrinsically more honorable and enjoyable than wealth and social status: "When guilty Ambition writhes upon its couch, why should bare-foot Integrity repine, tho' it's [*sic*] sweet sleep be canopied with a rugged hovel!" (Colman [1796] 1981, 71).

The de-Gothicization of Godwin's text further demanded that the Caleb character be conceived along altogether different lines from those of Godwin's antagonist. Thus Colman's Wilford is naive, gossipy, and inquisitive, but he lacks the sophistication to toy with his patron's sensibilities. Caleb, on the other hand, admits conducting "experiments" on Falkland while feigning the guileless adolescent. His remarks, he boasts, had "an air of innocence, frankness and courage," and his manner indicated "an apparent want of design" (108). His description of Falkland as "a fish that plays with the bait employed to trap him" suggests that in his own mind a role reversal has already transpired even as he enacts the underling. Wilford, in contrast, does not perform the part of the willing servant—he *is* a willing servant—his soliloquies reveal nothing more than a simpleminded curiosity about the contents of the iron chest. He never demonstrates a rebellion against his allotted role. Paradoxically, Godwin's text evinces far more interest in the duplicity, role-playing, and theatricality of master-servant relationships than does the stage adaptation—which would have been the logical forum in which to exploit the theatricality of Godwin's novel. Thus Wilford emerges in Colman's play as nothing more than an uncomplicated youngster whose inveterate newsiness calls down upon him the wrath of the master. Colman's Wilford is a simple victim.

Moreover, he is a melodramatic victim. The cosmos of *The Iron Chest* is not the implacable universe of *Caleb Williams.* Wilford never suffers like Caleb; he is never utterly bereft and abandoned—even at his lowest moment, his sweetheart pleads for him, believes in him. As melodramatic victim, Wilford need do nothing in his own defense because an all-seeing, all-just Providence will ensure his vindication. And it indeed does just that. Fitzharding, on the point of condemning Wilford, spies among the jewels planted in Wilford's trunk "a paper of curious enfolding" (122). As he lifts the paper to inspect it, a blood-stained knife clatters to the floor. Mortimer's (Falkland's) obvious distress then incites Fitzharding to read the wrapping paper—which turns out, appropriately enough, to be Mortimer's murder confession. It might also be noted that Fitzharding, much more sentimental a figure than Forrester, bestirs himself throughout on Wilford's behalf. His decision to unwrap the mysterious-looking parchment is prompted as much by a lingering hope of acquitting Wilford as it is by curiosity.

Godwin's dramatic and disturbing confrontation of master and servant never materializes in Colman's play. Our attention is deflected to the victim's hairbreadth escape. As Mortimer is carried off in convulsions, Wilford is surrounded and congratulated by the community from which he had never really been excluded. No revolt has taken place, nor is there any need for one. The somber and disconcerting issues that Godwin raises are thus brushed aside, glossed over. The final chorus nicely illustrates Colman's (and the melodramatist's) solution to the human misery of "things as they are":

> Where fever droops his burning head
> Where sick men languish on their bed;
> Around let ev'ry accent be,
> Harmony! Harmony!
> A soft and dulcet Harmony! (127)

The "harmony" alluded to here is not simply of the musical variety. Colman's harmonious society is one in which everyone knows his or her role and plays it contentedly. No jarring notes of rebellion should be discerned beneath the groundswell of universal satisfaction. The melodrama refuses to admit the victim-victimizer power structure without tampering with it, without breaking the cycle. There is never any indication in melodrama that the revolutionary cycle is about to be resumed, that the rescued-in-the-nick-of-time victim is about to metamorphose into a tyrant. Whereas the Gothic discloses disequilibrium and instability, the melodrama proffers stability and "dulcet harmony"—at least in the long run. The triumphant Wilford registers nothing but a solicitous concern for his master and a pious gratitude to the Supreme Master. His master may have done wrong, but he is master still. Unrectified usurpation, mob riot—these are impossibilities in melodrama.

The Gothic sensibility, on the other hand, "celebrates" political rage, fulminates against the status quo—and then insists that, in the end, nothing changes, that nothing can. And so Gothic victim and victimizer remain locked in a power struggle, exchanging roles occasionally, yet essentially powerless to break the cycle. There is no liberation in the Gothic cosmos; if it occurs at all, it is quickly unmasked as an illusion. "The way things are: is terribly cruel," insists the Gothic, but that is the way "things" are.

As will become evident, this configuration of Gothic power, which continually materializes in Gothic narrative texts, reappears almost intact in NeoGothic drama. The performing tyrants of Stephen Poliakoff's *City Sugar* (1975), Peter Weiss's *Marat-Sade* (1965), Peter Barnes's *The Ruling Class* (1969), and Roberta Athayde's *Miss Margarida's Way* (1977), initially secure in their roles, inevitably begin to manifest symptoms of the oncoming role exchange. In *Miss Margarida's Way* the tyrant's imminent collapse into the role of victim is most evident; however, all NeoGothic dramas imply, even if allusively, that, for the victimizer at least, a role reversal is ineluctable. In its portrayals of the support-ing players, the NeoGothic drama does envision the possibility of a role ex-change, but, unlike the Gothic fantasy, rarely represents the moment of revolt. In most cases the NeoGothic stage servant resembles fairly closely his or her narrative counterpart. Although several of these spear-carriers exhibit a surly discontent with their roles, their metamorphosis into spear-hurling mob is not, with the exception of *Marat-Sade,* represented. Thus, once again, *Marat Sade* continues to offer the most comprehensive example of all elements and configu-rations of the Gothic power struggle.

As a kind of prelude to discussion of the performing tyrant, it may be useful to consider the phenomenology of stage performance as an intrinsically risk-laden, taxing undertaking. Bert States helpfully offers a view of the actor which is decidedly at variance with the cliché of the egotist who uses the stage as a vehicle of exhibitionism. States provides some unusual and insightful reflections about the nature of theatrical performance:

> [In] the theater our sympathetic involvement with the characters is attended by a secondary and largely subliminal line of empathy born of the possibility that the illusion may at any moment be shattered by a mistake or accident. For the most part, this is a low-risk investment, but it is a crucial quality of the phenomenological quality of stage performance. It is our creatural bond with the actor who stands before us in a vulnerable place. . . . The theatre offers the actor no saving net; the play is one long danger. (1985, 119–20)

States clearly shares Artaud's sense of the contingency of the stage produc-tion, and he articulates more clearly than Artaud just how it is that onstage performance can be said to be a "cruelty" to the performer. "The actor," States reminds us, "risks the stage" (122). He or she "teeters constantly on the verge of catastrophe—that is, of becoming one of us," of tumbling "into the lower, or nonabsolute world of the audience" (121). This odd danger makes of the actor—even the bit-player—a daredevil figure, a high flying risk-taker. The inevitable cost of performing under, as Kierkegaard phrases it, "the prodigious burden" of "the weight of everyone's eyes" (77), is, however, more profoundly manifested in the spotlighted lead player. The NeoGothic drama compounds the stress of Gothic antiheroism with this stress which States describes. Not only is the NeoGothic stage tyrant climbing a ladder which is constantly descending, everyone is watching him do it. It is no accident that the metaphor of a vertiginous fall appears both in Wilt's discussion of the Gothic anti-hero and in States's analysis of the actor. Both teeter "on the verge of catastrophe."

Stephen Poliakoff's *City Sugar* (1975) presents an appropriately updated Ambrosio, now a secular preacher-priest. Leonard Brazil, teacher-turned-disc jockey, is *the* voice of Leicester, "reaching out, spreading across the whole city, . . . swooping into cars on the motorway and down chimneys and through brick walls and across pylons" (76). His methods of crowd control are adapted to the proclivities of his listening audience—an endless stream of soothing patter designed to lull the listener into mindless complacency. "Not to worry" is the gospel preached by Brazil to his "sweets." A wise-cracking, Machiavellian tyrant, Brazil knows how to cajole his audience into decorous passivity:

> And now I've something to say, folks. (*Gentle tone*) To all of you, I have a little message from our little friends, the Po-leese. They say a lot of people in this fair city of ours have been taking what doesn't belong to them . . . and our little friends in blue have had to go into the schools and shops . . . so they can catch them purple-handed. I know times are hard, but keep out of trouble, won't you? (44)

The debris left after an outdoor concert is euphemized as "rather a mess," which the untidy mob is asked to avoid at future gatherings. Chastisement is mitigated by an unctuous rhetoric that consistently soft-soaps its target. Brazil does not have to be told "what they want."

Off the air, however, Brazil drops this pose, revealing himself as a weary, contemptuous performer who despises the audience he manipulates. This backstage view of Brazil discloses a tyrant on the set who exacts unflinching obedience from his crew. He insults them, threatens them—"I do it to everybody who works for me," he explains cheerily. When he decides arbitrarily to truncate the station's newscast in mid-broadcast, the astonished announcer readily capitulates: "All right then—if that's what you want. If *you* say so" (70).

Oddly enough, this absolute lack of resistance galls Brazil. The more sycophantic members of his staff qualify for particular abuse. At such moments Brazil's tirades fall just short of the paroxysms of a Gothic antihero:

> I need somebody who's going to think, *think*. . . . Not just a callous, unquestioning secret police vegetable. . . . You're an abortion really, aren't you?—with absolutely no imagination. Nothing! A complete abortion. (55)

It is off the air too that Brazil's venomous loathing for his audience emerges: "If there was an earthquake today or a full-scale revolution, those girls wouldn't notice, not a chance." Even though he dismisses "the golden days of 1967" as so much "romantic crap" (53), he is even more disgusted by the mid-seventies climate of apathy. His disdain is apparent in this description of the crowd which had attended a weekend rock concert:

> It was vile . . . a gray, shabby echo of the time when festivals really were celebrations. Everybody was lying about in lifeless heaps, mumbling apologetically. . . . You could have turned them over with your foot, and they wouldn't have been able to get up. (53)

This figurative life-in-death quality becomes almost literal in his gruesome description of one concert goer whose face and lips were "sort of swollen and completely ashen, almost blue . . . as if she was actually physically dead" (53).

Like a frustrated teacher, Brazil prods his torpid listeners, hoping to detect some faint signs of life—even hostility is preferable to utter inanition. He therefore devises a contest, a "Competition of the Century," which becomes, ultimately, his means of proving to himself what he has surmised for quite some time—that, fed enough hype, the swinish multitude will swallow anything.

Brazil deliberately concocts ridiculous rules and demeaning regulations for his contest. The "prize"—a personal interview with any member of the latest, hottest rock group—is pathetic since "The Yellow Jacks" are even more insipid and boring than their adoring fans. To win this sorry jackpot, each contestant must first compose an essay explaining why he or she wants to win. Like some sadistic schoolmaster, Brazil reads, with a sarcastic, running side-commentary, some selected essays over the air. Since all the entries are equally execrable, Brazil arbitrarily chooses the first-round winners. Inventing the rules as he goes along, he ponders what he'll "make them do next." He next decrees that the semifinalists must each prepare a life-sized dummy of one of the "Jacks."

The cruelty of the contest escalates, however, when the two finalists show up for the final round, which is to be broadcast live. Brazil now takes on a metarole as a manic gameshow host. Without warning, he begins switching and reswitching the rules, barraging the bewildered contestants with screwball questions which have no relevance to the contest and which serve only to point up the finalists' status as ill-trained seals and his own as sadistic emcee. He needles the girls, demoralizes them with loud buzzers and bells, turning their real distress into a piece of showmanship. He stages this pitiful duel, calculatedly granting the opponents equal points so that he can, with a theatrical flourish, turn the final decision over to the listening audience, who can phone in their votes. Of course, the contest has been rigged from the start; Brazil had chosen his runner-up even before the contest began. He explains (off the air, of course):

> I picked you out, do you know that, homed in on you. . . . I picked out that voice, that slightly dead, empty sort of voice. Picked it out as Miss Average. . . . I let it get through each stage, let you clamber up here, because I wanted to see it. (75)

As the winner departs to claim her award—a ride in the car with "the boys' cook and the luggage" and "a half hour's chat at midnight with them in a motoring craft"—the loser remains behind with Brazil. Off the air once more, he sheds the mask of joker and confronts his victim directly:

> I glanced at you before the last question and saw that stare, that blank, infuriating gaze, and then it just happened. I wanted to see how far *I could push you,* how much you'd take—I was hoping you'd come back . . . that you'd put up a fight, Nichola. That you'd explode, Nichola, you'd explode. . . . [W]hy didn't you, why don't you? . . . What's the matter with all you kids now? (74)

"What's the matter" is that such worms lack the energy to writhe; there are no entrails to be crushed. Enraged by such vacuity, he seizes the girl, "holding her by the arm in front of him"—as Heathcliff held young Cathy. But he immediately realizes that even cruelty cannot provoke the spark of resistance, the flash of animation that he desperately desires. Degeneration has become so profound, so pervasive that "Metaphysics," even of the Artaudean variety, cannot penetrate such thick-skinnedness. As this last, flickering half-hope dies, Brazil consigns Nichola to the subhuman category of the zombie: "You almost feel, Nichola Davies,—as if you're from another planet" (74).

Brazil, NeoGothic antihero, is surrounded by creatures who mindlessly perform his bidding—a Gothic tyrant's dream come true, one would think. He has inherited what Gothic victimizers long for—a community so pliant that it will submit to every whim, will obey every command except the injunction to assert itself. *City Sugar* offers a portrait of a Gothic power-wielder alone in a world that contains nothing but horribly docile bodies, terribly willing victims. In the midst of his power, Brazil too doubts, doubts that such power could really be tolerated. Yet his worst suspicions are confirmed. The real horror of this revisionist interpretation of the Gothic power structure is this community of the almost-dead. It is Brazil's lucid terror that makes him cruel.

This grim lucidity and its withering contempt for the victim is likewise very much the through-line of Weiss's Sade. An even more overtly theatrical victim-victimizer relationship is that of Weiss's Sade and the nameless, hapless paranoiac who portrays Marat. Sade's persecution of the Marat-actor usually passes unnoticed because the audience's attention is diverted by his obvious persecution of the Marat-character. This more subtle harassment consists of a series of innuendoes designed, as Suzanne Dieckman contends, to implant "in the fertile field of the paranoiac's mind the suspicion that the assassination will be real, that the patient playing Corday will actually be permitted to stab him"

(1978, 56). This specifically theatrical formulation of persecution rests on a parodic revision of the theatrical convention by which an actor, a director, and an audience implicitly recognize that whatever happens onstage during the course of a play is not real. This revision is made possible by special conditions obtaining in the staging of Sade's play: since the actors are mad, there is for them no firm distinction between what happens offstage and what happens on. Hence this poor lunatic actor is even more vulnerable than Poliakoff's Nichola.

Dieckman proposes that Sade's persecution of this actor is an outgrowth of his hatred for the Marat-character. One could argue though that this persecution may be motivated by sheer sadism. In *Marat-Sade* (as in *City Sugar*) the theatrical cliché of the tyrant on the set, the taskmaster-director, is enacted, brought to monstrous life.

Dieckman identifies several of the strategies whereby Sade unnerves his helpless actor. These strategies in concert work to fuel the paranoid actor's anxiety. Dieckman interprets the Marat-actor's flight from the bathtub as an instance of his breaking character in his own real terror. Finally Dieckman asserts that the Marat-actor, given his precondition of paranoia and given Sade's demonically clever manipulations, does come to believe that he, while performing the role of Marat, will actually be murdered by the somnambulist who plays Corday.

Thus Dieckman's reading retheatricalizes what might otherwise seem merely an abstract tug-of-war between two antithetical political ideologies. Her discussion allows us to superimpose theatrical nomenclature onto Gothic political roles: the victimizer becomes a cruel *auteur*-director, and the victim an actor.

Our last glimpse of Sade is that of a man perched on a chair "laughing triumphantly." We can never know if that laughter is the laughter of gratified malice or whether it is the manic laughter of the deranged; nor can we be sure whether Sade has himself succumbed to madness, or whether he is supremely in control, signeurially detached from the turmoil breaking out all over the set.

The strain of playing the tyrant may or may not be beginning to tell on Sade. In this respect too there are antecedents within the Gothic narrative tradition. Though most Gothic anti-heroes self-destruct or are smashed to atoms, a few, like Melmoth, are not so unambiguously decreated, as Wilt observes.

> Maturin is strangely ambiguous about Melmoth's end. Are those cries of supplication or cries of blasphemy that issue from the Wanderer's chamber on the last night? . . . Is death . . . something he desires or fears? . . . [T]hough they find on the crag below the handkerchief Melmoth had worn, no trace of the man himself is found. (Wilt 1980, 57–58)

In Weiss's play, the subtext of that Sadean laughter forever eludes us. Sade may well be at the apex of his power; he may also be the only sane being in the halls of Charenton.

These questions do not trouble us when we bring them to bear on Poliakoff's play. As Brazil departs for the "large, large audience" of London, there is every reason to believe that he will conquer there with an ease that will only intensify his rage. That rage may twist itself into madness and self-destruction, but the tone and temper of *City Sugar* suggest that, if there are cracks in the facade of this Machiavellian anti-hero, they remain the tiniest of fissures. The stress of playing the tyrant is not so readily apparent in Brazil.

Such is not the case, however, with mad Jack Gurney of Peter Barnes's *The Ruling Class*. Although the play exhibits much the same Gothic power structure as *Marat-Sade* or *City Sugar,* there is an unequivocal insistence that the role of performer-tyrant is already, by definition, an insane one. There is here, as in the Weiss and Poliakoff plays, an explicit association of theatrical illusion-making and political manipulation. Stage presence, the ability to overawe and bedazzle, is, in *The Ruling Class,* a most formidable weapon in the arsenal of the ruling class. Yet, as will become evident, the play also demonstrates that the unending maintenance of such a posture, the nonstop putting on of the good show, the strain of being forever "on," leads inexorably to crackup.

Jack's initial interpretation of the role of performer-tyrant is, like Falkland's, benign. A paranoid-schizophrenic, Jack believes that he is Jesus Christ. This delusion, however, whether benign or otherwise, is clearly delineated as a consequence of his membership in the ruling class. As Bernard Dukore remarks, "Jack's delusion that he is God relates directly to the syndrome of the ruling class. His lunacy is an extension of the lunacy of his class . . . from 'my lord' to 'my Lord'" (1981, 15). As "JC," Jack preaches the equality of all people. He scandalizes his colleagues by insisting that: "The mighty must bow down before the pricks of the louse-ridden rogues" (Barnes [1969] 1981, 28). It is not, however, the obscenity that galvanizes his listeners into conspiring against him, but the "Bolshie" mass-levelling he proposes.

Jack's benign rendition of the tyrant role is subjected to a severe trial when he is forced to confront a rival interpretation in the person of the mad McKyle, who styles himself the "High Voltage Messiah," the "Electric Christ," the "AC/DC God." McKyle, who might have tumbled out of the pages of Hogg's *Confessions,* renders a decidedly Gothic version of a tyrant God: "I made the world in mae image. I'm a holy terror. Sae that accounts for the bloody mess it's in" (72). The Love-God that Jack has been enacting so charmingly is no match for McKyle's chthonic, death-dealing God. As Jack begins to succumb to McKyle's electrifying performance, the scene is interrupted by the spectacular entrance of a terrible, yet perversely comical-looking intruder:

There is a clap of thunder, the french-windows fly open and with a rush of cold wind a monstrous eight-foot beast bursts in. It walks upright like a man, covered with thick black hair swept out from each side like a gigantic guinea-pig, and is dressed incongruously in high Victorian fashion: morning coat and top-hat.[6]

A grotesque conglomeration of Frankenstein Monster, Wellsian ape-man and top-hatted Mr. Hyde, the creature attacks Jack "pummel[ing] his victim with a series of vicious wrestling holds" (74). None of the other characters are able to see this beast; only the audience shares Jack's bizarre, violent hallucination. The scene is unabashedly Gothic. As Jack lapses into unconsciousness, the thing "raises its hat, grunts and lurches out the way it came in" (74).

The creature's effect on Jack is not readily apparent until the next act wherein we discover that the Earl seems to have regained his sanity; more accurately, his madness has merely assumed a new, more insidious form—he now believes himself to be Jack the Ripper, aristocratic scourge of East End vice. He has been transformed into the genteel, well-heeled monster of Victorian fiction. It is a role he relishes:

> See how I marshal words. That's the secret of being normal. . . . I've finally been processed into right thinking power. They made me adjust to modern times. . . . I'm Jack, cunning Jack, quiet Jack . . . not the Good Shephard, not the Prince of Peace, I'm Red Jack . . . Jack from Hell. (90)

Thus the benevolent dictatorship of the "Prince of Peace" gives way to a reign of terror. As it turns out, Jack's adoption of the persona of the Ripper signifies his fitness for the role of victimizer and his acceptance of the ruling-class ethos. The historical Ripper, in preying on wayward women of the poorest classes, achieved almost mythic status as an arch-chastiser of aggressive sexuality in the lowborn; this sexuality, with its undertones of social mobility, of access to the upper class, converted such women, in the mind of a panic-stricken aristocracy, into covert working-class revolutionaries. Thus Jack, in assuming this role, achieves solidarity with his coterie.

In Barnes's play it is not the revolutionary crowd that is imaged in Gothic tropes but rather the ruling class. The House of Lords is a house of horrors, its inmates "mouldering dummies" with "bloated stomachs and skull-like faces" (117). It is an assemblage of great old ones, desiccated Gothic fathers, determined to retain power, determined to crush the upstart, the poor, the deviant, the weak. Jack's address here, thunderously applauded, publicizes his transfer of allegiance from childlike submissiveness to murdering fatherhood: "*God the Son* wants nothing but to give freely in love and gentleness. It's loathsome, a foul perversion of life! . . . *God the Father* demands, orders, controls, crushes. We must follow Him, my noble lords" (118).

If the world of *The Ruling Class* is a Gothic abyss, Jack has at last come to see "what the world's really like" (40). There is no lucid voice in this mad,

Figure 2.    Scene from *The Ruling Class* by Peter Weiss
            (*Used by permission, Chris Arthur/Transworld Eye*)

dark world; Jack's final delusion perfectly harmonizes with things as they are. In *The Ruling Class,* as in the Gothic fantasy, the basis of power is brute force after all—a God who "flays, stabs, bludgeons, mutilates" (118). "Sheer presence," "star quality," "natural dignity" are simply the theatrical manifestations of that raw, blatant power.

Despite its zaniness, *The Ruling Class* is a dark vision of a cruel and dangerous cosmos. That bloodcurdling "single scream of fear and agony" that emerges "out of the darkness" after the stage lights have faded down is the play's final "word" and its signature. If *The Ruling Class* is funny, that funniness is strange, desperate, and brutal, much like the mordant humor of Beckford's *Vathek:* at the end of each, the joking stops.

The performance of cruelty, as Artaud recognized, is itself a cruelty to the performer. The strain of playing the arch-tyrant is manifested in Jack's madness and in the bodily enervation of the ruling class. They are all, as Bishop "Bertie" pronounces them, "doomed," "accursed," "another House of Usher" (102).

Thus even as the play's ending seems to confirm Jack in his power, the underlying insinuation is that "it'll happen" to him too one day because the performance of tyranny deforms and sickens the performer. Such a perception is not, or course, limited to the Gothic; it belongs also to the savage moral vision of Jacobean tragedy. But it differs from this vision in that the Gothic foresees no termination to the cycle of tyranny—there will always be another Gurney, an equally cruel understudy waiting in the wings, ready to step into the spotlight, ready to seize the role from the collapsing, burned-out superstar.

This congenital lunacy of the Gothic power-wielder is the animating impulse of Roberto Athayde's *Miss Margarida's Way* (1979), whose tyrant is simultaneously the most ferocious, yet the most vulnerable and pitiable of victimizers. Like Jack, Miss Margarida is mad from the outset, yet, unlike Jack, her loneliness and helplessness—her own status as a victim herself—is painfully, immediately evident. Miss Margarida, a crazily archetypical teacher, rules alone, with nothing but the sheer force of her performance to keep her class in order, to keep the mob at bay. In Athayde's play the cracks in the tyrant's facade have widened into gaping holes.

Like Jack, Miss Margarida plays both the benevolent and the savage dictator, though, unlike Jack, she oscillates between the two interpretations of the role. This manic, unpredictable alternation between sweet cajolery and ranting bullying is the chief symptom of her madness. (Brazil likewise alternates, but his interpretation is dictated by whether he is on or off the air.) Actually, Miss Margarida's ravings do make a bleak, awful kind of sense.

Miss Margarida presents her "class" with a Gothic-style history lesson: the "great principle of History" is the old familiar Gothic story—"everyone wants to dominate everyone else" (23). And the story goes on and on, everlastingly recycling itself: "It's always the same thing. Nothing changes. . . . Everything is always the same crap. . . . And *revolution* . . . is . . . two times nothing, *nothing*! It's nothing at all" (35–36). The infrastructure of Gothic power never changes even though new actors are continually conscripted, hustled on stage to play the familiar, unvarying Gothic roles. Similarly, her economics lesson is a dark parable of infinite want in the face of infinite scarcity:

> In this classroom there are only twelve bananas for thirty-five students. . . . What is going to happen? Well, the strongest student will get eight or nine bananas all for himself. The second strongest will get three or four bananas. And the 33 remaining mouths will be left *perfectly without bananas*. That is division. (27)

When performed in a totalitarian state, *Miss Margarida's Way* confirms what the hungry masses know only too well—the top bananas get all the bananas. On the other hand, the play, if performed in a state which prides itself on an ethos of justice for the underdog, appears dangerous and subversive, for it insinuates that, beneath the comfortable facade, all is not well. Neither *Miss Margarida's Way* nor the Gothic fantasy questions the existence of the human *desire* for freedom. What they doubt is the efficacy of any effort to achieve it, to break the cycle of domination. In the Gothic world, the rage against prisons is always counterbalanced by an abiding conviction of the futility of revolt.

Miss Margarida's lessons, however, are not only about Gothic power. She articulates in one form or another most of the cardinal points of Gothic ideology. Her madness drives her to an obsession with those areas of experience which the Gothic claims for its own—the unspeakable, the taboo. Even when she lectures on the simple and prosaic, she manages to make it terrible, complex, frightening. She can turn a simple stroll into a nightmare by describing in mind-boggling detail the plethora of choices that infests even this most routine of activities, pursuing her calculus of probability to absurd yet awful lengths— "Miss Margarida found 24 billion, 713 million, 433 thousand, 511 possibilities for her stroll" (72). To confront such overwhelmingness is to risk the paralysis of agoraphobia. Thus, freedom of choice, the liberty to chart one's course through the bewildering labyrinth outside one's doors, becomes a hideous dilemma about which it is safer not to think.

Her ongoing biology lesson is equally devastating: microbes sicken and kill; everyone "will end up in the cemetery or else reduced to ashes" (24); both life and death are forced upon us "willy nilly." In the Gothic we are all, as Punter remarks, "born into the world screaming" (1980, 400). Miss Margarida would concur, and so she describes the features of the Gothic landscape to her students: it is a hostile terrain, pulsating with its own alien life, gathering itself to pounce; plant life has a language of its own, rocks breathe, animals demand "equality in power" (52).

Miss Margarida's pedagogical methods perfectly suit her material—she insults, threatens, persecutes her "students." As in the Inquisition, her victims are bombarded with questions. And the student-victims must respond even though they will be abused if they do so:

> You don't participate in anything in this class. Not one goddam thing. I talk to you and you believe whatever I happen to say. I am the fucking teacher here. Silence! SILENCE! . . . I'll ram this greenboard up the ass of the first bastard who opens his mouth! (26)

Such virulence far exceeds the controlled nastiness of a Leonard Brazil.

Even so, Miss Margarida is the most crippled, exposed, and vulnerable of these performing tyrants. The strain of the role is so evident in her that she seems as much a victim as a victimizer; her repeated call for a "Messiah" or a "Holy Ghost" may be a plea or a challenge. One reviewer expresses the fragility of the character beneath the mask of the bully:

> Miss Margarida suddenly falls silent and collapses upon her desk. . . . And suddenly the grotesque, ridiculous figure is one of us. . . . [Miss Margarida] shrinks to a middle-aged woman lying there in a slip and the judgment against totalitarianism becomes suddenly complex, uncertain, and oddly moving. (Eden 1977, C16)

That complexity and uncertainty arise from the disturbing realization that Miss Margarida too has had her role inflicted upon her, that the role itself is draining, devastating, deadly. Her collapse onstage does not invite the round of applause which normally accompanies the demise of the melodramatic stage villain.

The strain of playing the role of the tyrant expresses itself not just in the collapse of the character but in the obvious demands it makes of the actress with temerity enough to assay the part. The role allows no respite; it requires, as one commentator put it, "the stamina of a dockhand and an awesome range of acting skills being visibly laid waste" (Kalem 1977, 108). The actress must be prepared for unscripted outbursts from her more exhibitionistic audience-"students." Even as the audience is goaded by the play itself into baiting their "teacher," she is nonetheless expected to keep her "class" in order. On the other hand, an overdocile audience impels the actress to exert more and more pressure on it to respond. So exacting is this role that an ill-prepared actress risks her career in playing it. The political, the Gothic, and the theatrical dimensions of tyranny are merged in Miss Margarida's performance—crowd control becomes a matter of dazzle, unerring timing, unflappable stage presence, and dauntless bluster. These are Miss Margarida's only weapons: the "Principal," who is supposed to be on her "side," never appears. She lacks the brute force, the economic clout that shores up Jack Gurney's power. She is, in the end, quite alone, with nothing but language—empty threats—to stave off the not-so-compliant.

Thus it is that *Miss Margarida's Way* presents the collapse of the performer-tyrant, an event that fails to transpire in *Marat-Sade, City Sugar,* and even *The Ruling Class.* While retaining the savagery of the Gothic tyrant, she reminds us that, in the Gothic cosmos, that role is as crushing, as punishing as the mirror role of victim. Even so, *Miss Margarida's Way* never romanticizes its antiheroine. Such a tack would run deeply counter to the Gothic's insistence on moral ambivalence.

Mastership in the Gothic is certainly a torment; servitude, however, is an indignity. While the NeoGothic drama's ensemble players may undertake either role—victim or victimizer—most commonly these bit-role-players remain submissive if surly vassals. As with the player-tyrant, we can observe the player-victim's increasing discomfort with and restiveness in the role. This rebellion, however, only rarely manifests itself overtly. For reasons which will gradually become apparent, riot occurs more frequently in Gothic narrative than in the NeoGothic drama. We shall begin, therefore, with docile supporting players, watch them grow refractory, and finally, in *Marat-Sade,* observe them as they break out in the frenzy of mob riot.

Pinter's *The Dumbwaiter,* which many commentators have classified as an instance of "kitchen sink" realism, is "kitchen sink" indeed, but with a decidedly Gothic twist: this play about two docile kitchen servants rings a number of changes on the Gothic convention which associates domestic servitude with matters culinary. That the subject of food should remain central throughout is entirely in keeping with this convention.

The play's very title appears to ratify the Gothic linkage of servitude with stupidity. Ben and Gus obviously wait, but they are also waiters, that is, serving-men who dish out food. The epithet "dumb" is similarly equivocal as many readers have noted. The pair are, however, typically dimwitted Gothic servants. Their alternative identities as dumb, that is, silent, killers are not really explored.

Archetypal Gothic servants, Ben and Gus evince a lively interest in food. In the context of this grisly occupation, Gus's delight in the apartment's crockery seems incongruous until we realize that his tote bag of snacks is very much in the tradition of the food- and drink-obsessed Gothic peon. As observed earlier, tots of whiskey go a long way toward securing the cooperation of the lower orders: *The Monk*'s Cunegunda, the simpleminded duenna, is made pliable by a plentiful supply of cherry brandy. Dracula's coffin-haulers drop broad hints to his pursuers that their cooperation and other "dry work" is best rewarded by the impartment of liquid refreshment. It is, in fact, the unseen master's disregard for the physical comforts of his serving-men that fuels Gus's anxieties.

This anxiety has been read as existential angst by some commentators. But one could argue more simply, as does Austin Quigley, that Gus simply wants "assurance" (1978, 5). Gus is as equally docile a servant as Ben; he is simply a bit less secure in the role. Had his "comforts" been attended to, he would never have begun any line of questioning at all.

Once the dumbwaiter jolts into operation, however, the familiar Gothic money-shower, normally flowing downward upon the agitated crowd below (money, of course, a counter for food) is reversed. Now the upper realm (literal and figurative) exacts tribute from the lower, and that tribute is to be rendered, appropriately enough, in the form of food. The dumbwaiter becomes a hungry, mechanized maw which periodically demands the dainties of an upper-class table. Ben and Gus can send up only the junk-food slop of a poor man's kitchen—sour milk, stale crackers. The exotic cuisine requisitions mock the ineptitude and poverty of these two very dumb waiters.

Nonetheless, their rote response to the maddest demands from on high never flags. Ben's hat-in-hand mien in the face of such lunacy is a perfect instance of the unthinking, unswerving supineness of the Gothic servant: "(*speaking with great deference*): Good evening. I'm sorry to—bother you, but we just thought we'd let you know that we haven't got anything left. We sent up all we had" (111). Ludicrous it may be, "enough," as Gus remarks, "to make the cat laugh," but neither he nor Ben can even begin to explain their own frighteningly instinctive, mechanical obedience. They are not even on a par with Stoppard's "little men," Ros and Guil, who are at least articulate enough to rationalize their role as pawns.

This unwavering submissiveness, despite the fact that the flow of largesse has been reversed, bespeaks a very dark view of the serving class mentality. In the presence of the Gothic event, Ben and Gus stick to their old routines, taking orders just as always—only very dimly aware that the world has somehow gone strange. Such dogged (and doggie) loyalty to an alien and capricious authority is as frightening as the dumbwaiter itself. Ben and Gus's business-as-usual approach to the dumbwaiter suggests a terrible capacity of the human spirit to accommodate itself to immense cruelty, to any insanity forceful enough to assert itself.

While it is far from clear whether Ben, under orders, will shoot Gus, or even whether such a directive has been given, it is all too clear that Ben, and Gus too, will do as they are bid, no matter how silly, mad, obscene, or danger-ous the task, because they lack the imagination to interpret a command as anything other than a duty to be discharged. Like the marginal extras of a crowd scene, they will execute whatever the script decrees. As in Gothic fiction, that very inability to be frightened, that very paucity of imagination, that prosaic cloddishness, renders them the malleable tools of a master whose control over them is so absolute that he need not be present. No performer-tyrant need appear in *The Dumbwaiter,* for such loyal retainers have thoroughly internalized their subjugation.

As might be inferred, however, the physical embodiment of the performing tyrant does indeed suggest the presence of a less compliant victim than Ben or Gus. *City Sugar*'s Nichola, who, unlike Ben and Gus, does actually confront her tormentor, is more rebellious in the role of victim. As will become evident, Nichola, though a fairly cooperative supporting player, does exhibit a keener awareness and resentment.

The task Nichola is set resembles structurally the job assigned to Ben and Gus. She too is required to "send up" all she has. In forgoing her lunches (to save money to buy the paint to adorn her life-sized dummy), she too sacrifices her food. When the dummy must be stuffed, she strips her room, cramming her "posters . . . all her funny ornaments," in short, "everything" into the "stomach" of the dummy until "the torso is full" (50–51).

As already noted, Nichola is harassed and demeaned by Brazil during the final round of the "Competition of the Century." Shortly thereafter, she returns to the supermarket where she works as a clerk. It is by now quite late, and the store is empty except for one other shopgirl. The taciturnity that she had maintained throughout her persecution is now replaced by a "clenched violence inside" (75). In her fury she considers wrecking the store: "We could throw all this out if we wanted. . . . *Tear through it if we wanted*" (75–76). Susan, the other clerk, is astonished. Unlike Susan, Nichola has been backstage; she's heard Brazil's raging off-the-air voice. Yet she senses that the words to tell her own story will elude her. She insists, as do many Gothic tellers, that words are doomed to fail, that one can only "tell," that is, know as opposed to report, what such an experience is like. This decision not to tell her story, not even so much as to try, prepares us for her subsequent evasions. When the opportunity to revolt presents itself, Nichola backs down with the rationalization that "[i]t's not worth it really" (76). A rampage through the store would accomplish nothing except a wastage of food and the loss of her own livelihood. She will continue to be what she has always been—the sucker, the dupe, the taken.

Unlike Pinter, Poliakoff does envisage the possibility of revolution, but the resistance of the victimized can be expressed only as an inarticulate, pent-up rancor. Nichola cannot envision any other role for herself. Her sense of futility, that all movements amount to nothing, is very much in keeping with the tradition of Gothic politics. "Maybe next time," she mutters, but these fractious rumblings are drowned out by Brazil's voice booming out over the deserted supermarket. It is the master's voice—"It's him all right" (76).

The supporting player's confinement to the role of victim is equally evident in *The Ruling Class*. Neither exponent of the serving class—Grace Shelley, Jack's low-born wife, nor Tucker, Jack's aged manservant—can bring any real political vision to bear on their predicament. Grace's single *raison d'être* is to gain ruling class status and power, to "watch 'em creep and crawl at Harrods" (59). As for Tucker, Bernard Dukore's assessment is judicious: Tucker "as his name hints . . . is *tuckered,* his rebelliousness too exhausted to manifest itself effectively" (1981, 15).

Tucker, who is an articulate spokesman for the toiling class, accounts for its stoic endurance in this role:

> Fear and habit. You get into the habit of serving. Born of a servant, see, son of a servant. Family of servants. From a nation of servants. Very first thing an Englishman does, straight from his mother's womb is touch his forelock. . . . I know my history. Masters and servants, that's the way of it. (31)

Though Tucker casts himself in the role of servant spy—"Anarchist—Trotskyist—Communist Revolutionary" (31)—his undercover work amounts to nothing more than ineffective potshots: "spitting in the hot soup, peeing on the Wedgewood dinner plates" (31). For the most part, Tucker functions as the consummate butler, serving up food, drinks, and an occasional wisecrack. Despite the late Earl's bequest of 20,000 pounds—more than enough to retire in luxury—Tucker lingers on, continuing to play the servant. Later, when Jack frames him for Clare's murder (the butler did it—after all, who has better reason?), Tucker, bowing and scraping, plays the loyal retainer to the hilt: "You always was my favorite, Master Jack. . . . I could have gone but I stayed" (107).

Tucker mouths revolution—"[U]pper class excrement . . . needs kosher killing, hung up so the blue blood drains out slow and easy" (107)—and he performs his own creaking carmagnole over the corpse of murdered aristocracy, but his revolution, like that of Caleb Williams, is so much fustian. "I don't *do* anything," he admits. "I just pays me dues to the Party and they send me pamphlets, under plain cover" (105). Tucker cannot conceive of any power structure other than the one of victim and victimizer, master and servant. The pornographic photos mixed in with his Leninist pamphlets suggest their equivalence for him. The wrathful rising of the proletariat and the concomitant carnage of that event is for Tucker only a naughty fantasy.

While Tucker turns in an unconvincing portrayal of an underground revolutionary, Grace makes no pretense at fomenting revolution. Instead, all of her energies are directed toward a playing of the role of victim in order that she might escape it. Imposture being her métier, Grace is hired to impersonate Marguerite Gautier, the dramatis persona to whom Jack believes himself married. As guttersnipe, hireling, sometime actress, and kept mistress, Grace emerges as an avatar of the acting profession, an occupation which was for centuries condemned as profligate, depraved, if not downright satanic. Historically, as Jonas Barish reminds us, actors had been lumped with prostitutes as "public sinners" (1981, 192). In her dependence on the Gurneys, Grace likewise figures forth the historic condition of the actor as a servant dependent on the protection and patronage of aristocracy.[7]

By playing the victim, Grace hopes to evade this degrading role once and for all, so that she, in her turn, may make other creatures "creep and crawl" to do *her* bidding. But whereas Grace perceives the role as a temporary imposture and one deliberately assumed, the Gothic mechanisms of the play are conspiring to lock her into this role. Despite her native shrewdness, Grace never realizes the dangers of this role she has lightly undertaken, perhaps because she cherishes the common but misguided belief in the invincibility of the actor: "On certain nights. In front of the right audience. When the magic works. I've known what it is to be a God" (47). To the perils implicit in playing the role of madman's wife, she remains oblivious. She forgets that she is a hireling who, once she has produced an heir (a "little devil" who can "steal the show"), will have outlived her usefulness. Although she stages her own little revolt, loftily informing Sir Charles that he's "stuck [his] aristocratic schnozzle into [her] affairs for the last time" and that it's "a new deal all around" (88), Grace eventually discovers that the "new deal" is very much the old deal and that she, like all Gothic pawns, will never be a big deal. "[Y]ou'll never be a Gurney," Charles retorts. Grace may only play at being one. In the end she is forced back into the role she thought she had left behind for good—"Annie," streetwalker, battered toy. Grace's last role, a bit part after all, is that of one of the "Ripper's" murder victims.

Though neither she nor Tucker ever constitute any real threat to the sway of the ruling class, both are "punished" with a savagery that far exceeds the indignities inflicted on Nichola or on those Pinterian dumbwaiters. And as is usual in the Gothic, the ability to articulate the condition of victimization does not ease that condition even though it does betoken a more sharply focused discontent, an increased degree of restiveness, a heightened awareness of injustice and persecution.

Not the least of the downtrodden class's sufferings is that the escape into madness is the exclusive prerogative of aristocracy. Only "rich nobs and privileged assholes," as Tucker puts it, "can afford to be bonkers" (40). Though in one sense the play identifies insanity as a syndrome of power, a penalty for its possession, it also establishes lunacy as an index of sensibility. *The Ruling Class* pushes the Gothic convention of aristocratic hypersensitivity to its furthest limits—the hypersensitivity of a Roderick Usher is hyperbolized into outright lunacy. The poor, on the other hand, can afford nothing but a clear-eyed sanity which allows them absolutely no respite from the miseries of their predicament. This presentation of *sanity* as a kind of curse is common to Gothic fiction. Melmoth, for example, taunts the helplessly sane Stanton: "You will say . . . 'my sanity is my greatest curse in this abode of horrors'" (Maturin [1820] 1961, 43).

In Gothic representations of lower-class victimization, in contrast, the escape offered by insanity is rarely needed by the servant-class because it is perceived as so prosaic, so thick-skinned, so unimaginative as to be incapable of the kind of intense suffering that either leads to madness or desires it. *Marat-Sade* is unusual in that it presents two distinctly opposing views of the ensemble players. On the one hand, Sade's "The People," portrayed by the Four Singers and the ensemble of Patients, are the conventional Gothic common herd—cynical, materialistic, shortsighted, earthy—*incapable* of insanity. The madmen-actors, on the other hand, represent what is usually, in the Gothic, the aristocratic view of insanity—the last resort of the tortured, sensitive soul.

The signal trait of The People of *Marat-Sade* is its disillusionment with Revolutionary cant: "We've got rights the right to starve / We've got jobs waiting for work" (11). During Roux's passionate, rabble-rousing appeal, the Four Singers who stand in as his audience quickly grow bored with his fiery demagoguery and turn, like disinterested students, to other amusement—drinking and dicing. Roux's tirade is mocked by the riffraff's obvious boredom. They answer Roux's litany of victimization with a refrain of their own: "We have nothing, always had nothing." Masters and servants, that's the way of it.

The People's undisguised contempt for what to them is nothing but high-sounding mumbo-jumbo is not, however, founded on any particular perspicacity or political vision. Rather, it stems from a surly disappointment that the Revolution has not served up *their* portion of the good life. The People, as conceived by Sade, do not seek to alter the power structure, but simply to trade places with their oppressors. Thus, for them, the Revolution is "a fish, . . . a new pair of shoes . . . the best soup in the world." They are simultaneously clear-sighted and myopic, piteously wretched and contemptible. Sade's People always speak of "our revolution" as if it were some sort of bash, a long-awaited party. Sade's People are the Gothic mob—avaricious, bloodthirsty, stupid. The role, as written, is an aristocrat's view of the mob.

The madmen-actors, however, are not to be confused with Sade's People. The victimization of these conscripted actors is much more immediate and apparent than is the victimization of the People, about which we only hear. The victimization of the lunatic actors is enacted not chronicled. In the light of the beatings, straightjacketings, and enchainment inflicted upon the asylum inmates, the complaints of The People dwindle into childish, unconvincing whining.

Who are these madmen "pressed into service" to represent The People? If we consider that, as Weiss reminds us, the inmates of Charenton were just as likely to be "socially impossible"[8] as certifiably mad, then *Marat-Sade* acquires yet another victim-victimizer dimension superimposed over the other one. The social deviance to which Weiss alludes need not have been very radical in the intensely conservative atmosphere of post-Revolutionary France. In this wise the inmates (at least some of them) now appear as casualties of social repression and intolerance. "Woe to the man who is different," laments Roux, and we pause to wonder it if is himself of whom he speaks—or whether it is Marat, or

Sade, or them all. Perhaps the Charenton cast is actually a band of outspoken nonconformists, political and social rebels who have been battered into psychotic behavior. Mohammed Kowsar urges just such a reading: "*Marat/Sade* is first and foremost a text that exploits the bodies of *alleged* lunatics by means of a coercion that is brought to bear on inmates turned into reluctant actors" (1984, 375).

From this vantage point, the patient-actors take on an additional collective role besides that of Gothic commoner. That is to say, they are apotheosized into a group of beleaguered individualists persecuted by a loveless, hypocritical society. Their prototype then becomes the deranged Caleb, driven mad by the cruelty of the so-called sane.

Even if we do not apply these considerations, we must still recognize the victimization of Sade's actors as distinct from the historical victimization of The People to which the play continually alludes—Sade persecutes not just the Marat-actor but his entire cast. Though many commentators have chosen to regard Sade as a species of liberator (Coulmier's foil rather than Marat's), others have countered that Sade deliberately incites the Patients, knowing full well that any self-assertion on their part will be swiftly and brutally stifled by the cudgel-wielding "Nurses." Kowsar takes up this point:

> In fact, the systematic persecution (both physical and mental) of the patients is so pervasive that any intent at the level of philosophical discourse aspired to by the text is rendered spurious. . . . Though DeSade knows only too well that the notion of therapy through art and education veils the same old cruelty toward incarcerated victims under new liberal premises, his own theatre practice sanctions this duplicity. . . . [T]he spectacle of patients being pummelled and pelted is central to DeSade's release of histrionic activity. The melange of farce, pantomime and the grotesque that turns the theatre into a circus is the other face of the torture chamber. (1984, 375–77)

In fact, the content of *Marat-Sade* is so volatile that the tensions bound up in the roles can vent themselves on the real-life actors who undertake them. The history of the 1964–65 Brook production furnishes evidence of several peculiar side-effects which manifested themselves both onstage and off. Ian Richardson, for example, who portrayed Marat, disclosed the fact that, during performance, the cast had experienced "actual physical violence of a very serious sort breaking out," that there had been "real blood up there, fractured teeth, unconscious people" (Schechner 222). The subsequent American run of the production (which, with its more ambitious performance schedule, placed even heavier demands on the cast) was plagued by "attrition, melancholia, misanthropy, and persisting miserableness of spirit" (Roddy, 1966, 110). Between Brook's draining rehearsal techniques and the inherent stresses of the roles themselves, even the most seasoned professionals began to experience offstage psychological disturbances. Wryly commented Glenda Jackson, Brook's Corday, "We were all convinced that we were going looney" (Trewin 1971, 145). These developments were not mere happenstance; they arose out of the pressures and stresses of performing a dramatic text that, like the Gothic fantasy, "deals darkly with dark things." This victimization of the actor *qua* actor in *Marat-Sade* is to date the most extreme instance of the Gothic power structure as it has been translated into theatrical terms.

Before turning to the very rare eruption of mob rule in the NeoGothic drama, we may close this consideration of the victimized ensemble player with the anguished protest of one unusually prescient "First Attendant." A plague-stricken, dying spear-carrier in Peter Barnes's *Red Noses* fulminates against the dramatic convention of the expendable bit-player:

> All the fault of writers. . . . Always writing stories where some characters are important and others just disposable stock—First Attendant, Second Peasant, Third Guard. . . . That's how itty-bitty people like me come to be butchered in battlefields, die in droves. . . . (1985, 20)

This diatribe goes unnoticed, of course, even as the poor slob topples over in mid-speech. The claim to be "important too" may be objectively valid, but in a Gothic universe no one, neither tyrant nor peasant, is unexpendable. Furthermore, although this analysis of the power structure is painfully accurate, its insight is no more of a defense than "health, strength, or moral well-being." In a Gothic cosmos, as Peter Brooks concludes, "Man's destruction—torture, murder—merely does nature's work" (1979, 217). Hence, this bit-player's worst enemies are not the "important" characters, but a malignant, "iceberg-faced" Nature.

Thus, despite a few such outcries, the NeoGothic drama sustains with great fidelity the power structure of the Gothic fantasy: most NeoGothic servants are docile, only periphally aware, like Nichola, of their powerlessness. Even those few, like Tucker and the "First Attendant," who do manifest an awareness of their victimized condition, nonetheless regard the status quo as unchangeable. Finally, the inmate-actors of Charenton, who often seem like so many quelled revolutionaries, seem to prove that such is indeed the case. In other words, even those performers who resist their roles seem doomed to go on forever playing the victim.

As has already been observed, outbreaks of mob rule do not always materialize in the Gothic fantasy, and when they do occur, their duration is momentary. The NeoGothic drama follows suit in this regard: incidents of riot are rare even if the potential for violence is plainly evident. However, and this distinction is crucial, the NeoGothic drama, unlike its narrative counterpart, displays a kind of furtive relish in, a half-hankering for, anarchic violence. While the

Gothic fantasy registers anxiety about the consequences of mass revolt, the NeoGothic drama is much more worried abut the implications of mob apathy. Like their fiction-writing counterparts, the NeoGothic dramatists readily presume the greed and boorish stupidity of the common herd; nonetheless, in contrast to the Gothic novelists, the NeoGothic dramatists regard mob activism (in whatever form it assumes) as a lesser evil than crowd passivity. As in *City Sugar,* the NeoGothic crowd is less beast than zombie—passionless, soulless.

In *Miss Margarida's Way* the peasant revolt is pathetically feeble and short-lived—a single student shiftily rifles through Miss Margarida's handbag in her absence. Like the traditional Gothic commoner, he "understands nothing of what he sees" in the bag—except for Miss Margarida's stock of candy. (Food, we may recall, is the Gothic underdog's ruling passion.) Although the ingredients for a role exchange and *coup d'état* are vividly incarnate in the "large and frightening gun" he discovers in the bag, the seizure of power, the role exchange, never transpires. Cowed by the mere possibility of Miss Margarida's reappearance, he slinks back to his desk empty-handed. What are we to make of this pathetic excuse for a mob revolt? Certainly Athayde's position is far from clear, but it seems safe to conjecture that such spinelessness is intended to be perceived as despicable and even frightening in its wider implications.

In the NeoGothic drama, it seems, the ensemble players are so enervated and inert that only the most extraordinary circumstances could provoke them. It would appear from a survey of contemporary political drama that only the mad can generate the frenzy of Gothic riot. Weiss's *Marat-Sade* alone enacts Gothic pandemonium.

Though many commentators have argued that the performance of Sade's play awakens (or reawakens) the inmates' will to rebel, there is equally strong evidence to suggest that they too "understand nothing" of what they see and say, that the play for them is nothing more than a license to cut loose, to act out their own mad desires and aggressions. Samuel Weiss, for example, argues that "the senseless shouting and the mad dancing of the patients" undermines any sense of a "growth of consciousness" on the part of the inmate-actors (1966, 128). The revolt-in-progress, with which the play "concludes," is not necessarily a conscious uprising against Coulmier and his regime. It may simply be a Gothic brawl—utterly directionless, completely aimless.

For Sade, maniacal behavior is not confined to the clinically insane. It is precisely his view that all humanity is instinctually, helplessly brutish. Such is the message encoded in his anecdote of the "gentle, cultured" tailor who, foaming and screaming, rips open the chest of another human being. Sade indicates no motive for the deed. In the Gothic, as for Sade, none is needed—human cruelty is as natural as it is motiveless. Marat, on the other hand, insists on rationalizing human barbarism—the looting, the dismemberment, the dancing over corpses—as the necessary, explainable, and justifiable revenge of The

People. The carnival atmosphere that prevailed during the height of the Terror (represented in Sade's play by the macabre sporting with the severed head) is a phenomenon that Marat chooses to ignore, but which for Sade is central. Leslie Miller suggests in this context that Marat's defense of the execution as "just punishment" is demolished by the "frenzied and ecstatic behavior" of the lunatics during the mimed execution:

> At one level the reaction of the patients of Charenton is but a heightened rendering of the appalling reality documented in eyewitness accounts of the mob's response to executions performed during the actual Reign of Terror. . . . Their hysteria tends to recover the underlying motivations for the executions from the rational sphere and to equate it with primitive instinct gratification. . . . [It] implies that his [Marat's] references to rational concepts such as social justice are irrelevant even if they are objectively valid. (1971, 44)

Thus Marat, Miller insists, "remains blind to the destructive forces within himself and the revolution he has helped to unleash" (1971, 55). In the context of the play, Sade's view of the mob, the Gothic tyrant's view, is as credible as is Marat's opposite view—that the patients are crushed revolutionaries.

The use of madmen to portray the Revolutionary mob merely literalizes what occurs figuratively in the Gothic. Moreover, the frenzied behavior of the inmates is not so far removed from the behavior of a populace that did go berserk during the Revolution. If we can somehow block out the beatings and straightjacketings, the Charenton cast becomes the Gothic mob—mindless, inhuman, savage. Readmit the brutality of their wardens, and the demented become once more pathetic, abused victims.

While it was not strictly necessary for Weiss to have actually staged the Gothic riot, having staged it, he did in fact endow it with the characteristics which the Gothic has traditionally accorded the crowd in its role as victimizer. In so doing, he most fully endorses the Gothic's darkest credo—that man truly is "a mad animal"—a doctrine which these other NeoGothic playwrights cannot wholly bring themselves to ratify.

As Wilt sums up, the Gothic community is "alternatively the tool and the master of the solitary spirit" (1980, 78). In both Gothic narrative and the NeoGothic drama, the former condition is by far the prevailing one. The final portion of this chapter will not in any way dilute this position; it will merely refine and develop the preceding analysis of the Gothic power structure by examining three plays in which the act of staging a performance, the putting on of a show, becomes a political event. The inset plays of Barnes's *Red Noses*, Brenton's *The Churchill Play*, and David Caute's *The Demonstration* are incendiary in content, so that their enactment constitutes a gesture of revolt. Each offers in its own way a theatricalized version of revolution Gothic-style.

*Red Noses* (1985) investigates the efficacy of laughter, specifically stage laughter, as a gesture of defiance in the face of the Gothic cosmos. The archtyrant of the play is the Black Death—stealthy, unpredictable, inscrutable, remorseless "Master Pestilence." During this tyrant's reign, as Artaud puts it, "[T]he theatre is born" (1958, 24). Barnes would probably endorse Artaud's linkage of plague and theatre: *Red Noses,* he claims, "is really about the birth of show biz" (DuKore 1981, 39).

At the height of Master Pestilence's reign of terror, one Father Flote hears a call to form a new, rather unusual religious order—an acting troupe to perform as "God's Zanies." The "Red Noses of Auxerre" are bidden to form a road company whose "jibes, jokes and jabberjinks" will "cheer the hearts of men" (19). Accordingly, their debut production, an upbeat adaptation of *Everyman*, features an oafish Death who trips over his cloak, likes pancakes, and wears hairpants because "[T]hey're more uncomfortable than the traditional hairshirt" (51). So inept is this Master Death, played by Flote, that he loses the dicing game with Everyman and so must report back to God, empty-handed and ridiculous. Flote's "Everyman" brings down the house; the audience roars with approval, even as some of its members, plague-struck, die laughing.

The Church authorities, in hiding from the Plague, decide that the "Floties" could be quite useful. Pontiff Clement VI shrewdly realizes that "there's liberation in the plague air as well as worms," that in plague, "the restraints, customs and laws of centuries buckle" (87). Flotism could divert the people so as to keep them insensible to these liberating effects. Thus the great old one sanctions the troupe even though he regards Flote as a fool.

In time the plague recedes. As it does so, the humanly engendered forces of oppression swing back into operation: "Now the Plague has passed, we must immediately limit, tame, subordinate, rule" (103). "Bring on the wolves," howls Clement, so that the "butcher work" of tyranny and persecution may be resumed. In the meantime, however, Flote has scripted a new play for this new era. This new venture is quite a departure from "Everyman." A Nativity play, "Christ and Kings" is a harrowing representation of atrocity. It enacts the biblical horror story of the Forty Innocents of Bethlehem slain by a fear-shaken, mad tyrant. Flote's audience is horrified and enraged. Their protest can be heard over the sound of the "babies'" screams: "We were promised soothing syrup. . . . Where are the jollies? . . . It isn't funny!" (103) Flote justifies his new play to the infuriated audience:

> No, it isn't funny. In the days of pestilence we could be funny but now we're back to normal, life is too serious to be funny. . . . It isn't funny when they feed us lies, crush the light. . . . Isn't funny now inequality's in, naming rich and poor, mine and thine. Isn't funny when power rules and men manifest all their deeds in oppression. . . . Our humour was a way of avoiding truth, avoiding responsibility. Our mirth was used to divert attention whilst the strong men

Figure 3.   Trinity Repertory Production of *Red Noses* by Peter Barnes
(*Photo by Mark Morelli*)

slunk back to their thrones and palaces where they stand now in their saggy breeches and paper crowns, absurd like me. (103–4)

Flote now refuses to play the money-shower game, to pacify the riffraff with "creamy bon-bons." From now on his theatre will be a theatre of rabble-rousing; he and his cast will no longer be Clement's wolves, creatures who do the tyrant's bidding. Flote has become an actor in revolt. Clement knows very well how to deal with that sort. Flote is declared "anathema," as actors always had been anyway, and, in short order, all the holy innocents of the Flote company are slaughtered.

*Red Noses* might well be described as a rehashing of the Marat-Sade debate, only it is as if Marat, rather than Sade, had written the inset play. Flote is very much a Marat, one who believes that, even if Master Pestilence can't be dethroned, other masters can. His Nativity play is one which would have received Marat's heartfelt applause. Flote's foil, Clement, is the Sadean figure— cynical, contemptuous, brilliant. His world is the tortuous cosmos of the Gothic anti-hero:

> Heaven is dark and the earth a secret
> the cold snaps our bones, we shiver
> And dogs sniff round us, licking their paws
> Monsters eat our soul
> There is no way back
> Until God calls us to shadow
> So we rage at the wall and howl. (106–7)

Though Flote is clearly the moral victor, the play's epilogue is very open-ended. We hear snatches of ghostly voices—Flote and his Players about to make their debut before an almighty audience. What sort of father, they wonder, will this great old one be? A "bad joker"? A Holy Terror? We wonder, like Beatrice Cenci, whether this God will not "wind" his victims "in his hellish arms" and work on them too "the same ruin, scorn, pain, despair" (P. B. Shelley [1886] 1970, 86). The epilogue leaves unanswered the question whether it is best to deal lightly or darkly with dark things. It does leave open the possibility, as do so many Gothic fantasies, that death is simply the prelude to a new cycle of agony.

Less cosmic in sweep and resolutely secular is Brenton's *The Churchill Play* (1974). Here the troupe of actors is not a religious brotherhood, but a ragtag assortment of concentration camp "detainees." The frame play presents a dystopian vision of Britain under martial law. The inset play is a howl of protest, a furious revilement of all prison walls.

The subtitle of the play recalls the unwieldly entitled Weiss play: *The Churchill Play: As It Will Be Performed in the Winter of 1984 by the Internees of Churchill Camp Somewhere in England* (1974). The Camp Churchill prisoners' play, like the Charenton inmates' play, is a play as much about themselves as about public events. Just as Sade's play had sought to demythologize the David portrait of Marat, "The Churchill Play" seeks to revise the legend of another "People's Friend," Sir Winston Churchill. Since the enframed play begins the play proper, we do not immediately recognize that it is a play-within-the-play. The scene is Westminster Palace Hall, three a.m.—the wake of Sir Winston. Four servicemen stand honor guard over the casket. In their boredom, they break military discipline and fall to chatting about the great one. Not all comment is approbatory, however. One sneers: "He was our enemy. We hated his gut. The fat English upper-class gut of the man" (12). In the midst of this discussion, the coffin shudders, and "Churchill" rises from the dead.

At this climactic moment, the frame play interrupts. What we have been witnessing is a rehearsal for the play the internees plan to present to a parliamentary prison-inspection subcommittee. This rehearsal is interrupted by the entrance of the camp commander. Like Coulmier, he is insistent that the inmates' play be purged of any seditious content: "Put a few . . . patriotic remarks [ . . . ] about England [ . . . ] in it. . . . Winston Churchill saved this country from one thousand years of barbarism; so no disrespect to the memory of that great man."[9]

The prisoners are divided among themselves about whether to stage the play at all. One, a particularly reluctant actor, explains his objections:

> I'm no bloody puppet scarecrow. To be stuck up before ladies and gents of the House of bloody Commons. . . . Want me to get up and to a turn 'bout Winston Churchill do they? Oh what a funny little man, they'll say. But how happy he must be, to stand up there. . . . And they'll think I'm being rehabilitated. Which is the word of the Government for total, abysmal humiliation. I mean what are we? Performing bears? To stand up in our chains? W' grins on our muzzles? (36)

Still another has prophetic misgivings about the whole project: "Gerrin up a play. Reckon it's good fer ye. Well it's not. It's bloody murder" (48). Their discussion is interrupted by the news that one of their fellows has been "dumped" (prison jargon for unofficial execution) for his impudence to an officer. The news galvanizes them—they'll do the play "for 'em. . . . To them. At them" (48). Moreover, their play will no longer be simply an aesthetic expression of protest; now it will serve as a cover for an escape attempt.

The next day the committee duly arrives. Its members, like the Coulmier family, "very well dressed," take their seats in front of the stage the prisoners have erected. The play begins as before. "Churchill" rises once more. The servicemen remain nonplussed, conjecturing that Churchill must be a vampire, just as "all leaders of the world" are and always will be "the living dead" (69–70). Oblivious to their contempt, the Churchill corpse reminisces: "They

Figure 4.    Scene from *The Churchill Play* by Howard Brenton
(*Photo by Joe Cocks Studio, Stratford-upon-Avon*)

were always fond of me. I always felt love rising from English crowds" (71). Yet he also muses on the syndrome of the ruling class, its dark legacy of cruelty to even its own: "As a young boy in the great Blenheim Palace library, little Winston Churchill, me, took down the dark books of the Spanish Inquisition. Read of the whips, the racks, the brands" (75). For a moment, the judgment against tyranny becomes once again as in *Miss Margarida's Way* "uncertain," "oddly moving." Even so, the figure of Churchill, like that of Marat, must be demythologized—the past must be correctly reenacted.

Accordingly, Churchill is conducted back in time to the London of 1940 where a man and woman are wandering amid the ruins of their bombed-out home. Their encounter with the "great man" is played twice. In the first version, the couple performs like traditional Gothic servants, loyally assuring the master that they "can take it" and urging him to "[g]ive it . . . back" to Hitler. But one of the honor guards, who has been observing this scene, objects: "Not like my Uncle Ern told it. . . . That were myth. This is like it was" (79). In the second version of the playlet, "Uncle Ern," the rebellious manservant, tells it "like it was":

> Aye, I looked across. At the myth. Standing there. . . . And I felt angry. . . . And I wanted to say. . . . Go away from this hole that were my sister Annie's house. We're alright, we'll come through, what else is there for us. . . . And I said, I swear to this day I said. . . . We can take it. . . . But we just might give it back to you one day. . . . And in his book he wrote it down as. . . . Give it 'em back. (80)

With this angry re-realization, the prisoner's play abruptly closes. An embarrassed silence ensues as the onstage audience realizes it has been "got at." The silence gives way to righteous indignation, and a sergeant is despatched backstage to marshal the offending players. A moment later the curtain is hoisted once more to reveal an unexpected afterpiece—the sergeant, at gunpoint, has been tied up by the prisoners. The prisoner-actors, still in costume, demand the keys to the armory and the surrender of their audience's valuables. As in *Miss Margarida's Way* the ravaging of a handbag becomes an emblem of the underdogs' revolt. And it is no arbitrary coincidence that this is so: the purse is not only the repository of material valuables, it is also the storage container for personal belongings. The fingering of their personal possessions is frequently a prelude to the downfall of the ruling class.

The little prison insurrection is short-lived, however. The would-be escapees are betrayed, it seems, by the overeagerness of one of their own—one of the company has fired a gun through the wall. Within seconds, the lights are cut and searchlights play over the aircraft-hanger theater. The actors have been caught in the act, and their staged protest and rehearsed breakout are alike futile: "Breakout we thought. Freedom we thought. . . . We go out that door and they cut us down" (89). The theatre of revolt dissolves into a "theatre of calamity." The final word of the play is a blaring roll-call/potential execution list as the hanger's doors are yanked open.

Brenton himself as recently as 1985 cited *The Churchill Play* as his "most savage and gloomy play to date" (1985, 9). One can readily see why. Tyranny, as *Red Noses* also suggests, tolerates art only when it promotes the status quo or distracts the mob. *The Churchill Play* reproduces faithfully the savagery of tyranny and the rage against prisons so typical of the Gothic genre. Its gloominess, its sense that the power structure is well-nigh unalterable is likewise in the Gothic vein. However, Brenton's ensemble players are not the anarchic mob of Gothic fiction, nor are they the zombie-like automatons of Poliakoff's play. They are simply desperate, wronged men. They exhibit nothing of the brutality, the mindless savagery of the Gothic horde. The world of *The Churchill Play* is indeed bleak, but since it is humanly made, it can be humanly redeemed. For Brenton, the structure might—just might—someday topple. Even if "The Churchill Play" has failed to alter the consciousness of its audience, *The Churchill Play* itself is plainly intended as a political vehicle, a call to arms. Its author is clearly of Marat's party.

In contrast, Caute's *The Demonstration* (1970), likewise a play about the staging of revolt, takes a decidedly dim view of The People, in this case a group of drama students at a large prestigious English university. It is circa 1970, and the university is in the throes of student revolt, with its marches, rallies, demonstrations, and takeovers. The theatre students are not immune to the pressure of public events; they are, in fact, in the vanguard. However, competing for their attention is the traditional end-of-semester production, in this case an original play, "Pentagon 67," written by their dramatics professor Stephen Bright. Bright's script, which is a study of antiwar agitation, civil unrest, and revolution, is not activist enough to suit his students. Since, as they contend, it "poses many more questions than it answers," it "go[es] nowhere" (17).

They therefore submit their own rival script, a play about themselves, about student activism, which they dub "The Demonstration." Bright objects to their play on the grounds that it "tries to make itself a carbon copy of real life" (18). The students' angry riposte is that society is "real," that the "authoritarian regime that runs this university is real," and that they are "real" (18). Unimpressed by this logic, Bright's rejoinder is that real-life revolutionaries "did not muck about in theatres" (18). But all his arguments fail to convince. So, reluctantly, he agrees to experiment with their script, to explore it in rehearsal and improvisation.

From this point onward, three planes of dramatic reality continually intersect and overlap—the student's play, Bright's play, and the frame play in which purportedly real, public, "outside"-the-theatre events actually take place during the last weeks of the semester. In this context, Caute's production note is especially relevant:

> The entire play should be performed within a single set. This set represents the stage of the University theatre. Whatever description a particular scene may be given in the text (i.e. "the office of the Dean" or "Trafalgar Square") it should always remain abundantly clear that the necessary or suggestive props have been superimposed on the basic set—the stage of the University theatre. (9)

In other words, whether it is one of the inset plays or the frame play which is being performed, the stage of *The Demonstration* is always insistently a university stage. As the play progresses, it becomes increasingly difficult to determine to which "play" any given scene belongs—partly due to the ever-present single set and partly due to the extraordinarily similar, overlapping content of all three plays.

For example, Ann's confrontation with the Dean of Women turns out to be a scene from "The Demonstration" even though it had initially appeared to belong to the frame play. We discover our framing error as Bright disgustedly interrupts the scene, declaring that the students have glamorized their own roles and transformed the "Establishment" roles into cardboard stereotypes. "Is this scene really authentic?" he challenges. "I have no love for the Women's Dean but I don't believe she would behave so stupidly" (31).

Bright seems uncannily modelled on the real-life then Dean of the Yale School of Drama, Robert Brustein. Brustein's study *Revolution as Theatre* (1971) relentlessly exposes the posing and posturing that passed for revolutionary activism in the 1960s and 1970s. His text captures that era's peculiar conflation of the revolutionary and the theatrical event:

> Instead of using their opportunities for the formulation of radical ideas and innovative programs, the media revolutionaries have instead been indulging in muscle-flexing and tub thumping, proclaiming their violent plans on all the major talk shows. . . . The result is not revolution but rather theatre—a product of histrionic personalities and staged events. (17–18)

He is particularly disparaging of student posturing:

> The more radical students identify themselves with dining hall workers, protesting their long hours and low pay, while continuing to eat and live in college comfort without lifting a finger to help them with the trays. (25)

One can almost hear Bright's (and perhaps Sade's?) applause and cheers.

The truth is, however, that "Pentagon 67" is just as polemical as "The Demonstration." The scene which follows the Dean of Women confrontation scene turns out to be one from Bright's play. It pokes fun at the ponderous didacticism of much agitprop theatre. "A bearded guerrilla" tries to radicalize

"Pedro," a peasant (portrayed respectively by two student-actors): "You are brutally oppressed by an evil system" (36). "Pedro" readily agrees but hastens to point out some rather unpalatable realities: "We also know that we are backward illiterates . . . still in the grip of obscurantist and quasi-feudal mystifications" (37). Practical Pedro proves to be more interested in locating his lost goat than in fomenting revolution. In Bright's play, the revolutionary posture is presented as so much strutting, preening, and mouthing of revolutionary pieties.

Not surprisingly the two apprentice-actors revolt. "The lines stick in my throat," protests the guerilla-actor. He won't do the scene Bright's way. "Actors are no longer obedient puppets," he loftily informs Bright, "nor are students" (39). In so doing, he appears to be carrying out the actor's revolution which Weiss's Marat-actor cannot accomplish.

From this point on, the intermingling of all three plays is so thoroughgoing that disentangling them is nearly impossible. It seems that the student-actors abandon their rehearsals altogether in order to devote themselves to "real" demonstrations—but perhaps these demonstrations are staged as well, or perhaps they belong to the scripts of the inset plays. In any case, the play grows increasingly surrealistic, or seems so, as these different planes collide and intersect.[10]

By the end of *The Demonstration*, all the configurations of the Gothic power structure have been represented. Both roles of the ensemble-player have been portrayed—pitiable victim as well as stupid, anarchic bully. For example, the scene in which a Vietnamese woman (or perhaps a student-actress portraying a Vietnamese woman) tells movingly of battle atrocities and mutilations is compromised by another scene in which the actor-students (either playing themselves or being themselves) attack a lone victim—a campus military recruitment officer.

Both roles of the lead player have been presented as well. The Women's Dean (whether of *The Demonstration* or of "The Demonstration" we cannot tell) exhibits a cruelty worthy of any Gothic great old one: she berates one of the students, pries into her personal affairs, threatens to have her expelled. By the end of act 1, however, the role change has occurred, and the administration officials assume the role of victim. Bright himself is distraught at the conversion of his beloved theatre into the students' headquarters.

As the play continues, it traces the full cycle of revolution. The students are transformed into the Gothic mob: hedonistic, undisciplined, destructive. Riot-making has become its own *raison d'être:* "We no longer have demands. This struggle has no objective. It is the objective." Although the students' revolt appears to be in shambles, the representation may be Bright's invention.

At this point, the most serious of the revolution-making students are dispirited and confused. Bright chooses this moment of vulnerability to present his bribe. If they will resume rehearsal on his play (Did they ever really cease? Have they already resumed rehearsal of "Pentagon 67"? To which play does this bribe belong?), the administration will withdraw the police from the campus. More tempting still is his other news, which, with studied casualness, he lets slip: that organizers for the "International Festival of Student Drama" are "in town" and "ecstatic" about the students' activism. If "Pentagon 67" were to be performed at the festival, who knows how many talent scouts might be there to observe promising young actors? At first the students are suspicious, but Bright brushes aside their charges of self-interest and sellout using the parlance of the Terror: "If there is a purge here, Bright's head will be the first to fall into the basket" (97).

The next scene proves that the money-shower has done its job: the stage directions indicate that "Pentagon 67" is once more in rehearsal, though these same directions also indicate that the student-actors should appear as none too happy in their roles. At the end of the rehearsal, there are sounds of a scuffle backstage. The cast emerges "held handcuffed not by Pentagon guards but by London police Constables." Bright, like any Gothic tyrant, has, it seems, betrayed his students. He explains:

> I wanted to prove how quickly you would betray yourselves. . . . What wouldn't you do in the name of your revolution? Steal a man's life's work? Close down his theatre? Burn down London? Very probably. But would you sacrifice your own futures, those rosy dreams of playing Coriolanus, Hamlet, or Rosalind at the Old Vic? No. The doctors, technicians, civil servants, and managers—their ambitions are despicable, not yours. (110)

Then in a *coup de théâtre* worthy of Melmoth's Father Superior, he "drops the dramatist" and offhandedly informs them that their arrest has been nothing but a staged happening. He directs the "constables" to uncuff the students. But no one moves. Growing agitated, he tries first to remove the policeman's "mustache" and then the University President's "makeup" but nothing comes off; it is as if Stoppard's dagger has suddenly, in a flash, "turned real." The world of the frame play has taken over, a world in which Bright is a character, not a controlling author. Bright, "stricken and immobile," has himself been had. As the lights dim and *The Demonstration* closes, the President of the University "advances on him slowly" (112). The revolution has come full circle.

Such is the finale of the play, but it is not the end of *The Demonstration* story, for there is a real-life epilogue. Here is Caute's rueful account of one production of his play:

> [A]fter six months of meticulous German preparations and four weeks of full rehearsals, [it] had been boycotted by its actors. Because it was politically reactionary. . . . The younger actors of the company insisted that *The Demonstration* would give comfort to a bourgeois audience. . . . [T]hat art had anticipated life was an irony not lost on me. . . . [I] inwardly

recall, and not without a grimace, a line spoken in the play by a young revolutionary student, one of the characters: "Actors are no longer obedient puppets. A threat to you no doubt." He is speaking to his professor—but also, it would now seem, to me, his creator, his author. (Burns 1972, 180–81)

His own "hideous progeny" had indeed come back to haunt him.

# Gothic Spaces: Stage and Scaffold

"No single aspect of plot, image, or mood says 'Gothic' to us so clearly," claims Wilt, "as the aspect of place" (1980, 276). For most commentators, Gothic space *was* the Gothic, its essence, its crux, its *raison d'être*. Thus, the Gothic landscape has been charted with a thoroughness that yet remains to be applied to other less visible manifestations of the Gothic.

While early commentary was content simply to catalog stock Gothic settings, the inquisitorial dungeons and ruined abbeys, more recent studies in the Gothic have devoted themselves to a search for *the* emblematic Gothic setting of which all Gothic settings are simply variant figurations. Mario Praz, for example, descries the inspiration for Gothic topography in the "mighty daedalean buildings" of Piranesi's *Carceri* (1968, 17). For Jan Gordon, the artifact upon which the Gothic setting models itself is the fragment. For Gordon, the fragment includes not only what has never been finished, but also that which was once complete and whole but which has now lapsed into ontological incompleteness. The abandoned house, the rusty lock, the crumbling grave are variant formulations of the ruin (Gordon 1983, 213). Jerrold Hogle proffers the crypt, "a carved out and labyrinthine space where vestiges of death are surrounded by symbolic artifacts," as an emblem of the Gothic place (1980, 330). Several other archetypal settings have likewise been suggested—the abyss, the vortex or maelstrom, the savagely beautiful, "sublime" Radcliffean landscape, the coffin—spaces which now cramp, now dwarf the human body.

Though each of these emblematic settings is certainly appropriate to a number of Gothic texts, no one setting is entirely satisfactory for all. The reason for this lack of consensus is that the Gothic setting, which originally *did* present rigid and readily identifiable features, gradually began to encompass environments that bore little resemblance to the settings of earlier texts. For example, Victorian Gothic fantasies frequently eschewed the exotic locale and deliberately exploited the familiar and contemporary. Pat Day elaborates:

After the 1820s, exotic settings tend to disappear from the genre. . . . In the last two-thirds of
the nineteenth century, the Gothic appears to indulge in elaborate shows of ordinariness. . . .
The wild intrigues of the Inquisition are less exotic and less of a signal of the strange discontinuous landscape of the Gothic than the appearance of Dracula at high noon in Picadilly.
(1985, 300)

As David Richter puts it, Victorian Gothic brought the Gothic "back home"
(1983, 300). Or, to borrow Stoppard's muddled but wonderfully apt metaphor,
"The skeleton in the cupboard [had] com[e] home to roost" (*The Real Inspector
Hound* 1968, 20). The Burkean sublime gave way to the Freudian uncanny as
the wild and exotic Gothic setting became instead distressingly, disquietingly
banal.

James Keech addresses this difficulty attending the mapping out of the
Gothic terrain. He contends, and rightly so, that Gothic space is not bounded
or defined by "a set of rigid trappings and devices" (1974, 130). He instead
proposes that virtually any setting can be said to be Gothic, provided that it
conveys an atmosphere of ominousness: "With the proper atmosphere a child's
playhouse can be chillingly terrifying and a castle safe, warm, beautiful and
romantic" (1974, 134–35). Day concurs, asserting that "the Gothic world in its
purest form [is] all atmosphere and no substance, all suggestion, possibility,
inference, and suspense, totally without certainty" (1985, 30).

As the reader may readily perceive, we have strayed far afield from explicit
locale to some unspecified space that evokes in an indeterminate way fearful
anticipation and anxiety. While this shift from actual setting per se to the spirit
of place (atmosphere) allows greater tolerance and inclusiveness (that is, it is
less dismissive of settings which do not conform to stock formulas), it does
have the disadvantage of vagueness.

One way of solving this dilemma is to extract from the many-featured
Gothic setting certain consistent traits which work in concert to produce this
atmosphere that is so palpable yet so resistant to analysis. Therefore, rather than
embark on yet another quest to capture and label the quintessential Gothic
setting, I will instead survey what seem to be the salient features of this
shrouded, shifting landscape, and I will demonstrate how these characteristics
generate Gothic atmosphere. If Gordon is correct that Gothic form and thematics
are "remarkably synchronous," we should be able to perceive Gothic space as
an embodiment both of its formal structure and of the dynamics of Gothic
power.

One can begin by noting that Gothic space is binary, double-realmed, consisting
on the one hand of humanly engendered architectural space and on the other of
the inhuman kingdom of Nature. However, it is the interior, architectural space
which is most often represented. Alan Liu's description of the world of *Vathek*

as a universe "almost wholly architectural" (1984, 188) applies equally well to most Gothic texts. Therefore, I will defer discussion of outdoor Gothic space and begin with a tour through the winding corridors of the Gothic mansion.

Interior Gothic space, its architecture, is an emblem of the tyrant's power. Both Judith Wilt and Robert Kiely speak of the Gothic house as "charged." Writes Wilt, "The empty passages crackle with the presence of the Gothic antihero, the great old one . . . whose field of force, whose in a sense mystical body, this is" (1980, 10). Liu makes this identification of house and tyrant even more explicit in his discussion of *Vathek:* "Architecture in this work . . . is also organism, an incarnation of the hero" (1984, 188). Kiely pushes this notion even further, arguing that the Gothic structure absorbs the tyrant's power to such an extent that it becomes a sentient presence. Of *Otranto's* castle he writes, the "architectural construct . . . seems to have more life than the characters who inhabit it" (1972, 40). Paul Zweig similarly concludes that *Otranto*'s characters are "little more than puppets, manipulated by the cavernous presence of the castle" (1974, 173). So comprehensively and intensively is the tyrant's power infused into his space that his own actual presence may become superfluous. Thus the Gothic mansion itself comes to suggest, as David Morse notes, "the massive strength and intransigence of power and authority" (1982, 14). He cites *The Italian*'s Inquisitorial Chamber in this context:

> Vivaldi found himself in a spacious apartment, where only two persons were visible. . . . A book with some instrument of singular appearance, lay before him. Round the table were several unoccupied chairs, on the backs of which appeared figurative signs, at the upper end of the apartment, a gigantic crucifix stretched nearly to the vaulted roof, and at the lower end, suspended from an arch in the wall, was a dark curtain. (Radcliffe [1797] 1968, 201)

Here the chamber itself has become so overwhelmingly present and dreadful an entity that the Grand Inquisitor is himself upstaged. He has become in effect part of the scenery.

The interior Gothic space can become so intensely alive, so sentient, that the Gothic victim experiences it as a knowing, watchful presence—the very walls have eyes and ears. Not the least of the Inquisition's terrors is the prisoner's awful certainty that he is under constant surveillance by the house that tyranny has built.

Gothic structures can soak up so much power that they retain this power even when their owners have been dispossessed. Gothic tyrants may be ruined, but Gothic ruins endure, "still capable," as Wilt points out, "of infusing terror and awe" (1980, 243). The sacking and burning of monastery and convent is the dismemberment of the monastic-tyrant body, but the smoking ruin remains alive, if dormant. This endurance of the ruined house of power and the spell exercised over the perceiving imagination by it is attested to by the pervasive presence of the ruined abbey in so many early Gothic texts. Writes Wilt: "Solid and enduring theatres of tyranny . . . they were in fact 'dissolved' . . . dissolved but not entirely wiped away" (1980, 140).

So it is that *Dracula*'s postscript records the fact that all that has been (plot) and he who has been (tyrant) are now only memory, whereas the castle (place) endures, dwarfing the human creatures intrepid enough to picnic in its shade. It stands "as before, reared high" (Stoker [1897] 1965, 382), the erected structure remaining like a beast poised to strike.

Indeed in many Gothic plots the virulence of the house eventually supersedes that of its owner; the two can become enemy doubles. Zweig insists (and he is not alone in this perception) that in the Gothic fantasy, "the principle character . . . is not human at all. It is the castle, dark and complex, ruined but all powerful, the work of man's hands, now turned against him, threatening his frail psyche and defeating it" (1974, 168). Thus it is not at all unusual for the Gothic mansion to perform its own ceremony of decreation, to topple its own walls upon the "human center."[1] *The Fall of the House of Usher,* for example, may be read as a Gothic parable of house-turned-tyrant. Usher's enervation parallels the intense dynamism of a structure so powerful that it can generate its own weather (atmosphere qua atmosphere).

Wilt interprets these structural collapses as so many impositions of punishment: "the walls . . . crumble, crash, go up in flames, as though power itself were being rebuked for locating itself too long in one place" (1980, 277). Yet this explanation does not altogether satisfy, for in the world of the Gothic, as we have already seen, punishment is so entirely dislocated from crime as to be completely arbitrary. Rather, having engorged the power of their possessors, these Gothic mansions have merely become vessels of the Gothic cosmos and thus operate in accordance with that universe's savage, immutable laws. Gothic dwellings that crush their masters are acting out the role of the tyrant; they turn on the Gothic antihero himself, much in the same way that he has crushed his victims. Thus this decreation is not to be understood as the working out of poetic justice.

Another way of apprehending this mutilation of the human inhabitant by the Gothic structure is to perceive it as yet one more instance of Gothic parody. Such mutilations and persecutions are monstrous perversions of the domestic function of houses—shelter, warmth, hospitality. Gaston Bachelard expresses a poetics of the domestic fortress: "Faced with the brutal hostility of the storm . . . [the] house acquires the physical and moral energy of a human body. It braces itself to receive the downpour. . . . It is an instrument with which to confront the cosmos" ([1958] 1964, 46). The Gothic, on the other hand, deconstructs the sacrosanct domestic hearth; it converts the house into an instrument *of* the cosmos. A fine instance of such deconstruction occurs in *Dracula.* Jonathan Harker, having wandered into another wing of Dracula's castle, constructs a pretty fantasy of medieval domestic life: "I determined . . . to sleep here, where, of old, ladies had sat and sung and lived sweet lives whilst their gentle breasts were sad for their menfolk away in the midst of remorseless wars" (Stoker [1897] 1965, 45). As if this domestic idyll had summoned them, the three unhousewifely "ladies" materialize out of the dust. The obligatory dust which overspreads and the spiderwebs which festoon Gothic chambers are emblems not just of time's passage, but likewise of Gothic literature's insistent urge to make mockery of domesticity, an impulse which accounts too for the enduring Gothic cliché of the stranded traveller forced to weather the storm in a haunted house ("the-bridge-is-out-you'll-have-to-spend-the-night" formula). The guest quickly discovers that Gothic storms disallow any haven.

This notion of the domestic structure mutating into a monstrous, alien presence likewise animates the most recent figuration of the architectural setting—the infernal city. Seymour Rudin suggests in a brief speculative essay on twentieth-century Gothic film and literature that the blighted landscapes of half-demolished cities serve not only as settings for the emergence of the monstrous, but are themselves its actual spawning grounds (1984, 115–26). James Keech locates the beginnings of this sense of the urban topos as Gothic setting in the novels of Dickens: "The images of misery and Gothic fear are similar: decay, death, darkness, disease; they belong as much to slums such as Tom-all-Alone's as they do to castles and dungeons" (1974, 138). Wilt likewise discerns a Gothic "antipastoral" vision in the "plague-cities" and "prison-cities" of nineteenth-century mainstream novels (1980, 298). The razed slum is the inevitable descendent of the dissolved abbey—dissolved, but not entirely wiped away.

The urban scrapheap of a half-demolished city as setting incidentally presents a useful correlative to Gothic narrative texture. As has been demonstrated, Gothic narrative itself is in many ways a haunted junkyard, a trash heap of used bits. Similarly, the ravaged urban topos can be thought of as a representation of the Gothic compulsion to deconstruct all ideologies.

Whether demonic city or ruined castle, however, power—power residing in place, power *of* place—remains an enduring feature of Gothic architectural space. Unpredictability, according to Wilt the other crucial aspect of Gothic space, has to do too with power. Unpredictability, inscrutability—these are methods both of expressing and maintaining power. If we return to Radcliffe's Inquisitorial chamber, this relationship becomes apparent. David Morse explains:

> We are presented with intangibles, with gaps in the world waiting to be filled. The chairs are unoccupied, the signs are enigmatic, the purposes of the Inquisition obscure . . . the torment of the Inquisition is seen not so much in terms of torture as in terms of epistemological uncertainty. (1982, 71)

The unpredictability of Gothic space is rendered, as Wilt observes, in "hidden ascents and descents, sudden turnings, unexpected subspaces, alcoves and inner rooms" (1980, 10). The notorious penchant of the Gothic for dim lighting can best be understood as yet another manifestation of spatial unpredictability. Not only are the turns sudden, the alcoves unexpected, they are all, worse still, poorly lit.

The unpredictability of Gothic space often is rendered through intricacy and indirection. The organization of Gothic indoor space is devious, meandering. For example, the series of apartments which house the masque of Poe's "The Masque of the Red Death" are "so irregularly disposed that the vision embraced but little more than one at a time" ([1842] 1970, 360). Thus Gothic characters generally experience their environment as unnavigable—they wander in mazes, drift helplessly in circles. Just as Gothic narrative repudiates linearity, so too Gothic space is crooked, back-looping and multiframed. Jan Gordon makes an explicit connection between the narrative pattern of *Wuthering Heights* and the Heights as Gothic dwelling:

> The structural similarities serve to give *Wuthering Heights* itself a framed, mediated structure much like that of the house itself, with its snarling dogs inside progressively more interior corridors of the Gothic *penetralium*. These editorial explanations, which in reality constitute alternative beginnings, delay our access to the story by placing narrative impediments to the reader's progress in much the same way that the Gothic ruin impedes by its sequence of hidden doors, false closets, rooms within rooms. (1983, 216)

Intricacy, however, whether of setting or of narrative method, is, in Gothic tales, not always an expression of power. In some cases it simply represents the rational mind's defense mechanism against the onslaught of dread. Thus in *Dracula,* faced, in Wilt's words, "with plain tooth marks and the drained body," the common mind devises increasingly complicated explanations, rather than confront the "monstrously simple" (1980, 36). In spatial terms, the network surrounding the crypt keeps hidden unendurable primal truths. Death-chamber decor distracts the eye—the more fanciful, the more *outré,* the better. Insofar as Gothic travellers wish to evade their destination—that "carved out space," the "ominous crypt at the heart of the setting" (Hogle 1980, 330)—their landscapes can be understood as subjective representations of that desire.

A far more sinister hallmark of Gothic space, and one which has nothing to do with desire, is its thorough instability. The political, moral, social, and epistemological chaos that pervades the Gothic cosmos is embodied in the Gothic architectural setting. The Gothic space is a world in flux, a perpetual-motion machine. As Wilt pithily notes, things that seemed to be A are in fact B, "[just as] things that are A are also B, or soon will be" (1980, 136). Such continual metamorphosis, such constant reshuffling and redefinition of objects in space is shape-shifting on a grand scale. Classification of things, as well as of people, is a matter infinitely open to conjecture. There is no such thing as a reliable landmark on the Gothic landscape. (Even the ruin is not to be relied on since it assumes so many forms.) It is for this reason that Gothic characters so often undergo seizures of a kind of space-sickness, a disorientation so profound that directional indicators such as north or south, up or down, become for them virtually meaningless.

Gordon, like Wilt, perceives this wholesale loss of discreteness as endemic to the Gothic: "Such a fiction perpetually threatens the collapse of difference in one or more of several ways in order to create a univocity of being. . . . [In] the language of Gothic fiction . . . discrete objects . . . always threaten to coalesce and coagulate" (1983, 224). Day argues that this fluidity, this endless transform-ability reaches its apogee in a moment of fusion, recurrent in Gothic fantasy, between external, objective reality—the physical details of time and space—and the perceiving consciousness of the narrator. He contends that time and space (and all aspects thereof) become "not absolutes" but rather "relative functions of perception" (1985, 28). Such a reading suggests an absorption of the perceiving human consciousness by the setting—for instance, *Melmoth*'s Moncada and his prison-world become "the same thing" (Day 1980, 30). The perceiving self loses the sense of place as an entity distinct from the self. Put more boldly, the Gothic landscape is capable of engulfing all rival entities.

Such fusions, or engorgements, can occur, of course, in any setting, even in those not conventionally Gothic. More often, though, they occur, as Wilt claims, in places that convey extremity, places far removed from the "flat communal normal setting" (1980, 135). As in other respects, extremity is the norm in the Gothic—attics and cellars, peaks and pits. The Gothic castle rises massively, diminishing to insignificance the human figure at its base.

Yet the scale can be recalibrated so that the human figure is rendered outsized by a suffocatingly small space. Here again the "human center" is reduced, despite its bigness, to a helpless mote. What matters ultimately is not so much the size of the space, but rather its inescapability. And herein lies perhaps the most demonic character of Gothic architectural spaces—they are exitless. Gothic dwellings are claustrophobic; size does not really signify. From the narrow confines of Poe's coffin to the immense internal cavity of Udolpho, Gothic houses are Venus fly-trap-like containers—getting in is all too easy; getting out is nigh to impossible. Dracula's calèche becomes a Gothic container for poor Harker, a container whose escape-proofness is guaranteed by its encir-cling ring of ravenous wolves. Keech is quite right—virtually any housing structure can be transformed into a Gothic container.

Thus Gothic flights are exercises in futility: "narrow escapes," as Wilt points out, "lead only to worse imprisonments" (1980, 54). Hogg's Justified Sinner scurries from place to place only to discover that each hoped-for haven is a cheat and a delusion. The visual image of Wringham frantically struggling to extricate himself from the weaver's web is a kind of iconic representation of many of the features of the Gothic setting which have been discussed thus far—its intricacy, its perversion of the domestic, its inescapability, and its sinister insinuation of an unseen, monstrous spinner.

In *Melmoth* this web is figured as a labyrinth beneath the monastery, the "roots" of the "stupendous system" which *is* the monastery as institution and dwelling. Moncada threads his way through this maze and emerges into fresh air, freedom, and the embrace of a brother, only to discover that he has been betrayed. The System's tentacles drag him back down into the dungeons of the Inquisition.

However, the setting perhaps most emblematic of Gothic immurement is the madhouse. At once prison and antihospital, it becomes, in Mark Hennelly's words, a "macrocosm of the incarcerated mind itself" (1981, 671). A collection of solipsistic, tormented consciousnesses, it is anticommunal as well. The Gothic madhouse assimilates with demonic brilliance the political, domestic, and epistemological significations of Gothic architectural space.

Perhaps we have sojourned overlong inside the Gothic mansion, but it remains true that architectural space is more frequently invoked in Gothic literature than is the outdoor landscape. In fact, many Gothics seem to transpire almost entirely in an indoor realm. Robert Kiely confirms this indoor bias:

> Despite the increasing importance of vistas and shady groves, Gothic novels as their titles often suggest, are particularly concerned with buildings. In fact, the abbeys and castles of early romantic fiction appear to be designed to keep nature out.

Alan Liu observes of *Vathek* that even the outdoors is made over into an interior realm as Vathek erects screens and canopies to shelter his entourage (1984, 188). Even when Gothic writers did choose to depict exterior settings, they were drawn to topographies which were analogous to the architectural setting; thus the frowning cliffs, massive ice floes, and windswept wastelands can be perceived as so many variant renderings of the Gothic castle.

One major exception in this context, however, is the sublime landscape of Ann Radcliffe. Malcolm Ware contends that her painterly descriptions of outdoor scenery are intended to convey "a general feeling of repose, of a level of idyllic decorum" (1977, 187). Her characters, he holds, are not involved in these settings; they respond to Nature much as they would respond to a beautiful painting. Thus her heroine's souls are "highly elevated or sweetly soothed by scenes of nature" (Radcliffe [1797] 1968, 190). The effect of Radcliffe's scenes of Nature, even a Nature in tumult, is to shrink to a manageable size the troubles of the human observer. Her gazers return to their prisons refreshed, fortified and comforted. As Kiely notes, Radcliffean storms are "intermittent and ultimately harmless blemishes on the essentially placid, unchanging face of nature" (1972, 240). Radcliffe's landscapes serve as an antidote to indoor tyranny, the awful power which resides in the architectural cavity.

In most Gothic texts, however, the external world is experienced as hostile, alien, and terrifying. Most Gothic characters experience Nature as monstrous and terrifying. One wonders how "elevating" Ellena di Rosalba would have found a charred, lightning-struck corpse, or how "sweetly soothing" the storm which tosses the wrecked *Demeter* onto the sands of Whitby. In *Wuthering Heights,* as Eric Bentley points out, "the Yorkshire moors and the Yorkshire weather are 'the very devil'" (1965, 221). Human depravity is simply a pale imitation of the unrelenting malignity of Nature. In most Gothic texts, the Gothic world is, as Day describes it, "a *naturally* monstrous universe . . . unbounded by the laws of the material world and without divine or spiritual order" (1985, 37).

Nowhere is this strangeness, turmoil, and violence of Nature more evident than in *Frankenstein,* a text which seems at times to deconstruct, rock by rock, the Radcliffean vista. Peter Brooks's analysis of the natural world of *Frankenstein* is right to the mark:

> The novel dissents from the optimistic assumption that nature is support and comfort and source of right moral feeling. . . . Nature does not protect Clerval from its own malignant possibilities. It contains more than sounding cataracts and sublime mountains: there are also unaccommodated monsters and disseminated pieces of monstrous creation. . . . The fact of monsterism suggests that nature in *Frankenstein* has something of the radical amorality described by Sade. . . . [I]f one searches for an underlying pattern or principle in nature, what one finds is destruction itself. Therefore, man's destruction—torture, murder—merely does nature's work. (Brooks 1979, 216–17)

If we accept Brooks's reading, we must accept the Monster as a thoroughly natural creature. Indeed Day insists that Gothic monsters are not supernatural or contranatural creatures, but rather "products of the physical world called forth through thoroughly natural means" (1985, 37). Dracula is a perfectly integrated entity of this world. Such creatures as Dracula and Robert Louis Stevenson's Mr. Hyde are completely autochthonous, as *Dr. Jekyll and Mr. Hyde* makes clear: "This was the shocking thing; that the slime of the pit seemed to utter cries and voices; that the amorphous dust gesticulated and sinned" ([1886] 1978, 68).

This natural world of which Dracula is both avatar and ruler is chthonic, chaotic, malignant; furthermore, there is no other place—no numinous realm, no higher spiritual reality. Here is all there is. Thus in the most thoroughgoing Gothic fantasies, external landscapes, if they are rendered at all, are simply outdoor versions of inner space—Gothic containers writ large. They partake of the same qualities as the architectural structure—sentience, unpredictability, intricacy. The ubiquitous shipwreck in Gothic fiction serves as an emblem of the doubly imperilled human creature helplessly adrift in a storm-swept cosmos: the ship fails as shelter, becomes a prison in itself amid a writhing landscape which threatens imminent annihilation. Voyages in Gothic vessels lead inevitably to a descent into the maelstrom.

Although, as we have seen, Gothic geography encompasses a wide variety of landscapes, the theatrical setting was rarely represented. (Stanton's encounter with Melmoth the Wanderer in a crowded Restoration playhouse is an anomaly.) The Gothic Melodrama followed suit: stage carpenters and scene painters went to great lengths so as to transform stage space into the conventional Gothic settings—castle and cave. The *mise en scène* of the Gothic Melodrama was intended as a faithful "realization" of the source narrative's setting. The public, communal ambiance of the theatre was never exploited—was, in fact, negated by the concerted efforts of the Gothic Melodramatists.

Henry James's treatment in *The Turn of the Screw* of a theatrical image is telling: "[T]he autumn had dropped upon Bly and blown out half our lights. The place, with its grey sky and withered garlands, its bared spaces and scattered dead leaves, was like a theatre after the performance—all strewn with crumpled playbills" ([1898] 1966, 52). Here Bly is transformed into theatre-as-ruin, haunted by past performances and vanished performers; nonetheless, terror comes *after* the play is done—it is the desertedness of the theatre that is ominous. Now that a bare space has been cleared, the lights dimmed, and the crowd departed, the real horror show can begin. What is significant is that James does not correlate the eruption of the Gothic with the act of performance and indeed takes care to separate them.

As will become evident, such correlation does not occur until well into the twentieth century.[2] The Gothic Melodrama instead relied on stock devices unabashedly cribbed from early Gothic texts. One such device was the so-called "apparition scene," a visual extravaganza which thrilled the nineteenth-century playgoer. Here is one contemporary account of audience hysteria following a performance of Lewis's *The Captive* (1803):

> Never did Covent Garden present such a picture of agitation and dismay. Ladies bathed in tears—others fainting—and some shrieking with terror—while such of the audience as were able to avoid demonstrations like these, sat aghast, with pale horror painted on their countenances. (Mrs. Cornwall Baron-Wilson [1839] 1962, 1:233–34)

According to Joseph Donohue, Lewis, in several of his plays "employed the phantom figure with unexampled ingenuity" (1975, 100). It was in fact the apparition scene which made his *The Castle Spectre*, one might say, the hottest ticket of the 1797 season. It is important to bear in mind as one reads the following description of the apparition-scene that it is not the ghost as character that is frightening, but rather the ghost as *mise en scène* that horrifies:

> The set scene, in this theatre, had an oratory with a perforated dome of pure Gothic over which was a window of rich tracery, and Mrs. Jordan, who played Angela, being on the stage, a brilliant illumination suddenly took place, and the doors of the oratory opened—the light was perfectly celestial, and a majestic and lovely but melancholy image stood before us; at this moment, in a low but sweet and thrilling harmony, the band played the strain of Jomelli's *Chaconne*. . . . And the figure began to advance; it was the spirit of Angela's mother, Mrs. Powell, in all her beauty, with long sweeping envelopments of muslin attached to the wrist . . . Mrs. Jordan *cowered* down motionless with terror, and Mrs. Powell bent over her prostrate duty [sic] in maternal benediction: in a few minutes she entered the oratory again, the doors closed, and darkness once more enveloped the heroine and the scene. (Boaden 1831, 1: 347–48)

It was the spectacle of the apparition's blood-spattered gown which evoked the audience's titillation and inquietude. Their distress was based less on the fact that a ghost was being presented than on the fact that the spectre's accoutrements were so well calculated to achieve a horrific effect. Though Lewis's ghost was not a Gothic ghost, it was tricked out as one. Such scenes quickly became the focal point of the emergent Gothic Melodrama, "scenic pegs," as one commentator labels them, "on which to hang a commentary narrative" (Booth 1981, 63).

Like their narrative siblings, the gloomy settings of these early Gothic Melodramas were intended to arouse unease and awe. Nonetheless, as is the case with the apparition scene, some significant differences should be noted. For one, while "[i]t is amazing," as Eric Bentley points out, "what the nineteenth-century stage could do in the presentation of raging seas, mountains, glaciers, frozen lakes and the like . . . there were always much narrower limits than in a novel" (1965, 221). The stagecraft of the day simply could not fully realize the almost hallucinogenic settings of the Gothic fantasy. More significantly, unlike the tempests of Gothic fiction, these staged storms never annihilated the virtuous. Samuel Arnold's *The Woodman's Hut* (1814) offers a typical instance of this brief flirtation with natural disaster. In Arnold's play the innocent survive a raging forest fire by dashing across a burning bridge—this after having narrowly escaped drowning in a storm-tossed river. Only the vicious are struck by the Gothic Melodrama's very discriminating thunderbolt. Not surprisingly, Nature is rarely envisaged as innately malevolent. Baillie's Orra and Shelley's Beatrice are very much alone in their apprehension of the natural world as cruel and terrible. Gothic Melodrama's heroines do not, like Orra, perceive in a cloud formation a "warrior's plum'd head," a "portentous thing" (Baillie 1812, 3: 65). Nor have they any reason to do so.

Even more clear-cut evidence of the Gothic Melodrama's consistent taming of the storm is its treatment of the subject of shipwreck. Meisel pinpoints the crucial difference between the Gothic shipwreck and the melodramatic ship-wreck:

> In the affective iconography of the age, the image carried an unspecified charge of psychologi-cal and metaphysical disaster appearing . . . as the frozen analogue of metaphysical doubt and despair in the arctic imagery of . . . Mary Shelley. . . . Nautical melodrama . . . enlists the affective power of this image of disaster through spectacle and concurrently attempts to exor-cise or at least allay its terrors by a contextual domestication. (1983, 197)

Nautical melodramas (much like the 1970s disaster films such as *The Poseidon Adventure*) fused, as Meisel suggests, "perilous sensation" with "domestic feel-ing" (1983, 195). A convincing example of the nautical melodrama's proclivi-ties in this direction is offered by T. W. Robertson's 1867 *For Love!* Based on an actual maritime disaster in which the majority of the ship's passengers had perished, *For Love!* ensures that most of its onboard dramatis personae survive. Furthermore, the audience's attention is diverted from the fact of disaster by the tender reunion scenes of the survivors with their loved ones.

In the Gothic, however, the mere act of watching the spectacle of ship-wreck is a dangerous business. In *Dracula* the Whitby townsfolk gather on the pier to gape at the wretched, pitching schooner. They become so preoccupied with gawking at the spectacle of disaster that they become oblivious to their own peril: "It was found necessary to clear the entire piers from the mass of onlookers, or else the fatalities of the night would have been increased mani-fold" (Stoker [1897] 1965, 87). In *Melmoth* the merchant vessel bearing the Spaniard Moncada is dashed to pieces off the Irish coast. Not only does the ship go down with all hands on board, the onshore would-be rescuer is swept into the vortex: young John Melmoth, scrabbling up the cliff's face, loses his grip, and tumbles into the "roaring deep" which "seem[ed] to toss its ten thousand arms to receive and devour him" (Maturin [1820] 1961, 50).

The interior settings of the Gothic Melodrama also functioned differently from those of the Gothic novel, even though superficially they did seem to be faithful illustrations of the Gothic tale's crypt and castle. One striking difference is that, in Gothic Melodrama, places of sanctuary remain inviolate. For exam-ple, in Edward Fitz-ball's *The Devil's Elixir* (1829), the villain, once he enters the shrine of St. Anthony (where "no evil spirit can take advantage of mortal innocence") succumbs to the spell of the place and relinquishes his purloined bride. Pursued by a demon, he flees to the altar. However, "[T]he steps crumble beneath the Demon's feet. . . . The Demon is stricken with a thunderbolt—the shrine falls and overwhelms him in flames and ruins" (1975, 35–36). The next scene reveals that the wicked Francisco has survived the catastrophe and mended his ways. Ostensibly, Francisco is saved by his own repentance; however, the implication is that his remorse is due to the magical properties of the sanctuary-shrine.

Whereas the Gothic Melodrama observes the inviolability of the sanctuary, the supposedly sacred sites of the Gothic fantasy are repeatedly desecrated and rendered unsafe. As Howard Anderson remarks apropos of The Monk, "[P]laces of safety are transformed into places of danger" (1973, x). In Lorenzo's dream, the cathedral of Madrid metamorphoses into a vestibule of hell:

> Antonia shrieked. The monster clasped her in his arms, and springing with her upon the altar, tortured her with his odious caresses. . . . Instantly the Cathedral seemed crumbling into pieces . . . the altar sank down, and in its place appeared an abyss vomiting forth clouds of flame. (M. G. Lewis, [1796] 1973, 53)

Over and over in the Gothic, hallowed resting places—altars and biers—are transformed into so many Procrustean beds.

In contrast, the victims of Gothic Melodrama are not persecuted by their environment; they are victimized solely by the tyrant. Power in the Gothic Melodrama does not reside in place; power remains an adjunct of character. The stage settings (at least the interior ones) serve an illustrative function only. Usually, they are not active entities. They do not generate events; they merely provide a literal and figurative backdrop. (Even in those few cases where they do generate events, as in *The Devil's Elixir*, their influence is benign.) The environmental trappings of the Gothic are indeed obvious and present, but they are just that—obligatory decoration.

Oddly enough, a more Gothic treatment of interior setting is to be found in an 1840 harlequinade by William Bradwell, *The Castle of Otranto: or, Harlequin and the Giant Helmet*. Its inchoate atmosphere is more in keeping with the alogical cosmos of Walpole's *Otranto* than is Jephson's sane, Providentially ordered one, this despite the fact that the events and characters of the novel become barely recognizable as the figure of Pantomime appears and transforms the *Otranto* characters into those of the harlequinade. Now as helpless clowns, they find themselves in a room which sets about its own demolition. Here is how one reviewer described the scene:

> [C]hair after chair slips through the wall or floor, fire-irons find their way up the chimney . . . window curtains dissolve to naught . . . chimney ornaments fling themselves at the clowns, and the huge looking-glass falls on its head with a fearful smash, leaving them standing in melancholy astonishment in the empty frame. (*London Times* 1840, n.p.)

Booth's discussion of this cosmos of the Regency harlequinade reveals its peculiar resemblance to the cosmos of the Gothic fantasy:

In the Regency harlequinade, man's plight is often created by the transformation, misbehavior and relentless hostility of objects and mechanical devices. Things are not what they seem to be, or rather they are, but then they change frighteningly to something else. Nothing can be relied on; the very ground itself dissolves under the feet of the helpless characters. Such comedy is almost cosmic in its implications. . . . As is usual in extreme forms of comic theatre, a terrible seriousness underlies the jollity. ([1969] 1980, 155–56)

Perhaps the distinction between such comedy and the Gothic is the difference between "misbehavior" and "relentless hostility." When objects are no longer merely cantankerous and have become actively malevolent, we have entered the realm of the Gothic.

In essence, the characters of the Gothic Melodrama, unlike their fictional counterparts (and unlike those of the harlequinade), negotiate their spaces with relative ease. They do so because, while the settings of Gothic Melodramas may look Gothic, these settings do not operate as such. Natural disasters there are aplenty, but earthquakes and floods vanquish only the guilty; ruins collapse only on tyrants. In the Gothic Melodrama, environment simply is not the real problem. Objects are what they appear to be—signifier corresponds to signified. There is none of that ontological slipperiness so characteristic of Gothic narrative. Chimney ornaments do not suddenly convert themselves into self-propelled missiles. Thus one can say that in this respect the Gothic Melodrama was not faithful to its narrative source. And it was here, in the domain of space, where theatre and fiction most visibly intersect, that the Gothic Melodrama fell once again short of the mark. Never, for example, is the native "transformability" of the stage—its ability to stand "for any signified class of phenomena"—exploited (Elam 1980, 13). The inborn slitheriness of the stage prop, its capacity for inexplicable identity shifts, even "without structural modification" (Elam 1980, 12) is never turned to account. The Gothic Melodrama even in its earliest manifestation could easily have capitalized on the seeming self-motility of the stage, the manner in which stage objects seem to move of their own accord, even as the viewer's reason reminds him that unseen stagehands pull ropes and levers. None of this occurred because the theatre had yet to be freed, as States suggests, "of its servitude in mimetic signification" (1985, 101), of the "tyranny of reference" (1985, 109).

That realization, nascent in the dramas of German Expressionism and of Strindberg, surfaces full-blown in the NeoGothic plays of Pinter, Poliakoff, Beckett, and Stoppard. We shall first examine plays which, like the classic Gothic texts themselves, can be said to have lost the sense of an outdoor realm, plays whose worlds seem most akin to the airless, exitless, interior demesne of Gothic fiction. Next, we shall observe a play which transpires entirely in a hostile, exterior environment. Through this analysis it will become apparent that the characters of the NeoGothic drama are, like their narrative counterparts, engaged in a frantic search for shelter. We will turn, at this juncture, to an "asylum" play—*Marat-Sade*—a play which demonstrates the cruel betrayal by the false shelter. Finally, the last haven to which the Gothic character flees, his or her last resort for refuge and sanctuary, is the stage itself. In this context we will consider what might be termed "scaffold" plays—*The Swing* (Edward Bond), *Laughter!* (Peter Barnes), *Rosencrantz and Guildenstern Are Dead* (Tom Stoppard), and *Marat-Sade*—plays which demonstrate that the stage too is an antisanctuary. The full significance of this ultimate betrayal by the stage of its own creatures will become readily apparent: we will observe stage space revealing itself as the false haven it has always been.

In *Rosencrantz and Guildenstern* outdoor space seems to have disappeared altogether. The area to which the play's creatures are confined is resolutely and insistently interior, a domain in which, yes, there might be draught, but certainly no wind, a play in which autumn has "nothing to do with leaves" (Stoppard, *R & G*, 1968, 94). The play is most suggestive of the claustrophobic, architectural setting of Gothic narrative. Gillian Farish explains:

> Stoppard makes the characters and the audience aware of their physical boundaries and isolation by verbal and visual images. Four of the images that Stoppard uses . . . —box, boat, bag and bowl—all have initial labial plosives[,] sounds suggestive of the pent-up nervous energy of the characters trapped literally and figuratively by these "containers." . . . Hope of escape is too tenuous to talk about. (1975, 25)

As we have already noted, Ros and Guil have absolutely no sense of direction. They experience that space sickness that perennially afflicts Gothic travelers. Completely "at sea," confounded, disoriented, they are utterly incapable of getting their bearings: north or south, up or down—every way is the same way. They, even more than Hamlet, are "at the mercy of the elements," unable to steer, to plot a course, "slipping," as Ros, panic-stricken, realizes, "off the map." Thus they are victims not only of their circumstances but of the space they inhabit. The play is permeated with all sorts of indexical, directional references which crisscross and cancel one another out. Everything in this ill-defined zone is unanchored, adrift.

Not surprisingly, this is a world in which one simply cannot get comfortable. "I want to go home," whines Ros, who cannot find so much as a stool to perch on. It is a most inhospitable place, "the worst of both worlds"—the constriction of the domestic structure combined with the unflagging persecution of the Gothic cosmos.

Thus Ros and Guil are actually relieved when they discover themselves apparently on board a vessel at sea. For a while Guil convinces himself that "[b]oats are safe areas in the game of tag" (100). The truth is that there is no "safe area" and no place to break out to. The coalescence of "in here" and "out there" is evident in the following exchange:

| | |
|---|---|
| *Guil (pause)*: | No, somebody might come in. |
| *Ros*: | In where? |
| *Guil*: | Out here? |
| *Ros*: | In out here? |
| *Guil*: | On deck. (100) |

They realize eventually, of course, that their getaway cruise ship is bound for their point of departure, and that they are being carried back "as inexorably as the wind and current" (122), back to wherever it is they've always been.

In essence Ros and Guil occupy a theatricalized Gothic cage. The ever-present sense of surveillance which maddens Gothic inmates is likewise fore-grounded in *Rosencrantz and Guildenstern*. Ros and Guil suffer from a condition of permanent visibility in which they can be seen but in which they cannot discern who it is that observes *them*. It is, as Ros puts it, "like living in a public park" (75). Their very unprivate lives are ever on display, constantly open to inspection. The "fourth wall" may be invisible, but Ros and Guil apprehend its gaze as a disquieting presence. They sense that they are indeed being watched.

This sentient surveillance by the Gothic structure is embedded too in Stephen Poliakoff's work, although it is evoked through different means. Here surveillance is carried out by stage vehicles and stage lighting. For example, Nichola of *City Sugar* works as a supermarket clerk under the watchful scrutiny of a rotating camera. She and her co-worker Susan speculate about their unseen monitor: "Maybe he's staring at us, right at this moment, smacking his lips—about to jump" (41). Lighting on a Poliakoff set is rendered as an unrelenting, pitiless glare which maddens and torments. D. Keith Peacock points out that "Poliakoff's plays are full of stage directions which call for 'explosions' of bright neon light" (1983, 497). Remarks Susan, "glanc[ing] up at the strip lighting, 'Anyway, I start thinking funny thoughts after a bit. If you stare at those lights long enough, it does that'" (40).

Most often, in Poliakoff's plays the cosmos is rendered as more than simply watchful. It is represented as malevolently sentient—"about to jump." Peacock comments on the monstrous, hostile animism of the Poliakoff landscape:

Largely by means of the accretion of similar references—mostly to dirt, decay, noxious substances, intrusive noises and fungoid growths—the language creates a web of almost tangible and disturbing imagery which communicates a grotesque vision of contemporary "consumerist" society. Much of this imagery is based upon some kind of *activity*, animal or vegetable; and the image of a monstrous growth, pervasively and inexorably penetrating and corrupting society, is predominant. . . . Inanimate objects often reproduce themselves or come threateningly to life. (1983, 498)

It is to be noted that the corruption, whose source remains mysterious, is not of a moral nature, but more properly a kind of contamination or defilement.

For many of Poliakoff's characters, holocaust is imminent, the natural world is dangerously out of kilter. Mike of *A Shout across the River* (1979) presents several disaster scenarios:

> I read somewhere the Arctic is going to melt quite soon and the whole of Europe is going to be drowned. . . . And if that doesn't happen . . . something that is definitely going to happen will be the Thames. It's going to overflow. . . . There's a new disease too from Africa. A fly or something that eats through your skin . . . it's spreading to Europe, eating its way through hundreds. (24)

Ralph of *Hitting Town* (1978) shares this paranoiac vision of a world that really is out to get him:

> I got this idea, rather crazy really, that when I was walking along the pavement if I stepped on the lines a steel mantrap would spring up and get me by the leg, right there—honestly. I was sweating, just walking along. . . . And you know, the day before yesterday I saw a car parked. And I knew just like that it had a bomb in it, you see. It was a dirty green mini, vicious looking. . . . All the streets . . . and the buildings began to look, you know—dangerous, all of it. (29)

Poliakoff's characters exist in a defiled landscape of roadside cafes, sleazy restaurants, and cramped, ill-constructed flats. There is a prevailing sense that the outdoor world has been roofed over, and that the sun has been replaced by brash neon, that all sound has been subsumed by "The Sound of Muzak," that all "Strawberry Fields" have been cemented over. All of this may very well sound like a polemic against environmental pollution, but in Poliakoff's work, as Peacock points out: "There is no analysis of its [environmental pollution's] economic and social causes" (1983, 496). As is true of the Gothic writer, Poliakoff "does not advocate anything at all." The contamination of the earth is simply a given—a pretext for the engendering of the monstrous.

Poliakoff's plays belong to the subgenre of the Gothic antipastoral described earlier. The sense of the urban trashheap as spawning ground of the monstrous is quite clear in *Strawberry Fields*'s (1977) apocalyptic vision of the ruined motorway cafe:

> *Kevin*: Filthy here, isn't it in this cafe. . . . Imagine when the holocaust comes and these places are all deserted and there are thistles growing on the motorway [ . . . ] and there's grass growing over the jukebox. [ . . . ] . . . And of course there'll be a new sort of beast that hatches its eggs in the stale chips, yeah, in the chip trays, it lays its small blue eggs everywhere, all over, this new beast, and suddenly [ . . . ] and then suddenly it emerges from the fryers, this monster covered in batter, whole body in batter, and it goes after the last humans, catching and eating them.[3]

The café itself is a perversion of the traveller's shelter, with its stained table-cloths, crumbs, odors, overflowing trashbins, and out-of-order telephones. Yet the return to nature, the falling to ruin is likewise imaged as a monstrous event. The inhospitable, alien, threatening character of the Poliakoff landscape is augmented by sound effects as well: "loud, irritating noises during blackouts, tannoys, radio announcements, the insistent ringing of telephones, traffic noise and, everywhere, 'Muzak'" (Peacock 1983, 497). Poliakoff's forte is the exploitation of the disturbing within the commonplace. John Spurling clarifies this point:

> Although he writes straightforward, contemporary stories, . . . Poliakoff's characteristic effect is nightmarish. One seems to be looking at nothing more than an ordinary slice of life, but as it were in a lurid light; it is like seeing familiar faces and buildings turned slightly ghastly by neon. (1982, 641)

If Stoppard's and Poliakoff's plays seem obsessively architectonic, Beckett's *Happy Days* (1961) represents the opposite Gothic extreme—unrelenting exposure. Beckett's Winnie is a creature stuck outdoors. No architectural structure is anywhere in sight: "unbroken plain and sky reced[e] to meet in far distance" (7). And, like the monstrous, alien landscape of *Frankenstein* the world of *Happy Days* is one hundred percent "genuine pure filth" (19). It is emphatically not the sublime Nature of Radcliffe's exotic landscape. "*O felice giorno*," cheers Paolo at the wedding which closes *The Italian* (Radcliffe [1797] 1968, 415). "Another heavenly day," responds Winnie from her barren mound.

Winnie's space is "light-filled," like the world of Poliakoff's characters, and her light is equally, as James Knowlson suggests, "hellish" (1979, 93). She is divested of even the slight, pitiful shelter provided by her parasol as the poor thing disintegrates in spontaneous combustion. One thinks of a camping expedition (the urban flight to the "great outdoors") gone inexplicably bizarre, mad, terrible.

The "sun" that illuminates this barren landscape is also very much a theatrical sun—that is to say, it serves no order-making functions. This unblinking, harsh white light reminds one of nothing so much as a spotlight, which in fact it is: it sheds light, it directs one's gaze, it makes the actor sweat,[4] but it has nothing to do with marking time. *Happy Days* is a shadeless play, utterly without "blackouts." In *Rosencrantz and Guildenstern*, the sun has ceased to operate as a trustworthy point of spatial reference; in *Happy Days* it has also ceased to serve as a temporal referent. Thus to say "day after day" as Winnie does is to speak, as she admits, in "the old style." And to ask for the sun to rise and set, well, one might as well be "asking for the moon" (29).

Instead, Winnie's time is parcelled out by the arbitrary ringing of a bell whose clanging determines when she's to sleep and when to wake. Winnie has no idea how long in any given session she has been allowed to sleep. It may have been five minutes—or five hours, or five days. Even if she does not suffer sleep deprivation, her condition is still akin to that of the tortured captive who is disoriented by the repeated, deliberate disturbance of natural body rhythms.

As in *Rosencrantz and Guildenstern* and in the Poliakoff plays, this constant bombardment of light also suggests surveillance. Winnie does sense that she is being watched: "Strange feeling that someone is looking at me. I am clear, then dim, then gone, then dim again, then clear again; and so on, back and forth, in and out of someone's eye" (40). Knowlson speculates about Winnie's silent observer:

> For who, after all, can be "looking at [her]." . . . A hypothesized God-observer? Willie himself? Or just the hundreds of eyes from the audience, who are even less able to do anything to help Winnie in her plight than her husband can do. (1979, 100)

David Alpaugh perceives this "brutal, destructive sun" as the eye of some "diabolical" God (1966, 207). Thomas Whitaker makes more explicit the role of the audience as spy and sadistic voyeur: "We seem much less human than she as we sit securely in our seats, vicarious devils in charge of her hell" (1977, 20).

Unlike the Poliakoff and Stoppard landscapes, though, this space is insistently an external landscape. Winnie's ultimate enemy is the good earth, the "old extinguisher" (37). The dust sucks her down into its depths as surely, if more slowly, than the infamous Gothic maelstrom. It is a landscape in motion, though glacier-like, maddeningly slow. Despite its sterility, it is alive. "What a blessing nothing grows here," remarks Winnie, as if she'd just seen a Poliakoff play, "imagine if all this stuff were to start growing" (34).

Much has been made of the immobility of the human body on the Beckett stage, and rightly so, but equally important is the fact that in such a world there is no place else to go—even if one could "rattle about," as Guildenstern remarks of life on boats. In the NeoGothic drama, someplace else, whether the interior of a shelter or the free expanse of out-of-doors space, is, as Guildenstern puts it, "just a conspiracy of cartographers" (107).

The preceding discussion suggests that when the NeoGothic drama takes on the project of presenting Gothic space, it remains faithful to the structural organization of the environments of Gothic narrative, even as it discovers ways and means of theatricalizing those structural traits. It might also be added that, while outdoor space may indeed by represented, as in *Happy Days,* the NeoGothic drama shares the Gothic narrative's predilection for enclosed, architectural environments. This preference may be explained by reference to Laurence Kitchin's notion of "compressionism," which he defines as "a marriage between modern man's prison complex and the proscenium stage's aptitude for boxing actors in" (1963, 12). Thus the proscenium stage itself may be regarded as yet another potential Gothic container.

There exists finally a subcategory of the NeoGothic drama, a group of plays which chronicle the Gothic dweller's search for sanctuary, a magic circle, that "safe area in the game of tag," a shelter against the Gothic tempest. This group is well represented by Pinter's *The Caretaker* and *The Dumbwaiter*. In both, the proffered haven turns out to be itself a menacing, dangerous environment. In this context, we shall also consider the NeoGothic "asylum" play, that is, a play in which the victim is housed in an institutional Gothic shelter—the madhouse of *Marat-Sade,* for example.

The final portion of the chapter will attend to the most extreme form of the sanctuary subgenre, a small, specialized group of plays, which I shall refer to as "scaffold" dramas. In these plays, the stage itself, which appears to be an absolutely inviolable place of sanctuary, becomes, in classic Gothic fashion, the most lethal place of all.

*The Caretaker* is a story of Gothic guesthood. Such a reading does not, at first, seem justified since, as Ronald Hayman observes of the settings of Pinter's early plays, "The setting is nearly always a realistic representation of a room" (1979, 128). Aston's place may be messy, but, admittedly, it does resemble rooms we have seen, and in any case it seems innocuous enough. Certainly it seems to be a snug enough retreat for a storm-tossed traveller like Davies.

In fact, however, Aston's dwelling will exhibit the carceral brutality and malefic antihospitality which is the trademark of Gothic houses. This place will "mess" Davies about "from here to breakfast time."

It has become a critical commonplace to speak of Aston's room as an embodiment of his disorientation. Bernard Dukore's assessment is typical: "The scenic clutter and disarray reflect the mind of the room's occupant, the absence of an orderly world in which everything has a place" (1982, 53). Certainly this is a point which need not be debated, but the further implications of this "disarray" do need to be attended to. This sloppiness is not the cheerful disorder reflective of a too-busy, otherwise engaged occupant. Rather it is a miniaturized version of the urban scrapheap—slum pickings, filthy bric-a-brac. Secondly, the room makes no pretense at being inhabitable, let alone comfortable. The nonfunctionality of the stove and sink emblematizes the antidomestic character of this room. This is a chamber in which one sleeps, as Dracula cryptically warns Harker, "unwisely," a chamber which gives its sleepers "bad dreams."[5] Thus Davies's simpleminded, illogical distrust of the stove begins to make perfect sense. It *would* be perfectly in keeping with the nature of Gothic houses-pace for Aston's oven to "blow-up"—disconnected or not.

To make matters worse, the immediate surroundings of this room—"up the landing," "downstairs" and "the house next door"—are "closed up," "out of commission." Ewa Byczkowska-Page labels such spaces in Pinter drama "*locus horridus,*" places "impossible to explore, incomprehensible, mysterious and terrifying" (1983, 29). These diegetic zones remain inaccessible to Davies. They are as forbidden, as off limits as Bluebeard's Blue Chamber or the "other part" of Dracula's castle. As for the realm from which he has fled, it is clearly an urban jungle, a zone of coldness, persecution, hunger. Davies's space, once so vast, has now shrunk to the parameters of this tiny room. Here has become, in classic Gothic fashion, all there is. Davies will make the same discoveries that every Gothic guest makes: enclosure does not constitute safety and the weather outside is not going to "break" (16).

Within this space all objects, regardless of their ostensible domestic function, are latent weapons, instruments of torture (hence the attack of the Electrolux and the smashing of the Buddha statuette). Moreover, objects in the Gothic world operate with or without human agency. Even though it is obvious that it is, after all, Mick who pushes the vacuum cleaner, *The Caretaker* is permeated by a sense of shelterlessness and environmental hostility that can best be described as Gothic. Bert States puts the case differently, but his view is essentially the same: "Pinter's characters . . . are forever waging war with things" (1985, 66). To this one could add that the "war" amounts to nothing more than a poorly conducted, foredoomed defense.

This ferocity of place is given clearer expression in *The Dumbwaiter*. Here the setting becomes a strangely alive, hostile entity—so alive, in fact, that the tyrant-owner does not and need not appear. This "dump" too is one in which one sleeps poorly. Gus complains of a restless night and unclean sheets, and he rails against his unseen host, who should have seen to it that "there was enough gas for a cup of tea" (101). Even more disturbing to him is an overwhelming sense of being confined: "I wouldn't mind if you had a window" (84).

However, the most unsettling feature of this apartment is the way its adjunct facilities seem to be self-propelled and self-motivated.[6] The toilet "decides" when and if it is going to flush; the dumbwaiter rumbles into life. Charles Carpenter's commentary on this phenomenon inadvertently suggests some provocative parallels to *The Castle of Otranto* harlequinade discussed earlier. He maintains that the world of *The Dumbwaiter* is the "nutty, unlifelike, non-analogical world of farce" (1973, 281). One of his major underlying premises for this argument is the way in which "mechanical objects suspend nature's law and follow theirs" (1973, 281). As I have already indicated, whether one classifies *The Dumbwaiter* as farcical or Gothic depends largely on whether one construes the activity of the inanimate object as malevolent or simply obstreperous.

Whichever reading one espouses, the choice is purely arbitrary, for Pinter, characteristically, does not provide enough data for us to favor one reading over the other. *The Dumbwaiter* may indeed be "haunted-house farce," as Carpenter contends, but it may also be read as haunted-house Gothic, a species of Gothic in which human visitors are engorged or annihilated by the powerful Gothic structure that they attempt to inhabit. We do not know if Ben will do the house's bidding, nor do we know the nature of the command itself. So it is that *The Dumbwaiter,* poised precariously, like *The Castle of Otranto,* between a guffaw and a scream, elicits terror—and laughter.

While Pinter's plays depict the movement into the Gothic structure as voluntary (though ill-advised), the asylum play presents this movement as an involuntarily executed *fait accompli.* In the NeoGothic asylum play, the victim's status as helpless prisoner, involuntary "guest," is immediately apparent. The extraordinary number of contemporary plays with prison or prison-like settings is well documented and verified by Carol Rosen's 1983 *Plays of Impasse.* However, only a very few of these "plays of impasse" transform the carceral setting into Gothic space. In most cases, the indignities or brutalities which the inmate suffers are clearly attributable to a human source whose motives are discernable and common. Unlike Gothic fantasies, most of these plays are indictments of a merely human authoritarianism: petty tyranny or mindless bureaucracy. The enemy in *The Churchill Play,* for example, is not the barbed wire itself, but rather the human beings who erect it and who "dump" uncooperative "detainees." We are rarely invited to view space itself and objects themselves as power-charged, persecuting entities.

*Marat-Sade* is singular in this regard, for it does succeed in rendering "institutional containment" (Roberts 1986, 118) in Gothic terms—the dreaded antihospital. Marat's tub is the domesticated analogue of Winnie's mound. One human artifact after another has been made over into a weapon of the institution, an instrument of torture: waistcoat becomes straitjacket, the housewife's apron becomes a butcher's apron, the lowly household bucket brims with blood.

The significance of the bathhouse-madhouse setting is that it perfectly embodies the institutional asylum: the madhouse is the public, institutional figuration of the false shelter, and the bathhouse implies the perversion of the domestic. Herein lies the essential distinction between the private false shelter and the institutional one. In the former, the perversion of the domestic is accomplished through the imagery of dirt, decay, refuse, and disorder; in the latter, the perversion is indicated by the opposite extreme—an inhuman cleanliness, an enforced formal order that categorically excludes the freewheeling, the messy, the spontaneous. Hence the flailing arms of the incarcerated one are pinned in place by the straightjacket. The institutional asylum is horribly sanitary, the inmate scrubbed to within an inch of his or her life. We have, of course, already seen this equation of housewifely neatness and torture in *Kaspar.* *Marat-Sade*'s madhouse-bathhouse setting is the incarnation of hygiene Gothic-style.[7]

The institutional false shelter can be even more insidious than the private one. In *Marat-Sade* it is the patients who furnish the *traditional* Gothic effects— it is they who are terrifying. By comparison, the bathhouse setting appears to be harmless. In fact, Coulmier's hydrotherapy seems benign, just the thing to soothe fevered imaginations. Thus Marat's watery confinement seems a well-meant kindness, a humane treatment for his burning flesh, so much so that Sade, as part of his persecution of Marat, can sneer at the safety and comfort of Marat's bath, comparing its water to "the pink water of the womb."[8]

Marat, on the other hand, in his ravings of bloodbaths and of the purgings of the Reign of Terror gives voice to the horror behind the cool, neat, antiseptic facade of the institutional asylum: in torture, as Elaine Scarry concludes about real-life instances, "[T]he domestic act of protecting becomes an act of hurting" (1985, 41). While the Marat-character in his fanaticism acquiesces in the catharsis of bloodshed, the Marat-actor adumbrates his rage, his helplessness and terror: such cleanliness is the furthest thing from godliness. The beatings and whippings administered in the name of order belie Coulmier's assertions of benevolent care for his "guests." As Ruby Cohn asserts, "The large bath reflects the smaller one" (1967, 480)—and surely vice versa.

Otto Reinert asserts that *"Marat-Sade* obviously has nothing in common with the small, claustrophobic, quiescent worlds of Beckett and Pinter" (1970, 930). On the contrary, *Marat-Sade,* its quality of spectacle notwithstanding, has everything to do with the worlds of Beckett and Pinter. Size, as has already been demonstrated, does not signify. Marat is fixed in his tub as securely as Winnie is fixed in her mound. Should he once more attempt to scramble out, he will again be promptly escorted back to his watery confinement. For him, as for her, there is no place else. For him, as for Pinter's waiters, sanctuary is an illusion.

In their flight from the cosmic storm, NeoGothic dramatic characters seek but fail to obtain refuge in Gothic structures, both private and institutional. Their last resort, the one to which they turn in their extremity, is the stage itself. In such "scaffold" plays, the Elizabethan synonym for the performance platform is resurrected and reinvested with its sinister original meaning. In Barnes's *Laughter!*, Bond's *The Swing, Rosencrantz and Guildenstern,* and *Marat-Sade,* the stage becomes a literal scaffold, an execution platform while still retaining its function as performance arena. In the scaffold play, the stage is not content to "needle" its inhabitants; it seeks nothing less than a complete annihilation. The magic circle of the "wooden O" is transformed into the locus of dread.

Before turning to the plays themselves, it is useful to note that the stage itself has traditionally been perceived as a place of sanctuary and to consider the reasons for this perception. In this regard, Bert States's ruminations on the collapse in mid-performance of two legendary actors—Kean and Molière—are most helpful:

Consider . . . two legendary facts from the history of theater: Molière and Kean were stricken in performance and died soon after. One always hears these events recited with a certain degree of awe and pride. . . . But surely we can go deeper. . . . I think the fascination takes us to the very core of the theater experience. . . . [H]ow impertinent of nature to shatter the illusion of art, to touch these two men when they were not, so to speak, themselves. . . . Had Molière collapsed in rehearsal, the event would lose its phenomenal significance and become a detail in his obituary. The mystery rests, rather, in the fact that the event took place in the theater, under "the weight of all those eyes." Surely here, of all places, Moliere should be guaranteed a temporary immunity to the laws of nature, somewhat like a criminal in the sanctuary of a church.

This sense of the stage as a territory where only unreal deaths occur underlies Guildenstern's contemptuous dismissal of the Player's death-scene throes: "You! What do *you* know about *death*? . . . Actors!" (83). This notion of the stage as an inviolable zone is given explicit expression in Ronald Harwood's *The Dresser*. "Sir," about to enact the role of Lear, dares the blitzkrieg itself to violate his theatre-sanctuary:

The night I played my first Lear there was a real thunderstorm. Now they send bombs. [ . . . ] Bomb, bomb, bomb us into oblivion if you dare, but each word I speak will be a shield against your savagery, each line I utter protection from your terror. (1981, 51)

This convention of the stage as a "safe area in the game of tag" is demolished by Peter Barnes's epilogue to his *Auschwitz* (the second half of *Laughter*). Barnes presents us with two "hollow-eyed" concentration camp inmates who perform an abbreviated—more accurately, an abruptly terminated—vaudeville routine as part of the "Extermination Camp Christmas Concert" (410). The voice-over announcement advises us that this performance is to be their "farewell appearance," and we discover shortly that these words are to be understood literally. In the midst of their black comedy banter about pain and slaughter ("*Bierberstein*: Bernie Litvinoff just died. *Bimko*: Well if he had a chance to better himself. *Bierberstein*: Drunk a whole bottle of varnish. Awful sight but a beautiful finish" [411]), the background tune of *On the Sunny Side of the Street* gives way to "a hissing sound" and the "follow-spot begins to turn blue." Lighting and sound become stage vehicles for the representation of hydrocyanide gas. Even as these elements of *mise en scène* are transformed into a medium of execution, they remain just what they are—accoutrement of the stage.[9] Gasping and coughing, the "Boffo Boys of Birkenau" invoke a theatrical metaphor which is now literally, shockingly true: "this act" really is "dead on its feet" (411). These two song-and-dance men die, like Stoppard's helpless pair, with the fade of the spotlight. Although we understand that some human hand pulls the switch that releases the "gas," no human agency is presented or even implied. Death seems to emanate from the stage itself, a stage that is simultaneously a structure belonging to an extermination camp and a platform erected for the purpose of performance. The act of performance—the jokes, the songs, the dances—is too fragile a defense. It provides no more protection than does Winnie's parasol or her "story." So much for the sanctuary of the stage.

Equally savage, and, if possible, more bizarre is Edward Bond's one-act piece *The Swing* (1976), part of a double bill composed on the occasion of the American Bicentennial. As the play begins, the audience is directly addressed, in Brechtian fashion, by a character who purports to provide a brief synopsis of the play:

> In the fall of nineteen eleven in Livermore Kentucky a blackman [*sic*] was charged with murder. He was taken to the local theatre and tied to a stake on stage. The box office sold tickets accordin [sic] to the usual custom: the more you paid the better you sat. The performance was this: people in the pricey seats got to empty their revolvers into the man. People in the gallery got one shot. An [*sic*] pro rata in between. Course he died very easy compared t' the style of some lynchin's [*sic*]. What you're gonna see is substantially true. (37)

We find, however, that the plot summary does not accord with the subsequent enacted events. For example, the charge is not murder but rape. The actuality of the crime is questionable since the victim is unable to identify her assailant and, in fact, unable to articulate her experience. Nonetheless, the lack of witnesses and the confusion of the victim do not deter the townspeople from selecting a suspect. The play takes its most pronouncedly abrupt detour away from the above synopsis when the accused turns out to be a white man. The expected political statement about racism in America fails to materialize. Comments one critic, "The play is very wide of the target as [a] comment on the racial problem in the United States today" (Kerensky 1977, 26). Bond's target is not (surprisingly) racism, but the shibboleth of the inviolability of performance space. Thus what we are confronted with is an arbitrarily chosen victim whose execution will furnish a spectacle.

In classic Gothic fashion, without the formality of a trial, the condemned is hustled onto the stage by the theatre's regular stagehands and hoisted onto a rude sort of trapeze. A circus-act motif begins to emerge as one character assumes the role of a tent pitchman while another dons the baggy pants, white face, and "bulbous nose" of a clown. "White with terror," Fred, the victim, believes, like the Marat-actor, that he is about to take *his* final bow. Yet our expectations are subverted when the clown aims his "pistol" and "shoots" the tethered suspect with water: "(*Fred laughs with hysterical relief.*) O fellas. Fellas. I thought it was real. I thought you were goin—(*Laughing weakly.*) I thought it was real. I thought it was real" (75). And in a flash, his imaginings, like those of James's governess, do "turn real." The clown fires a pistol that *has* somehow become real, and the audience quickly follows suit. In the original production of the play, according to Tony Coult, the live theatre audience "in awed silence" listened to "their avenging counterparts (on tape . . . ) cheer, scream, and empty their revolvers into Fred" (1977, 52). The stage directions which describe the execution are uncompromisingly brutal:

> Fred spins, twists, jerks, screams. After screams, blood spurts. . . . The audience noise seethes in a crescendo. . . . Last volley. Audience noise explodes. Fred has keeled over. He swings slowly and silently upside down. Blood falls and swishes over the stage. (76)

Coult believes that *The Swing* contains "the most terrible act of violence in all of Bond's works," that it is "a play that offers no way out" (1977, 53). Much of its shock value can be ascribed to the grim visual image, the horrible parody of the young man on the flying trapeze. But part of it too can be explained in terms of this violation of the convention of the stage as a sanctuary. The zany, showbiz antics of the clown, the ambience of the circus, tend to impart a false sense of security, to which even the victim briefly succumbs. When that security is shattered, when the magic circle is proven pregnable, we are doubly startled and disturbed.

It turns out, after all, Guildenstern's disbelief notwithstanding, that the stage *does* know a great deal about dying—at least as much as it is possible to know. The actor who "dies" onstage, must, as Robert Egan observes, "give living form to all he knows of death: bewilderment, fear, waves of physical pain; the fading of speech, of consciousness, and finally of breath. He must tax to the full his own observations (and thus his most painful personal experiences)" (1979, 68). This is a task that is not only taxing for the actor but potentially terrifying.

*Rosencrantz and Guildenstern*'s Player has known this task and its concomitant terror. However, he also knows the predispositions of theatrical audiences: "Audiences know what to expect and that is all they are prepared to believe in" (84). What they believe in is the sacrosanct inviolability of the stage to real death. The Player's anecdote about the actor-thief whose execution he inserts into a performance underscores the invalidity of that belief while at the same time demonstrates the audience's stubborn persistence in that belief. We should not let the airy dismissiveness of the Player deflect our attention away from the fact of a human being, "white with terror," dying under the weight of all those unconvinced, irreverent eyes.

And finally, there is the "lucky" paranoiac who has been conscripted to portray Marat. In an agony of uncertainty, he worries whether Corday's knife is a stage prop or a real weapon, whether his tub will be his coffin, whether the final tableau will for him be indeed final. He cannot know to what lengths Sade might go to make this death both convincing and theatrical. Having heard Sade's rhapsodic rendition of the execution of Damiens as well as his bored denunciations of the "anonymous cheapened" death by the guillotine, the Marat-actor need not be paranoid in order to fear that this, his stage debut, may also be his "farewell appearance." Thus the scaffold play touches, probes, a taboo of theatrical representation—the enactment of real death on a self-consciously real stage. John Perlette, in discussing *Rosencrantz and Guildenstern,* observes that we would react to real death on a theatrical stage with "incredulity" and "total alienation" (1985, 667). In between "incredulity" and "total alienation" is a moment "white with terror."

# Other Gothic Spaces:
# Offstage Space—Gallery and Wings

"With defilement," writes Paul Ricouer, "we enter into the reign of terror" ([1967] 1969, 25). "What thing am I," wails Shelley's father-ravished Beatrice, and her keening echoes across the century. "Unclean," shrieks *Dracula*'s Mina Harker, as if in answer. And the other question—"What have I done?"—on the lips of both defiled ones, is central to the Gothic defiled ones, even though defilement is not the consequence of wrong-doing, but rather the condition of total, absolute victimization.[1] In defilement, according to Ricouer, "The ethical order of doing ill has not been distinguished from the cosmo-biological order of faring ill" ([1967] 1969, 27).

In its accounts of defilement, the Gothic mode's predilection for commingling and fusion joins forces with its maniacal insistence on tyranny and injustice. The penetrated, defiled body of the innocent one becomes in itself a source of terror to its owner. This body of the defiled is experienced as alien, other, and awful, for it has been converted into the body of the defiler. Thus Beatrice intuits that her veins are "contaminated," that her blood is no longer hers but Cenci's. Mina Harker apprehends that to herself and to her beloved she is now the "worst enemy" (Stoker [1897] 1965, 290). Defilement is not simple invasion and plunder. It is, rather, a takeover, a makeover, that is stunningly, ruthlessly thorough. In this sense the body of the defiled one can be likened to the plague-struck body. Ricouer explains the prevalence of the language of illness in portrayals of defilement: "The representation of defilement dwells in the half-light of a quasi-physical infection that points toward a quasi-moral unworthiness" ([1967] 1969, 35). Thus it is no accident that, when the Gothic tells stories of defilement, it refers again and again to the language of infection and epidemic. Thus Lucy Westenra's decline into vampirehood is documented as the process of a wasting disease. Thus too Poe's archetypal fable of invasion, "The Masque of the Red Death," repeatedly invokes a language of pathology.

This contamination in the Gothic spreads outward from the violated body, infiltrating the body's environment, both public and private. Dracula's appropriation of his victims' bodies is paralleled by his disregard for the privacy of the boudoir and also by his acquisition of real estate. Each property is transformed into Dracula-space by the implantation of an infected coffin-box of home soil, which, in order to be reclaimed, must be "sterilized." Stealthily and steadily, Dracula works from the inside, accumulating the territory and the bodies which will constitute his own counterempire.

Dracula's utter indifference to humanly engendered boundaries, his ability to trespass at will, sets in motion the transformation of ordinary space into Gothic space. Geoffrey Wall describes this process:

> All secrecies, all privacies, all territories and rules for contact between bodies are unravelling. Much masculine ingenuity is devoted to the creation of sealed and impregnable spaces, where what is in stays in, where what is out stays out. Bedrooms with charmed windows, asylums with locked doors, coffins with lids screwed down, graves properly inhabited and accurately inscribed, diaries tied in blue ribbon: all in vain. Windows are broken, locks are picked, lunatics escape, coffins open. (1984, 21)

Wall's observations indicate that Dracula's empire is indeed, like Roderick Usher's, a "kingdom of inorganization." Boundaries are collapsing, walls are becoming permeable membranes, inside and outside are no longer clearly demarcated.[2] It is as if the seizure of a single cell infects the whole organism, setting off a chain reaction in which all cells become increasingly nondifferentiated while taking on the characteristics of the viral invader. This process of viral-like invasion and contamination is a common mechanism in Gothic texts. Thus, for example, in *The Monk,* Matilda's successful penetration of Ambrosio's conventual cell leads inevitably to the defilement of Antonia.

A more spectacular rendering of invasion and defilement is set forth in Brown's *Wieland.* The elder Wieland erects a sanctuary, "a circular area . . . cleared of moss and shrubs and exactly levelled" ([1798] 1973, 18), in the midst of the encroaching wilderness, a hallowed spot where he can commune with his God. "Suddenly," his daughter's narrative tells us, and for no apparent reason, he is stricken with anguish and a sense of impending doom. His "inquietudes increased" until one night, in the midst of his devotions, his temple is invaded by a mysterious, alien force. The first witness to arrive on the scene perceives an indistinct, nebulous entity which he can describe "no better . . . than by saying it resembled a cloud impregnated with light" (25).

Wieland, barely alive, is scorched and bruised; his defilement becomes evident when his wounds begin to fester. "More terrible symptoms" ensue—the contaminated body becomes a foul object of disgust and fear; "Insupportable exhalations and crawling putrefaction had driven from his chamber every one whom their duty did not detain" ([1798] 1973, 26). The elder Wieland's "imperfect account," the tale delivered in delirium, shortly gives way to utter silence.

Years later the adult Clara is troubled by the inexplicability and pointlessness of her father's terrible death. She speculates about this mystery, wondering whether this death had been caused by internal or external agents: "Was . . . this the stroke of a vindictive and invisible hand? . . . Or was it merely the irregular expansion of the fluid that imparts warmth to our heart and our blood" (27). But the etiology here is even more insidious, for, as Clara seems to have forgotten, her father has years before been *out there* in the savage wilderness from which he has returned "with a constitution somewhat decayed" (18). Clara neglects to consider that her father has somehow been infected, contaminated by something out there, that his disorder has already been established within, that the fiery explosion and the subsequent symptoms are but the manifestation of some alien malaise contracted in the world beyond the circular clearing.

Whatever the causes, in classic Gothic fashion, the contamination spreads outward from the stricken body: Clara's mother lapses into a mortal illness, an ailment that Clara attributes to "shock." Years later the younger Wieland, *his* brain "scorched to cinders," is transformed into a psychotic killer. And there is nothing the Wieland children can do. Whatever was out there is now lodged within.

*The Turn of the Screw* would seem to have little in common with Brown's lurid tale, but actually it conforms fairly closely to the same dynamics of Gothic defilement which Brown's text exhibits. *The Turn of the Screw* is a sustained exploration of defilement, a defilement to be understood as physical, spatial, and metaphysical.

The intrusion of Quint into the hothouse-stronghold of Bly is conveyed as a sequence of closings-in. He appears first on the outside—on the roof; later he materializes just outside a window. Soon enough he is within. Quint too is no respecter of boundaries; he is a "bounder," refusing to stay put below stairs —or within whatever zone it is to which he had been banished. It is significant that Quint is so often enframed, first figuratively in the governess's description and then literally by an actual window frame. Like Dracula he is a "border being," belonging to that category of creatures which, according to Christopher Craft, "abrogate demarcations" and who move with ease between "exclusive realms."[3] Accordingly, these encounters with Quint are rendered by the governess as so many invasions of privacy: "We had been, collectively, subject to an intrusion; some commonplace traveller . . . had made his way in unobserved" (James [1898], 1966, 18). Predictably the tone quickly escalates to the hysteria of defilement—"someone" has "taken a liberty rather monstrous" (18).

Eventually, however, the governess comes to believe that it is not she who has been interfered with, but rather the two cherubic innocents entrusted to her care. The imagery of defilement now defines the "little wretches" who are "mad" and possessed." Even the house itself is now "poisoned" (49). Meanwhile, her own role, as she sees it, is to provide a border, a barrier—to serve as the wall, the "fence," the "screen" which the "outsiders" must not breach.[4]

By now, the parlance of disease has infected the narrative. Miles appears to her as "some wistful patient in a children's hospital" (63). Shortly thereafter, Flora, in a fit of choleric temper, denounces her would-be protectress—and promptly falls ill: Bly has "ceased to agree with her" (81). Miles too exhibits symptoms, alternating, like Lucy Westenra and Flora, between the hectic flush of fever and the pallor of anemia. The earlier movement from outside to inside is reversed: the inside is working its way out. Yet, as Miles and the governess are, so to speak, having it out, Quint appears, once more enframed by the window casing, "like a sentinel before a prison" (85), as if to keep bound fast the defilement within.

As in *Wieland,* the dispossession, the emptying out, is rendered as a cryptic, "imperfect account," which shortly gives way to utter silence. Like the landscape itself which falls so deathly quiet in Quint's presence, Miles, having said it all, having got it out of his system (the colloquialism seems so apposite here), lapses into silence, his blood stilled. The story, like Quint, recedes, disappears back into darkness and silence. This subtle interconnectedness of articulation and disease is recognized by Geoffrey Harpham:

> Life is synonymous with articulation and death with silence, with the condition of having "nothing left to say." Perfect health is similarly inarticulate. . . . Tales narrate trouble, the mid-region between the silence of health and the silence of death. (1982, 117)

By the end of the tale, inside and outside have become hopelessly enmeshed. Defilement is a contagious, palpable presence throughout, yet its origin remains hidden, unexplained. The imagery of disease in *The Turn of the Screw* cannot be readily translated into moral turpitude or social disorder, though we are invited, tempted to do so. On the contrary, there is nothing to be learned at all, nothing to be done. The Gothic exegesis of sickness is radically different from, for example, that of the medieval. As Susan Sontag explains, "In the Middle Ages, a leper was a social text in which corruption was made visible—an exemplum, an emblem of decay" (1977, 58). In the Gothic world, however, defilement, so often registered as illness, has nothing to do with transgression per se, nor does it serve as any sort of object lesson. Ricouer concurs: defilement is "a quasi-material something that infects as a sort of filth, that harms by invisible properties and that nonetheless works in the manner of a force in the field of our individually psychic and corporeal existence" ([1967] 1969, 25). It simply settles upon bodies and places, clinging and penetrating like a cloud of contaminating mist. Thus it is that both Shelley's Beatrice and Stoker's Mina describe their experience of defilement as an envelopment by a smothering, paralyzing fog. *Wieland* too sustains this metaphor.

Nowhere, however, is the phenomenon of Gothic invasion and defilement chronicled with more clinical precision than in Poe's "The Masque of the Red

Death." Harpham asserts the story's intense concern with boundary-making yet its simultaneous insistence on the futility of all boundaries:

> In locking himself within, Prospero has made a statement about boundaries, implying that the Red Death can be thwarted by the interposition of walls, as if it belonged to the same order of being as a mad dog or a cannonball. (1982, 113)

Harpham goes on to suggest that the story is "an allegory of the outside becoming inside" (1982, 118). One might add that the opposite holds true as well, that the two zones become inseparable, indistinguishable. The plague microbe, contained in the entrails of the reveler, is carried into the walled-off sanctuary. Once there, it begins to manifest itself: what is within comes out. Harpham perceives this showing forth, this unmasking, in terms that suggest the Gothic servant-spy: "Red . . . has followed them inside the abbey, has 'pursued' them down the corridors. . . . [It is] an undercover agent, obtaining employment in the duke's household, plotting his death" (1982, 113).

Construed thus, the Red Death no longer appears as the party-goers' well-earned punishment for crassness or arrogance. From the very first, the pestilence is imaged forth as inescapable, virulent beyond measure. Defilement is already there; space has been contaminated. Prospero's project, to establish an inviolable, sterile zone, a walled-in empire secure against the Red Death's counterempire, is, of course, doomed from the start. The disease is already within: to breathe is to be sick. These merry-makers are, as Harpham contends, "larval corpses" (1982, 113). The time of the masque is merely the period of incubation—the incubus is already within.

Like *The Turn of the Screw*, "The Masque of the Red Death" closes with a confrontation, the flush of fever, and then a ponderous silence. The Prince is hoarse, "convulsed," "reddened with rage" (Poe [1842] 1970, 364). (It is the flush of anger, we are told, but then "choler" and "cholera" are lexical cousins.) What is within now begins to surface even as the figure of the Red Death is itself encircled: the untenanted costume is framed by the "vast assembly . . . [which] shrank from the centres of the rooms to the walls" (365). The blood inside now surges out through the body's pores, and the halls become "blood bedewed" (366). As in grotesque art, Gothic narrative features this merging of an "alien outside . . . with its victim-mate-self to produce a condition of such exquisite disorder that it is impossible to distinguish host from parasite" (Harpsham 1982, 106). Poe's invasion story terminates with the establishment of an empire of "illimitable dominion" (Poe [1842] 1970, 366). In these two words are summed up the infrastructure of Gothic invasion—the dissolution of boundary-limits and the complete mastery of the invaded space: inside and outside are now one.

Both "The Masque of the Red Death" and *The Turn of the Screw* represent a complete takeover, a successful invasion. There are other texts, however, which, while they do portray the structure and dynamics of Gothic invasion, do not present that invasion as fully successful. In these texts, the virus is somehow resisted. These are texts into whose realistic narrative fabric the Gothic needle pokes small, quickly mended "black holes," "pockets of darkness," as Rosemary Jackson deems them (1979, 100–101). The invasion is represented, but defilement does not occur; the two fictive modes do not merge in "exquisite disorder." Such moments strike the reader as surrealistic tableaux, peculiar fissures, stoppages in the flow of narrative. Jackson elaborates: "Gothic episodes erupt into Victorian texts. . . . A predominantly realistic narrative is fractured, spiralling into surrealistic convulsions" (99).

Such a text is *Jane Eyre*. From behind the forbidden door, from the marginal zone of banishment, the topmost periphery of this "Bluebeard's Castle," a figure irrupts. Another border-being, like Dracula, like Quint, Bertha Mason Rochester is a trespasser of boundaries, a violator of private domestic space. Bertha, bursting her shackles, oversteps her boundaries and drifts, trailing the alien and strange behind her, into Jane's everyday world, the world of the not-Gothic. Jane apprehends this invader as huge, loathsome, threatening, other—the "vampyr." Gilbert and Gubar have argued convincingly that Bertha figures as Jane's angry other self, and such a view well serves an interpretation of the novel as a realistic, feminist text. Still, it does seem possible to take Jane at her own word and thus to regard Bertha's demonic dreadfulness as a manifestation of the Gothic world, as a temporary intrusion of the Gothic into a text whose concerns and business lie elsewhere. From this vantage point, Jane's revulsion is simply the visceral reaction of horror. Understood in these terms, Bertha is a literal monster, an embodiment of the Gothic, an avatar of Gothic invasion. The inferno which she makes of Thornfield may be likened to that other Gothic bonfire around which yet another monster performs a dance of fury.

Nonetheless, Bertha merely hovers over Jane. Brontë allows her heroine to survive her encounter with the demonic, to emerge unscathed and undefiled. In the world of *Jane Eyre,* there *are* other places to which one can go, even if they are uncomfortable and inconvenient; flight is a viable option. In texts such as *Jane Eyre,* Gothic power can be counted on to self-destruct. *Jane Eyre* is not itself a Gothic text, but it does, like Baillie's *Orra,* speculate on the nature of the Gothic.

Although *Wieland* presents a fully realized instance of Gothic invasion, it can also be placed here too, among those texts which image that invasion as a temporary intrusion into, rather than a total transformation of, ordinary space. Such precisely is Clara's own experience of invasion—the penetration of her home, her family, her very soul by the interloper Carwin. Carwin, with his eloquence, his lofty deportment, his Spanish sympathies, seems almost a refugee from *The Monk*. (His physical appearance anticipates that of Shelley's Monster, as Day notices [1985, 129].) He worms his way into the tightly-knit Wieland circle, ingratiating himself so thoroughly that he comes to be regarded "as a kind of inmate of the house" (Brown [1798] 1973, 90). But Carwin infringes upon the prerogatives of guesthood—he goes where he pleases.

The disembodied voice of Carwin invades Clara's private spaces—her summer house, her bedchamber. Her sleep is disturbed, like that of so many restless Gothic sleepers, by the presence of the stranger by the bedside. Soon no place is safe for her. Clara becomes a haunted woman, her home-space no longer her own: "All places were alike accessible to this foe; or, if his empire were restricted by local bounds, those bounds were utterly inscrutable by me" (99).

The fact that Carwin's motives are venial does not lessen our sense of this monstrous invasion of Clara's privacy. This pollution of her private space, in conjunction with the shock of her brother's madness, literally sickens her. Yet Clara is saved, remaining herself undefiled, like Jane Eyre, by the purifying flames that raze the contaminated house:

> This incident, as disastrous as it might at first seem, had, in reality, a beneficial effect upon my feelings. I was, in some degree, roused from the stupor which had seized my faculties. . . . My habitation was levelled with the ground, and I was obliged to seek a new one. (267–68)

Luckily for her, Clara too has access to someplace else. Still, one's lingering sense of *Wieland* is that of a charade, a game of playacting so intense that the game is transformed into a shattering reality. Though not concerned with theatricality in any overt way, *Wieland* does participate in the Gothic's abiding sense of the danger of the theatrical project. Thus, *Wieland* moves us closer to the conditions which obtain when the drama enacts Gothic invasion. It is precisely the disembodiedness, the there-but-not-there quality of Carwin's voice that invests it with such awful power; that is, Carwin's power reaches its apogee when he is, so to speak, offstage. Thus *Wieland* inadvertently offers us a preliminary model of leakage from offstage space, a phenomenon to which we shall soon return.

If *Wieland* illustrates the terrifying effect of "noises off," George Eliot's *Daniel Deronda*, while not a Gothic novel, offers a striking little vignette in which onstage space is invaded by an ocular element. The tableau-vivant scene of *Daniel Deronda* represents a startling distillation of all the elements we have been discussing—here the Gothic intrudes into a realistic setting which just so happens to be overtly theatrical. The little sketch performed by Gwendolyn and her cousins is to be "something pleasant" ([1874] 1967, 90), nothing more than a light entertainment for family and friends. Everything is "answering perfectly," when the unexpected (always possible in the theatre) disrupts the rehearsed:

[B]efore Hermione [Gwendolyn] had put forth her foot, the movable panel, which was on a line with the piano, flew open on the right opposite the stage and disclosed the picture of the dead face and the fleeing figure, brought out in pale definitiveness by the position of the waxlights. Everyone was startled, but all eyes in the act of turning towards the opened panel were recalled by a piercing cry from Gwendolyn, who stood without change of attitude, but with a change of expression that was terrifying in its terror. She looked like a statue into which a soul of Fear had entered: her pallid lips were parted; her eyes, usually narrowed under their long lashes, were dilated and fixed. (91)

The movable panel, de riguer accoutrement of haunted mansions and theatrical sets alike, springs open, seemingly of its own accord, and the face of Dread intrudes into the artful, pretty world of Gwendolyn's masque. Gwendolyn responds to this intruder in classic Gothic fashion: her terror is absolute.

It hardly matters that the panel's apparent self-propulsion can be attributed to "the sudden vibration from the piano" (92). What does matter is what Gwendolyn sees and the context in which she sees it. The "dead face" and the "fleeing figure" of the painting belong both to offstage space and to the alien world of the Gothic. Gwendolyn has known this terror before, "occasional experiences, which seemed like a brief remembered madness, an unexplained exception from her normal life" (94). But such experiences had, until now, occurred only in "solitude" in a "wide scene"; heretofore she had always recovered, "found again her usual world" as soon as "someone joined her" (95). Now this experience of dread has occurred in a public setting, onstage, in "well-lit company" (49). The donning of a costume, the assumption of a role, does not immunize Gwendolyn any more than had the outrageous masks and "wild apportionments" protected Poe's masqueraders. No place is secure, not even the well-lit stage, from the Gothic invader waiting in the wings.

Poe, in the Dupinesque mood of his "The Philosophy of Composition," transforms backstage space into a metaphor for the plain hard work, the tricks even, that underlie poetic composition. In this exposé, "behind the scenes" becomes the realm of unvarnished, even tawdry reality, the zone of "wheels and pinions . . . step-ladders and demon-traps," those crude mechanisms which raise ghosts and stir tempests out front (Poe [1846] 1970, 529–30). It seems that nothing could be further removed from what we know about Gothic space.

There is, however, another way to conceive of Gothic space. The distinction Poe makes is a distinction between zones of theatrical space and zones of dramatic space. Michael Issacharoff, writing on the semiotic dimension of stage space, defines the former as a matter of architecture and the latter as "space as used by an individual dramatist" (1981, 212). In other words, as theatrical space, backstage is precisely what Poe claims it to be—a very prosaic realm inhabited by stage managers and the like. As dramatic space, however, backstage or wing space is another matter entirely. As dramatic space, the backstage area is a "diegetic" realm, that is, as Issacharoff suggests, a space that is "referred to by the characters" but unseen by the audience (1981, 215). Strictly speaking, diegetic space is purely a verbal construct. Nonetheless, as Issacharoff points out, "[D]ramatic tension and interest can often arise from the interplay between mimetic [onstage] space and diegetic space" (1981, 215).

In Gothic drama, both old and new, this "interplay" assumes a very specific character. In the nineteenth-century Gothic Melodrama, the most common pattern is the movement of some dramatic character from diegetic space into the mimetic zone, a movement that effects a temporary (and reversible) transformation of the mimetic space. Invasion is merely an episode. In contrast, in the NeoGothic drama, the intruder is not a character in any ordinary sense; it is inhuman, a thing, most commonly a disembodied voice or an invasive prop. Moreover, the foreign entity accomplishes an absolute and enduring alteration of mimetic space. Thus, even if it is driven back into its old haunts, the territory it has touched is irrevocably, significantly transformed. The NeoGothic invasion drama, conforming more closely than the Gothic Melodrama to the infrastructure of Gothic invasion, likewise retains the imagery of pathology; the Gothic Melodrama does not. That is to say, in the nineteenth-century stage piece, the invader is perceived as simply villainous, unsound of soul. Whereas the Gothic Melodrama (with the remarkable exception of *The Cenci*) was concerned with the representation of moral turpitude, the NeoGothic drama seeks to represent defilement. A close examination of some specimens of each of the two forms will confirm this diagnosis.

The nineteenth-century stage interloper erupts into festive gatherings much as Gothic episodes erupt into non-Gothic narrative texts. He most frequently turns up as a gate-crasher at an in-progress celebration, usually a wedding feast. This pattern, which Peter Brooks designates as the "violated banquet," was provided its stage inauguration by Pixérécourt's *Coelina*, a play which shortly thereafter resurfaced in England as Thomas Holcroft's *A Tale of Mystery* (1802). (This pattern appears earlier in Gothic fiction. In fact, a violated banquet launches the first Gothic novel.) Like Poe's masqueraders, the merrymakers are "disconcerted" by the striking of the hour, a sound which augurs the ingress of the unwelcome guest:

[*In the midst of the rejoicing the clock strikes; the dancing suddenly ceases; the music inspires alarm and dismay.*]
   *Enter Malvoglio.*
   [*He stops in the middle of the stage. . . . All express terror. . . . Malvoglio then presents a letter to Bonamo, with a malignant assurance. . . . Bonamo opens the letter and reads with great agitation. . . .* ]
*Bonamo*: No more of love or marriage! No more of sports, rejoicing and mirth. ([1802] 1975, 21)

As in realistic fiction, the Gothic invader is construed as an alien, dangerous character who must be and can be destroyed, or at least exorcised—contained, driven back into marginal spaces. The Gothic Melodrama permits this complete expulsion and indeed bends all of its energies to that purpose.

It was not uncommon for the nineteenth-century Gothic invasion play to conclude with a corrective nuptial to underscore the return to communal wholeness. A number of variations were wrought on this pattern. For example, in Edward Fitz-ball's *The Devil's Elixir* (1829), a "false" celebration is in progress, false in the sense that the bridegroom is the true bridegroom's identical twin. The entrance of the real bridegroom at the height of the festivities brings the party to a complete standstill. The apparent invader is in this case a liberating force since the real interloper has gone unrecognized. Desperately clinging to his assumed role, the false bridegroom casts his brother in the old, familiar role—the "stranger . . . that stealest thus unbidden to our feast" ([1829] 1975, 28). Despite this stratagem, the ceremony remains unconcluded. The play's final scene gestures toward a replaying of the exchange of vows, but with the false bridegroom once more playing his original role of pious friar, in which capacity he will join in wedlock his brother and the woman who is no longer his bride but his "sister." The proper ceremony seems intended as an antidote to the ill-founded one which preceded it. (This pattern of the ill-omened and interrupted un-marriage, which is eventually amended by a proper and propitious one, seems inherited from Radcliffe, since, in the more radical, more thoroughgoing Gothic fantasies such as *Frankenstein* and *Melmoth,* the remedial marriage ceremony never transpires. In *Otranto,* though duly provided, the ceremony seems spurious and its therapeutic value is patently questionable.) The revival of the pattern in *Jane Eyre* is another piece of evidence linking the nineteenth-century Gothic Melodrama to those realistic Victorian texts which contain and repress Gothic intrusions.

The permanent, full-fledged transformation of space, the contamination of defilement, does not transpire in the Gothic Melodrama. Since the Gothic intrusion is envisioned as episodic and temporary, the two realms, the inside and the outside, are never allowed to mesh. The significant posture of the melodramatic stage, regardless of Gothic subject matter, was one of boundary affirmation.

One Gothic Melodrama that does approach this degree of permeability in its treatment of invasion, and thus serves as a transitional piece, is Lewis's *The Bells,* which we have already encountered briefly. *The Bells* manipulates the invasion theme in a manner that approaches Gothic narrative treatments.

That the play does so is partially attributable to the fact that its invasive element is accorded so little in the way of human characterization as to seem scarcely human, but, more significantly, it is because the play makes some commitment to aural representation of the invader. The invasion theme is announced by that familiar Gothic sound—the smashing of window glass. Furthermore, this commitment to the aural is carried on through the identification of the invader with the sinister tinkling of sleigh bells, a noise which invariably disconcerts Mathias, who alone can hear them. The sound of these bells becomes an invasive force, a disembodied "voice" that hounds Mathias, much as Clara Wieland had been haunted by her voices. Although the play urges us to construe this sound as the voice of conscience, as "standing for" Mathias's guilt, we do well to remember that the sound of the bells is pure, inarticulate noise, unfreighted with ethical signification. Act 2's curtain helps to clarify this point. In the midst of the strains of the wedding waltz (the music of fellowship), the ominous jingle of the sleigh bells intrudes. In a *coup de théâtre* remarkable for its day, the two sounds—one joyful and public, the other horrifying and private—clash and compete for dominance.

Moreover, pure sound suggests the invisibility, the undetectability of the Gothic viral-invader. Like Poe's Prospero, Mathias foolishly believes that if he can surround himself with enough sound, enough happy noise, he can hold the invader at bay. *The Bells* presses us to translate Mathias's fever, thirst, and faintness into retributive punishment—faring ill because of having done ill—but there is also a lingering sense that he has been the unlucky recipient of some demonic visitation.

A final and convincing reason to read *The Bells* as prototypical of NeoGothic drama (as opposed to Gothic Melodrama) is that it concludes with an interrupted wedding; no remedial nuptial restores communal wholeness. Its final "word" is a disarticulate keening. The contaminated gold pieces that Mathias feared to pass on to his children are still there, securely lodged within. Though Lewis's play is overtly concerned with wickedness and chastisement, its unusual reworking of the Gothic invasion theme moves it closer to the literature of defilement. For fully realized treatments of Gothic invasion, dramas wherein barriers are ruptured to the point of becoming permeable membranes, we must look to the NeoGothic dramas of Pinter, Ionesco, Shepard, and Berkoff.

Pinter's *The Hothouse* (1980) presents an extraordinarily faithful rendering of aural (and to some extent, tactile) Gothic invasion. At first glance, this play seems more properly a NeoGothic "asylum" play. The title itself evokes the romanticized image of the deranged as so many sensitive plants who, since they wither in the harsh sunlight and chill of ordinary reality, must be sequestered for their own protection. Still, on the other hand, "hothouse" also suggests the barely contained explosiveness of the pressure-cooker. As Frances Gillen observes, "Heat . . . becomes an important metaphor in the play, indicating the build-up of pressure beneath the enforced order" (1983, 91). One can think even more literally than this though. The heat of which the characters complain is oppressively real, and it emanates from diegetic space. It seems that somewhere in the deep recesses of the Hothouse there must be a boiler running amok, a machine whose manic activities cannot be regulated.[5] Despite the fact that it is the dead of winter, the inside temperature is that of a "crematorium"; so hot has this mimetic space become that the snow of the play's other diegetic zone has "turned to slush" (90).

From a peripheral zone likewise emanate the sighs, whispers, groans, and laughter of the mad. Thus aural leakage reminds us irresistibly of the unnerving laughter that filters out of Thornfield's attic. Unlike *Jane Eyre,* however, *The Hothouse* maintains the incorporeality of the voices. Gillen relates that in the original manuscript of the play the patients do appear. He speculates that, during the rehearsal period, Pinter shifted to a less naturalistic treatment (1983, 92). In any event, Pinter eventually chose to present the breakout of the inmates exclusively through lighting and sound cues:

> *The lights go down on the office.*
> *Darkness.*
> *A low light on the stairway and the forestage.*
> *Squeaks are heard, of locks turning.*
> *The rattle of chains.*
> *A great clanging, reverberating, as of iron doors opening.*
> *Shafts of light appear abruptly about the stage, as of doors opening into corridors and into rooms.*
> *Whispers, chuckles, half-screams of the patients grow.*
> *The clanging of locks and doors grows in intensity.*
> *The lights shift from area to area, rapidly.*
> *The sounds reach a feverish pitch and stop.* (145)

In *The Hothouse* the Gothic invasion is imaged forth as an inundation of sound. The rattlings and clankings, obligatory trappings of the Gothic ghost, are reinvested with the old primal terror they had all but lost. The effect is remarkably akin to the closing of Poe's "The Fall of the House of Usher." The sound effects which punctuate the Usher narrator's recitation of the "Mad Trist" of Sir Lancelot Canning seem just too predictable, too heavily laden with stock associations to be anything other than amusing camp—one hardly knows how to stifle one's laughter. Yet for all their tendentious overdoneness, the noises *are* a faithful orchestration of what is going on below stairs. In *The Hothouse,* as in "Usher," the clankings and scrapings, no matter how absurd, *are* reliable semiotic signals that a barrier is being smashed and that the monstrous is about to be unleashed. The "whisper" that Roote claims he can hear "in the basement" unerringly tells him that "something is going on" (128). Paul Lewis remarks that Poe's work "[g]enerally acknowledges [that] the last act of the human drama is slaughter" (1981, 320). The silence which ensues after the noises have reached a "feverish pitch" is the profound quietude after the massacre. Likewise, in *The Hothouse,* mass slaughter is what happens in that momentary interval of flickering lights and noises off.

Despite the heating up, though, no inferno ensues, no purifying flames raze the asylum. This fact has led more than one commentator to conclude that *The Hothouse* is satiric in intent, that it is a condemnation of the bureaucracy and insensitivity of the institutional mind. Gillen, for example, responds to the play in these terms, arguing that it is a parable of suppression and of suppression's inevitable consequences:

> [T]he organization quickly absorbs such moments of violence and moves on, almost of its own momentum. . . . The organization is all, and presumably will go on just about as before until the heat builds up again, the cries of whatever is suppressed to that order are heard, and new violence erupts. Then names of those in authority may change as they do here . . . but the organization will go on. (1983, 93)

One can read the play in such fashion, of course, as does Rudolf Stamm, who deems it "Pinter's Tribute to Anger" (1981, 290). But then one can read "The Masque of the Red Death" as a didactic tale of arrogance and retribution. From a Gothic perspective, though, a different pattern emerges. Pinter's characters in *The Hothouse* are no more pitiable than Poe's masquers; they *are* all "gargoyles," as Martin Esslin complains (1970, 106). The point remains that they are victims of Gothic invasion.

The monarch of this enclave, Pinter's own Prospero, is Roote, who tries unavailingly to keep the messiness of organic life from intruding into his clockwork domain. The news that a birth and a death have occurred "on these premises" sends him into a panic. His distress at first seems ludicrous, as silly as Prospero's rage that an uninvited guest has infiltrated his by-invitation-only orgy. Yet Roote's anxiety turns out to have been well founded. While Gibbs "can't see that the matter is of such extreme significance," Roote "smell[s] disaster" (38).

From this point on, the physical edifice evidences the symptoms of a malfunction: "Everything's clogged up, bunged up, stuffed up, buggered up" (102). Typewriters are out of order, the intercom will not work, radiators can not be turned off. As in Poe's "Usher," the imagery of pathology is grafted onto descriptions of the housing structure: Usher's house is sick; Pinter's "hothouse" has a fever. And the pathogenesis of this disorder is, as in Poe's tale, just as mysterious. Somehow, the red death, which is life itself, has made its way in on this Christmas Day.

The play's conclusion, which transpires outside of the Hothouse in the Ministry's headquarters, implies the beginnings of a new cycle of power exchanges. Stamm argues, for example, that: "[W]e . . . are left with the certainty that [Roote's] successor will be worse and that the wheel will continue to turn without alteration" (1981, 293). In the main, Stack is right, though for the wrong reasons; the cycle has nothing to do with the righteous wrath of the victimized or the deeper-dyed cruelty of the new tyrant: circularity is the informing structure of Gothic revolution; all the vest-wearing and lock-testing in the world is not going to make any difference. Eventually Gibbs too will go "down like a log," not because he is manipulative and deceitful—he is—but because that is "the way things are." In the Gothic cosmos, neither things nor people stay put.

While *The Hothouse* features an invasion that is primarily aural,[6] Eugene Ionesco's *Amédée or How to Get Rid of It* (1954) images invasion in uncompromisingly visual terms. The outsized corpse which thrusts itself into ordinary living space cannot help but remind us of the gigantic ghostly body which eventually appropriates the whole of Otranto's castle.

Actually, "how to get rid of it" seems a comparatively mundane dilemma compared to the questions "What is it? How did it get here? Why is it here?" Thus, *Otranto* is not at all helpful, really, at providing answers to these sorts of questions, as Stephen Sandy observes:

> Walpole makes no use of syntax or rhetorical device to introduce [the helmet] and he never attempts an adequate explanation of its origin. . . . It remains in the court, the agent of Conrad's death, . . . inexplicable, absurd. (1980, 35–36)

From here on, various gargantuan appendages and accoutrements keep turning up all over the castle. When the ghostly visitor pulls itself together, it turns out to be much too large for its container: the castle walls crumble as the figure, "dilated to an immense magnitude," bursts its confinement and rises heavenward ([1765] 1968, 145).

What are we to make of this huge unburied child? For Wilt, the Otranto ghost represents "remote, therefore magnified, punishment" (1980, 29). For Punter, it signifies "our past rising against us, whether it be the psychological past . . . or the historical past" (1980, 53). Day perceives it as "a purely formal representation of the supernatural, a representation so formalized that it is drained of content, except as an aspect of the Gothic world" (1985, 38). Despite the fundamental unknowableness of this thing that has inserted itself into Manfred's world, it is best understood as an avatar of the Gothic itself with all its inscrutability and blatant cruelty. Whatever the ghost is, once it is there, life no longer proceeds "according to schedule."

Ionesco's play seems almost to pick up where *Otranto* leaves off. It is as if the giant intruder has inexplicably returned, once more to plague the now middle-aged, never very happily married couple that was once young Theodore and Isabella. Their unwelcome guest is, like Alphonso's ghost, absurd and inexplicable. Amédée and Madeleine are unable to reach any consensus as to whose body it is and how it got there in the first place. "Did I really kill him?" wonders poor Amédée when Madeleine insists that he did—though her only proof is that she thinks that Amédée once admitted to the crime. The corpse is variously identified as that of Madeleine's lover, a neighbor's baby, a drowned woman.

The response of most critical commentary to all of this confusion on the literal level has been to suggest that the massive body represents a judgment of some sort on Amédée and Madeleine. Leonard Pronko contends that the dead body is a figuration of the couple's dead love.[7] Mary Ann Witt concludes that it "acts as both judge and jailer for them" (1972, 315). Linda Davis Kyle suggests that the corpse "could represent Amedee's dead creative energy—both as an artist and a lover" (1976, 284).

However, as is so often the case in the Gothic, goodness—or badness—has nothing to do with it. David Bradby, in opposition to most readers, insists that this corpse is an insistent "concrete presence" and that "any attempts to rationalize it as a symbol of something else" are bound to be frustrated. Thus this vast encroaching body is not a representation of "the death of their marriage or their ideals or the pressure of passing time" (1984, 64). It is, like Otranto's giant ghost, simply there, a Gothic invader. James Knowlson, even bolder than Bradby, proclaims *Amédée*'s affinity to the Gothic:

> *Amédée*, together with *Rhinocéros*, draws some of its inspiration from those deep inner fears of man that lie at the root of the Gothic romance, tales of mystery and imagination, . . . the continued growth of a long since dead body and the guilt felt at its presence and preservation; the transformation of man into beast by changes in his appearance and behavior. All of these elements recall numerous examples of the genre, in particular tales by Poe, Stevenson and Wells. (1972, 178)

Although we are never sure as to how the play's diegetic zone has been invaded, it is quite clear that the mimetic zone is going to be taken over as a result of the ungovernable growth of the dead one's remains. "He's got geometrical progression . . . the incurable disease of the dead," explains Amédée (178), not perceiving that his peculiar house guest *is* a disease, a parasite which is eating up every particle of space.

Once again, as in the tales of Gothic invasion, allusions to infestation and disease insinuate themselves into the text. Madeleine oscillates from fever to chills, while Amédée feels "so tired" and complains of indigestion and bloating.[8] Counterpointing this talk of human unwellness are constant references to the mushrooms ("poisonous, of course"), saprophytic plant life, evocative of fungoid malignancy and grave mold, spawning itself everywhere, converting homespace into an alien landscape. We should not be surprised that to Madeleine's anguished "[w]hat have I ever done to deserve this . . . to be persecuted like this?"—no answer can be made, any more than could be made to Beatrice Cenci or Mina Harker.

Predictably, as in the Gothic, boundaries begin to give way, signalled by the smash of a pane of glass, the Gothic's alarm signal of invasion. The bedroom door collapses under the pressure of the dead thing's feet, and then the feet protrude themselves into the couple's living room. "It's *his* world," wails Madeleine, "not *ours*" (203), and her words uncannily echo the hysterical outburst of James's governess. In utter desperation and not without some misapprehensions, the two decide that they must somehow get rid of this "skeleton in our cupboard." But the creature, which has been "branching out," resists their efforts to uproot it. As sinuous as a Virginia creeper and "heavier than an oak," the vegetable-man almost brings down the set as Amédée and Madeleine drag him across the stage and attempt to shove him out the window, back into diegetic space.[9]

The concluding scene of the play, which transpires in the outside world, outside the walls of the shabby little flat, thus presents what had formerly been diegetic space. Here a curious thing happens: Amédée is lifted out of the playing area by the dead creature (which now functions as a sort of balloon) and is wafted off by it to some unknown destination. While most commentators perceive this event as an image of transcendence, George Wellworth maintains that "the burlesque and irony should not mask from us the essential despair of the play's conclusion. . . . [W]hat we are really witnessing is the extinction of a typical human being who has never really lived" (1982, 43). Actually it seems sounder to argue that Ionesco's ending is, in the classic Gothic tradition, inconclusive. The bits and pieces of Amédée that rain down—his shoes and cigarettes—remind us of Melmoth's handkerchief caught on a crag—oddly homely relics of a being who has jumped into, or been dragged off to, some other realm.

Sam Shepard's *Buried Child* (1979), despite its veneer of corn-pone Americana, resembles Ionesco's absurdist piece to a remarkable degree. It too harbors a cadaver whose origins, placement, and ultimate implications remain frighteningly mysterious. Though diminutive (unlike *Amédée*'s overgrown corpse), this body likewise effects a transformation of home-space into Gothic space, a conversion indicated, as in *Amédée,* by the germination of fantastical, impossible vegetation.

*Buried Child* also lures us into the same sort of detective mind-set that *Amédée* invites. Since, as in the Gothic fantasy, we are provided with only an "imperfect account," the same sorts of contradictions and confusion persist on the literal level: Is the corn there or not? Was there ever a real baby? Was this baby murdered? If the baby was real, was it the product of incest? And so on. These riddles in turn engender the same sort of symbol-hunting activity that Ionesco's play (and, incidentally, Pinter's *The Homecoming*) elicits. Hence, for Doris Auerbach, the buried baby is "the decaying corpse of the American dream" (1982, 54). Ron Mottram holds that the buried child "signifies a set of familial attitudes and relationships much more than it does an individual or a particular event from the past" (1984, 140). Don Shewey, arguing for an alogical reading, suggests that "Vince and the buried child are the same person, each one a fantasy of what the other might have been under different circumstances" (1985, 104). As Tilden puts it, "Everybody ha[s] a different answer" (Shepard [1979] 1981, 104).

However, once we apply the Gothic paradigm of invasion and defilement to *Buried Child,* these questions (and the answers they generate) become largely irrelevant. The tiny body is simply the matrix of—not the reason for—defilement. It is a kind of "fault" in the geological rather than in the moral sense, a crack in the otherwise seamless surface of things, from which shock waves radiate outward. To argue, as do Vivian Patraka and Mark Siegel, that "the land itself refuses to conceal the crime" (1985, 41) is to assume that a "crime" has been committed, an assumption which in turn rests upon the naive belief that Shepard's characters are providing reliable testimony.

No, the condition of the world of *Buried Child* is not one of guilt or punishment; it is rather the stricken, pre-ethical world of defilement. The little bundle planted "out back" is the viral cell of contagion. To speak of contagion in the face of what seems incontrovertible evidence to the contrary—the imagery of fecundity that permeates the play—may seem a willful misreading, though not all commentators draw sanguine conclusions from such imagery. Gerald Weales, for example, though he articulates the consensus opinion that the contagion of *Buried Child* resolves itself into cure, does go on to express some discomfort with this view:

> Conventionally, in the theatre a kind of purification takes place when the secret is uncovered, and life is presumed to go on in a different, healthier way. When Tilden enters carrying the corpse of the buried child, it could be the sign of a new beginning. After all, he has brought in corn, then carrots, although nothing grows on the property, and at the end, Halie's offstage voice proclaims a miracle, the crops bursting from the ground. . . . [Yet] even if we do not remember Dodge's earlier words ("Now you think everything's gonna be different. Just 'cause the sun comes out"), our last image is of Dodge, dead on the floor, and Vince, stretched out on the couch, staring at the ceiling, his body having assumed the posture of his dead grandfather. (1981, 43–44)

Actually, there is an antecedent, albeit minor, tradition in Gothic literature which associates overabundance, lush fertility with imminent sterility and illness (as in Christina Rossetti's "Goblin Market" or in Keats's "La Belle Dame Sans Merci"). Herbert Blau, in an essay provocatively entitled "The American Dream in American Gothic: The Plays of Sam Shepard and Adrienne Kennedy," follows this vein of thought, noting that the imagery of abundance in Shepard's plays signifies "a moldy superfluidity, . . . an economy of abundance grown maggoty, glutted with its own excess—a sort of overgrowth of nature gone to seed" (1984, 526). In any event, with such fertilizer, the salutariness of Shepard's crop is more than a little suspect. This tiny body, so fragile yet so potent, is more akin to compacted nuclear waste, contaminated and contaminating material for which there really is no adequate receptacle, no safe means of disposal.

From this shriveled, minuscule body, the contamination spreads outward. As in the Gothic tale, the presence of defilement is signalled by the language of pathology—the very first "word" of *Buried Child* is a cough. Though the imagery of illness is concentrated mainly on Dodge, all of the creatures of the play are maimed in some way—even Shelly is reduced to sipping broth. And, as in the Gothic, the last "word" is silence and a death.

It might be objected at this point that while *Buried Child* exhibits the dynamics of Gothic invasion, its invasive entity differs strikingly from the huge, monolithic figures commonly featured in Gothic literature. To be sure, the thing—"bones wrapped in muddy cloth"—is grisly enough, yet the figure of the child is simultaneously invested with a pattern of imagery which insistently maintains that the disgusting bundle was once a sweet, fragile babe.

Here again, however, there are precedents in Gothic narrative. We may observe how the Gothic transforms babyhood in this brief excerpt from *Melmoth:*

> Around the throat of the miserable infant, born amid agony and nursed in a dungeon, there was a black mark. . . . By some it was deemed as the sign impressed by the evil one at its birth—by others as the fearful effect of maternal despair. (Maturin [1820] 1961, 403)

Here is another dungeon baby from *The Monk:*

> [T]he want of proper attendance, my ignorance how to nurse it, the bitter cold of the dungeon, and the unwholesome air which inflated its lungs, terminated my sweet babe's short and painful existence. . . . It soon became a mass of putridity, and to every eye was a loathsome and disgusting object, to every eye but a mother's. . . . Hour after hour have I passed upon my sorry couch, contemplating what had once been my child. I endeavored to retrace its features through the livid corruption with which they were overspread. (Lewis, [1796] 1952, 393)

Thus the sweet newborn is simultaneously an object of horror and an acutely vulnerable, innocent victim. This bizarre combination of gruesomeness and pathos epitomizes Shepard's buried baby. The creature, though dehumanized into a disgusting "thing," nonetheless emerges as touchingly lovely and vulnerable. Thus we can accept Dodge's testimony at its face value—or, we can hear beneath his horrified account the equally appalling confessional subtext which narrates an infanticide:

*Dodge*:   It lived, see. It lived. It wanted to grow up in this family. It wanted to be just like us. It wanted to be a part of us. It wanted to pretend that I was its father. . . . We couldn't let a thing like that continue. We couldn't allow that to grow up right in the middle of our lives. It made everything we'd accomplished look like it was nothin'. Everything was cancelled out by this one mistake. This one weakness.

*Shelly*:   So you killed him?

*Dodge*:   I killed it. I drowned it. Just like the runt of a litter. Just drowned it. (124)

Perhaps terror had made *him* cruel. Certainly this *enfant terrible* is as simultaneously piteous and terrifying as other ghostly waifs of Gothic fantasy—for example, the dream child who terrorizes Lockwood in *Wuthering Heights*. In other respects too, Shepard's play belongs with other theatricalizations of the Gothic invasion tale. The terror that has been hovering on the fringe of the clearing at last comes home to roost. By the end of the play, Vince's earlier distinctions between indoor home-space and that "taboo territory," the "verboten" diegetic realm where one "disintegrate[s]" or becomes "mixed up" (like the Pinterian *locus horridas*), have been erased.

Although boundary-crossings in the Gothic are commonly constituted as invasions, that is, penetrations into marked-off space, occasionally the Gothic effects a species of colonization of this space by way of a movement that resembles more an ingestion rather than an invasion. This movement is characterized by elements being pulled in or suctioned from one realm into another. An overt narrative instance of this engulfing process is furnished by Poe's "Descent into the Maelström." Frederick S. Franks points out that the whirlpool "resembles a macabre mouth and throat of the invisible Gothic anatomy of a giant sea creature whose size rivals the colossal body of Alfonso the Great within the walls of Walpole's *The Castle of Otranto*" (1976, 89).

In such "ingestion" stories, takeover is imaged not in the language of pathology, but rather in terms of gastronomy and nourishment. Transformation receives less emphasis than envelopment and absorption. Thus the "maelstrom" narrator refers to the "embrace of the whirlpool" and notes with wonder the fantastical omnivorousness of the creature's appetite, an appetite which can accommodate whales, bears, ships, fir trees, and furniture. At the conclusion of its meal, the monster regurgitates the flotsam and jetsam, "chafed and roughed" or "disfigured," that it did not completely absorb. Thus, while the maelstrom is a fine example of the Gothic's hostile natural environment, it also offers a constructive illustration of the Gothic's suctioning movement.

As we have already determined, the invasive movement in the NeoGothic drama generally consists of an encroachment by the diegetic realm into mimetic space. The ingestion movement, however, appears as well. As Bert States makes clear, this movement entails an appropriation of off-stage space, both theatrical and dramatic, by the mimetic zone. In other words, the mimetic zone siphons material from the diegetic world of the play as well as from the real world, what States aptly designates "the driveway outside":

> Theater ingests the world of objects and signs only to bring images to life. . . . [A]ll that is on stage is art; but what enters the theater originates, so to speak, in the driveway outside. That is, among the various appetites of theater we find the need for a certain roughage of hard-core reality that continually nourishes the illusionary system. . . . One might describe the theater as an infinitely tolerant institution that can incorporate almost anything into its diet.

Obviously, this ingestion to which he refers occurs to at least some extent in virtually all forms of theatrical activity. The phenomenon is so commonplace, so much an accepted fact about the nature of theatrical production, that it scarcely arouses the same sort of alarm as does Poe's "infinitely tolerant" maw. The NeoGothic drama does not challenge this arrangement; however, it makes the centripetal force of the stage so evident that it appears to be sucking into itself the entire contents of that "driveway outside."

An interesting case in point is Steven Berkoff's adaptation of Poe's *The Fall of the House of Usher* (1974), wherein we find some particularly quirky stage directions regarding props and costumes:

> All props should be priceless and precious on stage. Irreplaceable [*sic*] and thus add a degree of tension by their vibrant delicacy and brittleness. The cheap will only coarsen, all costumes must be hand made and costly. (86)

These directions, which appear to be merely whimsical, if not downright pretentious, actually have astonishing ramifications. Berkoff's stage is not to be a kingdom of rhinestone diamonds: he wants real ones—from out there. The urge to hyper-realize becomes even more acutely evident in his subsequent injunction that the Usher-actor and the Madeleine-actress "should preferably be lovers, or about to be at some time during the rehearsals or at least tasted the pleasure of each other's bodies" (112). The implications here are extraordinary from a phenomenological standpoint: the beast must be fed whatever it needs to survive. The mimetic zone appears here as a parasitic entity no longer content with the mere scraps of reality usually flung to it. These stage directions imply that the stage world be permitted to consume choice bits of the real world, delicacies which that world has traditionally been denied. Berkoff's stipulations do not contradict States's observations; they simply exploit their more sinister implications. This *Usher* proposes the outrageous possibility that a play's appetite may become insatiable, even ghoulishly gourmet.[10]

Berkoff's play suggests that the devouring maw may just as easily be an art-object and that the eroded barrier may be the tenuous, fragile line that divides art from life out there in the driveway. We can see, therefore, that Berkoff is invoking the same Gothic aesthetic as that pursued by Wilde's *The Picture of*

*Dorian Gray*. Whether selectively or indiscriminately (like the maelstrom), the Dorian painting gobbles up the stuff of real life which Dorian willingly—or helplessly—provides it. Jan Gordon regards *Dorian* as a "logical predecessor" of such twentieth-century forms as living theatre, forms in which "the barriers separating life and art approach extinction" (1970, 83). In Berkoff's case, however, it is less a matter of the art content spilling out into offstage space as it is a monstrous ingestion of offstage artifacts by the mimetic zone.

This engulfment of stuff from the driveway is even more trenchant in Ionesco's *The New Tenant,* a play which might aptly be described as a hyperbolic rendition of the nightmare of moving-day. Gradually the stage is literally clogged with furniture and domestic accoutrements which are hauled in from offstage space. Performance of the play requires a stage with especially capacious wing-space, for the gentleman lodger keeps requisitioning effects and possessions which must be wrested out of a literal backstage space that becomes more and more identifiable with diegetic space. In fact, by the conclusion, onstage space has been converted into backstage space; everything that had formerly been wedged into wing-space is now crammed into the mimetic area. Even Aston's mess would look tidy by comparison. *The New Tenant*'s prop list is one likely to demoralize even the most imperturbable of stage managers. The striking of this set night after night is certainly a daunting prospect: the play concludes with a stage so crowded with objects that the "moving men" appear to be trapped on stage by the massive clutter:

> The two furniture movers, each still keeping to his own side, make their way, blindly and tentatively, to the back of the stage, towards invisible and problematical exits, Heaven knows where; for the door is stopped up and through the open folding doors you can still see the violently colored wood that blocks the way. ([1955] 1958, 2:266)

David Bradby perceives *The New Tenant* as a study of invasion: Le Monsieur is "followed by a stack of furniture that grows and grows to the point where he is first walled in and then literally buried beneath the mass of invading objects" (1984, 78). However, the operative dynamics of the play can more accurately be described as suctorial: the view we are offered is one from within the maelstrom. *The New Tenant* offers an oneiric vision of a vast diegetic realm being stripped of its contents, being sucked into the vortex of The New Tenant's room—the whole driveway is in imminent danger of being devoured by this insatiable stage:

> *Gentleman*: What is it that's left?
> *1st Furniture Mover*: Wardrobes. . . . And that's not all. There's more to come.
> *2nd Furniture Mover*: The staircase is jammed from top to bottom. Nobody can go up or down.
> *Gentleman*: The yard is cram-full too. So is the street.
> *1st Furniture Mover*: The traffic's come to a standstill in the town. Full of furniture.

..............................................................................................................................

*1st Furniture Mover*: Perhaps the tube's still running.
*2nd Furniture Mover*: No, it isn't.
*Gentleman*: No, all the underground lines are blocked.
*2nd Furniture Mover*: [to the Gentleman] Some furniture! It's cluttering up the whole country.
*Gentleman*: The Thames has stopped flowing too. Dammed up. No more water. (264)

Thus we are invited to imagine a cosmos in which all moorings have been snapped and in which every object joins the inconceivably long stream of things, all of which are being dragged inexorably toward the lodger's room. Never has the human propensity for feathering one's nest been parodied so thoroughly: the whole world is not enough.

Rather than invoking the language of defilement or even of ingestion, *The New Tenant* reverts to the language of domesticity, for it is a play about setting up housekeeping, a play punctuated by the running refrain, "Are you comfortable?" Paradoxically, the wholesale ingestion of the material world transforms the room into a claustrophobic box. The apartment comes to resemble nothing so much as a Pharaoh's tomb, stuffed to capacity with human artifacts. The play offers a kind of gloss on Poe's "Premature Burial," whose narrator, with his "charnel apprehensions," holes up inside his house and fits out his mausoleum with all the comforts of home.

To recapitulate then, we have discovered that the NeoGothic drama does formulate its own peculiar solutions to the problem of representing Gothic boundary transgression. In *The Hothouse, Amédée*, and *Buried Child*, we witness the transformation of mimetic space by some invasive element from the diegetic zone. On the other hand, Berkoff's *Usher*, and, more forcibly, *The New Tenant* represent engulfments of diegetic territory by the mimetic zone. What we are not provided, and for obvious, logical reasons, is a view from inside the diegetic zone. (By definition, once a diegetic zone is represented mimetically on stage, it is no longer diegetic but mimetic, even in the case of a play like Michael Frayn's *Noises Off!*, which purports to represent literal backstage space.)

The representation of an invasion of the diegetic zone by the mimetic can be carried out, oddly enough, only in nondramatic literature. This strange state of affairs is amusingly set forth in a short story penned in 1882 by Octave Mirbeau. Jonas Barish's encapsulation of the piece is worth quoting at some length:

Mirbeau recounts an imaginary interview with the retired matinee idol Frédérick Febvre. . . . Febvre confesses gloomily that he has fallen victim to a strange visitation. Everything in his life—all tangible and visible phenomena, his books, his furniture, his newly purchased clock, the sky itself—has turned into stage decor. "I live in a horrible nightmare," he laments. At this moment a servant appears to set lunch before Febvre, but the roast chicken that steams and sputters savorously as it is being carried in turns into a papier mâché prop as soon as Febvre tries to cut it, and the knife itself scratches spiritlessly against it, a stick of painted cardboard. . . . Meanwhile—in despair, the wretched actor drops a tear, but the tear, instead of drying up or wetting his cheek, condenses into a solid little ball which drops to the floor with a sharp click. At length Febvre disappears, "behind an illusionistic door-curtain," and the visitor listens for some time to the tears that rattle onto the floor like dried peas in the adjoining room.[11]

As Barish remarks of the story, everything in the offstage world "derealizes itself into stage trumpery, into canvas, tinsel and paste" (1981, 341). Mirbeau's vignette recalls Wilde's send-up in *Dorian Gray* of the retired melodramatic actress Mrs. Vane, so infected by the stage that real life to her seems like "a bad rehearsal" ([1891] 1949, 75) and whose every speech is played to "an imaginary gallery" (81). However, even as these and other fictions portray the incursion of stage life into real life, one might note that the invasive force is theatricality as a mode in itself—not the mimetic world of any given play.

The other category of offstage space which now requires our attention is that inhabited by the spectator. Here also, as will become increasingly apparent, boundary transgression is a common feature of the NeoGothic drama. In some instances the boundary violation is obvious and physical—actors and/or nonhuman elements infiltrate space that is normally reserved for audience use. In other cases, the transgression is subtler and consists of some violation of a theatrical convention, some form of linguistic pressure that is exerted on the offstage audience and that frequently causes that audience to experience "frame confusion," a phenomenon about which more will be said later.

It should be noted at the outset that the physical appropriation of audience space by the onstage world is not confined to the NeoGothic drama. Experimentation with encroachment upon audience space has been for the past twenty-five years a marked attribute of theatrical staging and is one significant manifestation of "the deliberate manipulation of distance," which, according to Daphna Ben Chaim, "is one of the distinctive features of twentieth-century theatre" (1984, 78). What should be pointed out, however, is that in the NeoGothic drama this takeover of the stalls is so designed that it is experienced by the audience as a disturbing phenomenon.

For audiences heavily conditioned to the substantial distancing provided by conventional proscenium staging, the mere close proximity of an actor or actress in performance can be a disquieting experience in itself. For such audiences, physical distancing and psychical distancing are inversely proportional—that is, as physical distance increases, the audience experiences greater empathy for the character while at the same time it experiences itself as emotionally protected. The audience under such conditions is involved but safely distanced. Once this distance is diminished, the audience begins to feel less secure.[12] As Kenneth Tynan puts it, "Nothing so quickly dispels one's sense of reality as a bedaubed and bedizened actor standing four feet from one's face and declaiming

over one's head."[13] Barish, musing over this confrontation in the theatre between live actor and live spectator, takes this notion a step further:

> [Live theatre] requires the onlooker to take account of another human being distinct from
> himself, with a prickly otherness that can never be entirely soothing, as the image on the screen
> can be soothing. . . . [A]udiences sense this underlying self-assertion on the part of the player
> and though exhilarated by it, find it alarming. They prefer the shadow-play of the screen, from
> which live human presence has been deleted, so that what remains is only a ghostly simulacrum
> of reality, a dance of wraiths . . . onto which they can fasten such feelings as will soothe and
> comfort them. (1981, 399)

As Ben Chaim concludes, we are "more sheltered in the 'dark room'" of the
movie theater (1984, 59).

The resultant decrease in distance between performer and spectator brought
about through nonproscenium staging intensifies this disquietude to which
Tynan, Barish, and Ben Chaim allude. As if in agreement, Gillian Farish,
describing the mid-seventies Young Vic production of *Rosencrantz and Guildenstern Are Dead,* observes that, when the actors playing Ros and Guil left the
stage to sit among the audience, "No matter how charmed the audience [was]
by this departure from tradition, it bec[a]me apprehensive as to what Ros and
Guil might involve it in" (1975, 21).

Such violations of audience space as that described above are relatively
benign. There was, however, during the 1960s and 1970s, in both Britain and
America, a movement to apply the Artaudean aesthetics of the cruel performance so as to implicate the audience as well. Moreover, it is obvious from
descriptions of such performances that Artaud's notion of cruelty was being
interpreted in a very literal way. Fringe historian Naseem Khan reminisces about
the early days of the alternative theatre movement in London: "The threat of
'participatory drama' spread some alarm and consternation among audiences.
Audiences could be (and were) locked up in cages, insulted, embarrassed and
manhandled."[14] The tactics of New York off-off Broadway theater were similar,
as Albert Bermel attests:

> Plays frequently were propagandistic, accusatory; they treated audiences as accessories to the
> political crimes of the times. The actors went down to them in their seats, cajoled or yelled at
> them, even reviled or challenged them. If it was a show dispensing love, they blew them kisses
> or broke bread with them. . . . In tactile theatre, actors made a point of touching their pa-
> trons. . . . The audience, who had not been warned, much less trained, as co-performers, often
> responded uncertainly or with hostility, especially [those] . . . who were used to sitting back
> anonymously in the dark. (1978, 45)

The point of all this jamboree, however, was in most instances political
consciousness-raising, and so most of these "happenings" and other forms of
confrontational theatre are not truly classifiable as NeoGothic drama—this de-

spite the intimidation and encagement of their audiences. Neither audience-baiting nor exhortation is a desideratum of the Gothic mode. Furthermore, it might be pointed out that this assaultive technique soon became routine, institutionalized. One set of conventions was merely exchanged for another. In short order, audiences who attended happenings came prepared for spontaneity. As Stoppard's cynical Player observes, "Audiences know what to expect and that is all they're prepared to believe in" (1967, 84). In any case, those who did not care to become coperformers quickly learned to stay away.

Yet, it remains quite valid to claim that a frequently recurring feature of the NeoGothic drama is some form of physical intrusion by the actor or some other element of mimetic space into the audience zone. The goal is in either case a kind of de-sheltering, the breeding of insecurity, of dis-ease in the inmates of "the house." We have already observed that the mere physical presence of the actor within audience territory, these encounters with a "prickly otherness," can disconcert the audience. A nonhuman entity can likewise effect an invasion of audience space although this phenomenon seldom occurs. Ordinarily, stage props remain affixed to onstage space: the stage rarely ejects its contents into the gallery. The same holds true for the NeoGothic drama—its props rarely penetrate audience space. (One spectacular exception is Howard Brenton's *Fruit,* which concludes with one of the characters "throwing a petrol bomb into the auditorium" (Itzin 1980, 194).)

For practical reasons the NeoGothic drama, when it does physically invade audience territory by means of nonhuman elements, does so in manner which unnerves the audience without actually jeopardizing its physical safety or subjecting it to defilement. Defilement touches neither Gothic audiences nor Gothic readers. Instead the reader or spectator experiences anxiety. In the theatre, the most common method of infiltrating audience space, aside from the intrusion of the actor, is the use of disturbing aural effects. Toby Zinman's description of a production of Shepard's *Fool for Love* indicates how an audience can be put on edge by pure sound:

> Shepard had the walls of the set of *Fool for Love* wired for reverberation and four speakers installed under the seats so that every slam of the door physically involved the audience. . . . [A]cknowledgement of the audience is . . . not politically overt as in Brecht or self-consciously witty as in Beckett, but [is] an assaulting aesthetic that demands our visceral engagement in the performance rather than in the plot. (1986, 425)

Yet even Beckett, Zinman's comments notwithstanding, will "acknowledge" the audience in a fashion that is equally assaultive and not at all "self-consciously witty." Beckett's stipulations about the tonal quality of Winnie's bell during the Royal Court production in 1979 carry a definite assaultive thrust: "I'm after a searing, cutting quality. It [the sound of the bell] should be brief and cut off suddenly, clean cut like a blow or a knife on metal" (Knowlson 1985, 141). Thus the offstage audience shares Winnie's torture. In fact, when the play is staged with high-intensity lighting, the audience must, along with Winnie, endure the glare.

The special ability of sound to "remain" on stage as a vehicle of meaning, even as it simultaneously overleaps the proscenium fence and infiltrates audience space, renders it especially useful to the NeoGothic drama. As we have already observed of Leopold Lewis's *The Bells*, a sound can serve equally well as a signifier and as a method of playing on its audiences' nerves. Of all NeoGothic playwrights, Poliakoff is perhaps the most noise-conscious. His plays reverberate with all manner of grating aural effects that bedevil both his characters and his audiences. Pinter's *The Hothouse* so adroitly manages its sound effects that the audience comes to occupy a position not unlike that of the Gothic victim who alone fully apprehends the ghostly origin of unearthly noises:

> *A long keen is heard, amplified.*
>
> *They look up.*
>
> *A laugh is heard, amplified, dying away.*
>
> *Silence.*
> Lush:     What was that?
> Roote:    I don't know. What was it?
> Gibbs:    I don't know.
> *Pause.*
> Roote:    I heard something, didn't you?
> Lush:     Yes I did.
> Gibbs:    Yes, I heard something.
> *Pause.*
> Roote:    Well, what was it?
> *Pause.*
> Gibbs:    I don't know.
> Lush:     Nor do I. (135–36)

The audience knows what it has heard, of course, even if its more obtuse colleagues on stage do not.

Not all invasions of audience territory are, however, physical. A less overt, but equally effective, ploy is the exertion of some form of linguistic pressure on the spectators, a pressure that emanates from onstage space but which does not manifest itself in the baiting and intimidation we have already noted. Instead, this pressure takes the form of some peculiar violation of a sacrosanct theatrical convention. Thus the audience experiences dis-ease not through an assault on its senses or through confrontation with a live actor, but through the stage's transgression of nonspatial boundaries, transgressions which either encourages the audience to make framing errors or else causes the audience to become confused as to what constitutes the parameters of the play itself.

Those NeoGothic dramas which utilize this strategy do not, as in the case of improvised theater, or "happenings," exchange one set of theatrical conventions for another. They do not flout standard theatrical conventions. Boundaries *are* maintained in order, as Todorov remarks of fantasy literature in general, "to furnish the pretext for incessant transgressions" ([1970] 1975, 116).

The offstage audience is particularly susceptible to this species of invasion for reasons that have to do with the phenomenological nature of theatre. The theatre, because it is experienced by the audience in space and time as a real event, is capable, despite its ontological status as prearranged make-believe, of evoking a more intense visceral response than that elicited by a nondramatic, unperformed text. Elizabeth Burns verifies this realness of the stage: "Everything that happens on the stage can be called real, because it can be seen and heard to happen. It is perceived by the senses and is therefore as real as anything that happens outside the theater" (1972, 15). Bert States puts the case more colorfully: "Put bluntly, in theater there is always a possibility that an act of sexual congress between two so-called signs will produce a real pregnancy" (1985, 20).

A second factor is that a theatrical performance is such a convention-bound, convention-ridden event. Keir Elam explains:

> This firm cognitive division [between what does and does not belong to the play] is usually reinforced by symbolic spatial or temporal boundary markers or "brackets"—the stage, the dimming of the lights . . . [etc.] which allow a more or less precise definition of what is included and what is excluded from the frame in space and time. (1980, 88–89)

However, these markers can be made problematic or indistinct; such, precisely, is the forte of the NeoGothic drama. It does not demolish the convention; it simply puts it at risk. The audience can be made to feel, even if very fleetingly, insecure, either because it fears to commit a frame error or because it has been lured into committing just such an error. Audience distress arises from the "incessant transgression" yet concurrent adherence to standard theatrical conventions.

Such violations may assume a variety of forms but are most easily apprehended through the disturbance of four cardinal conventions of the stage event: (1) intermission "belongs" to the audience; (2) the play is make-believe, not real; (3) the audience may leave at any time it so desires; (4) the audience will be provided a reliable "cue" that the performance is over.

Handke's *Kaspar* (1967) provides an interesting example of the concomitant breakage and upholding of the theatrical convention that intermission is audience time. Normally an audience is relieved of its "audiencing" duties during this interval. Handke both provides and withholds the intermission from his audience. In typical fashion as the first act concludes, the house lights are turned on and "the auditorium doors are opened" (112). The audience members are presumably free to refresh themselves, purchase drinks, chat, stretch their legs, etc. However, during *Kaspar*'s interval, its audience is subjected to an "intermission text" which consists of "tapes of the Prompter's speeches, sheer noise, actual taped speeches by party leaders" (112). The text is irritating because it consists of "mangled sentences" that either make no sense or become increasingly menacing and interspersed with images of physical violence. Accompanying this verbal text is "sheer noise," an almost unendurable barrage of "rattling, gongs, factory sirens" (116). Thus the audience is subjected to the same sort of disturbing aural phenomena it has had to endure throughout the first act. This verbal and nonverbal text that persists through the interlude is an encroachment upon the audience's space and its time. The audience is torn between attending or disattending to this apparently out-of-frame activity. Thus the audience has been granted and yet denied its well-earned rest; the play has been halted and yet continued.

In *Rosencrantz and Guildenstern* Stoppard momentarily alarms the audience by simultaneously contravening and confirming two conventions—that the play is unreal and that the audience may leave at any time. Apropos of nothing, Rosencrantz suddenly "leaps up and bellows at the audience, 'Fire!'" (60). The audience is jolted by the sheer volume and by the unexpectedness of the sound, especially since it breaks what had been a fairly lengthy silence. The audience is also taken aback by the semantic content of this shout. Its immediate response, before it has had time to invoke convention #2 (a *character* is shouting "Fire!" as part of his performance; there is *no real fire*), is to experience alarm. Indeed, through a few consciousnesses might dart a peripheral remembrance that theatre fires were once all too real and frequent events. (The lowered asbestos curtain in British theatres is a memento mori of such tragedies.) What promotes this consternation is the fact that Rosencrantz appears to be breaking character, for he does seem to be addressing his warning to the real, offstage audience. Nonetheless, the audience, well schooled in convention #2, remains more or less calmly seated. Then, almost immediately, Guildenstern performs the instinctual response that the audience has just repressed. He jumps up, shouting, "Where?"

At this point the convention snaps securely back into place. Rosencrantz is in character after all: he explains to Guildenstern his reason for shouting in the first place—"I'm demonstrating the misuse of free speech. To prove that it exists." The audience is once more relaxed and passive, waiting to see what will happen next, whereupon Rosencrantz appears once more to break character: "He regards the audience, that is, the direction, with contempt—and other directions, then front again." He seems to register what has in fact transpired. The audience has not stampeded for the exit doors; it is still there, watching him, waiting to see what *he* is going to do next: "Not a move," he comments acidly. "They should all burn to death in their shoes." Again the audience is disarmed, but since there is no question this time of there being any real danger present, the tension is relieved with laughter. Yet here too, the convention has been sustained. Rosencrantz has not broken character after all, for he regards "other directions" as well as the location of the audience; moreover, "they" is an ambiguous pronoun referent which could just as easily refer to other characters who happen to be offstage. ("They" in this play in fact frequently designates Hamlet, Claudius, and their retinue.) Despite their amused chuckles, the audience has been made aware that their framing error could have been fraught with dire consequences.

This same episode likewise defies and obeys convention #3—the audience may leave the theatre at any time. Rosencrantz's exclamation "Fire!" carries the implied injunction "Flee this place of danger." His text is semiotically reified by the clearly marked, brightly lit "exits" of the theatre, signs which are both indexical and meaningful. They point to the doors through which the audience must pass if it wishes to depart; they assure the audience that all emergencies have been provided for, that in an emergency such as a fire, the audience may exit quickly and safely. What occurs in this peculiar episode of performance-audience interaction is that convention #2 practically cancels out #3. That is to say, any audience member who madly dis-suspended disbelief in the play's reality, deciding to run first and rationalize later, would be placing himself or herself in an extraordinary predicament—he or she would become the butt of laughter. In that mad dash for the exit doors, he or she would be "on," the unwilling cynosure of all eyes. For this one very fleeting moment, the *Rosencrantz and Guildenstern* audience is *not* really free to leave even though those exit doors so plainly beckon. Thus the infringement of convention #3 constitutes not so much an invasion of audience space as it is a gesture of containment, of incarceration even.

The problem of knowing when one may leave, when one ought to leave the theatre, is the crux of convention #4—the audience will be reliably cued that the play is over. As we have already discovered, endings in the Gothic are always in some way problematic. This indeterminacy can be exacerbated by the conditions of theatrical performance. *Marat-Sade* offers a fascinating demonstration of the way in which the leave-taking ceremonies of the stage can be both undercut and insistently retained. As the orchestra launches into the finale music, the induction narrator Coulmier dismisses his audience ("let's close the history book and then / return to 1808 the present day" [99]) and the playwright Sade is congratulated. Meanwhile, the audience of Weiss's play observes these gestures of impending closure, still waiting for its own cues, unsure whether any of these activities have any relevance to them. At this point the play has gained so much momentum that, despite the closure cues, it has become incapable of stopping itself. This state of affairs is a trifle disconcerting to the offstage audience, but it is not unduly alarmed since it understands that, although one play has ended, the "other" is still in progress. From the moment Coulmier steps in to give "the signal to close the curtain," literally the last words of Weiss's play, each director is free to extemporize the play's closure; just because Coulmier signals that the curtain is to close does not mean that it will or that it must do so.

If the director chooses to close the curtain, the audience is still faced with an awkward dilemma. Here is the cue for which it has been waiting, yet the cue is ambiguous. Is the closed curtain an authentic signal that the play is indeed over, or is it simply part of the performance? (The fact that Coulmier has called for its closure suggests the latter interpretation, even though a closed curtain traditionally means "that's all, folks.") The Gothic reluctance to provide closure is thus directly experienced by the *Marat-Sade* audience as a frustrating, bewildering ordeal.

This discomposure of the audience was intensified by the Peter Brook production in 1964. Susan Sontag describes the production's finale:

> The inmates, that is, the "cast" of Sade's play, have gone berserk and assaulted the Coulmiers; but this riot—that is, the play—is broken off by the entry of the stage manager of the Aldwych Theater, in modern skirt, sweater, and gym shoes. She blows a whistle; the actors abruptly stop, turn, and face the audience; but when the audience applauds, the company responds with a slow ominous handclap, drowning out the "free" applause and leaving everyone pretty uncomfortable.[15]

Sidney Parham explains why this denouement so unnerved its audience:

> The discomfort the audience felt was the discomfort of the double-bind. All through Brook's production, the audience's sense of proper response was assaulted; they did not know quite what to make of the play. Then at the end of the play, the audience were sure that applause was the correct response—it always had been—but even that certainty was taken away from them. (1977, 245)

Brook himself describes his even more insidious finale staging:

> At the end of one performance *God Save the Queen* was played, but with this innovation: the tape was looped so that no sooner was the anthem completed than it began again. The interesting thing was that it took two complete rounds before the audience realized they were being fooled. The second time through they thought that it was a terrible mistake and they weren't going to embarrass us by drawing attention to it. When the third time came around they began to move toward the door very painfully, fighting against an umbilical cord that told them to stand still. (Schechner 1966, 229)

The "looped tape" which plays and replays is entirely in keeping with the recycling nature of Gothic endings. Brook needles his audience into going over the same old ground again and again. The interrelatedness of theatrical conventions is evident here also in that convention #3 is placed in jeopardy by convention #4's failure to operate properly. It is only by clinging desperately, "painfully" to convention #2 (the play is not real), that the audience is able to make its eventual departure. Even here, the audience has decided that "the Play"—the theatrical event at least—is still on. (In other words, they have concluded that the national anthem is part of the show, as opposed to being an element outside its parameters.) Thus we arrive back at the point from which we started—*when* is the show over? Terence Hawkes contends that every curtain call, "the ultimate Pirandellian moment which any play reaches," is both part and not part of the action, "the point . . . at which we see the 'edge' of the play before it disappears entirely" (1981, 356).

These few instances, though admittedly fleeting, do indicate that theatrical audiences can be profoundly misled and disoriented by boundary transgressions. As such, these transgressions constitute what David Bradby describes as "attacks on the spectators' sense of linguistic . . . proprieties as well as on their sense of what is important, logical or real" (63). The question remaining is whether this is always a one-way process, whether the mimetic zone can be penetrated by incursions from the audience's sphere.

At first, one is tempted to argue that of course the audience itself, as well as elements of audience space, can indeed intrude themselves into the mimetic zone. In terms of theatrical as opposed to dramatic space, this species of violation has been at various times throughout the history of the theatre a commonplace happening. One has only to recall the boos and hisses of the vociferous crowd that attended the Victorian melodrama, or the theatrical cliché of the rotten tomato pitched on stage by an obstreperous audience, to realize that the mimetic zone as theatrical space can be invaded with relative ease.

One is even tempted to conclude, especially in the light of such plays as *Miss Margarida's Way*, plays which deliberately court audience intervention, that the mimetic zone as dramatic space is equally pregnable. Upon closer inspection, however, we realize that such intrusions have in a sense been scripted and provided for. The coperformance of the audience has already been established within the parameters of the play.

On the other hand, how do we classify interruptive, spontaneous, unrehearsed audience intrusions? Elam suggests that such phenomena represent "out of frame activity," and as such are supposed to be "disattended," although he admits that in practice such disattendance is apt to be difficult for both audience and actors:

It is unlikely today that either a performer or spectator of a dramatic representation would be prepared patiently to discount the invasions of the stage, vocal participation by wits and actual outbreaks of violence known to the Restoration stage (events such as these today characterize other kinds of performance, such as soccer matches and rock concerts, where they are, indeed, more or less disattended). (1980, 81)

Certainly these sorts of out-of-frame activities can, if sufficiently disruptive, halt any given performance of a play. They can provoke a player into an unscripted outburst. But they do not, cannot—and this is the crux of the matter—invade the mimetic world of the play. That world remains pristine, untouched, intact, quite beyond the reach of any fist that attempts to puncture the barrier between the two worlds. No audience can truly effect an invasion of the mimetic zone, though it is itself very much at the mercy of the stage.

At its mercy also, as we have already discovered, are the performers. The Gothic, like the frame narrative, leaves no one out. In the Gothic, we all suffer, to invoke the description of Stoppard's Guildenstern, "a fine persecution." That horribly pristine world which cannot be touched, yet which touches so profoundly, mocks, like Dorian's sinister portrait, its beholder.

What Huet claims as true of theatre in general is true in a special and urgent way of the NeoGothic drama:

[T]he theater gathers into an irremediable fusion everything that everyday life already contains in the way of cruelty and profound perversity. . . . [T]he theater . . . catch[es] hold in . . . a rather mysterious way, of the strangeness of the real. (1982, 106)

The NeoGothic drama, like the Gothic fantasy before it, refuses to let buried things, dead things lie. Always there must be a dredging up, a going over the same old ground, for in the Gothic there is no peace, no rest, only an everlasting same old next time.

I have sought to give this "mystery theater," this "strange new form," of which Katherine Worth speaks, a lineage and a name. In so doing, I have concluded that the form is neither unfamiliar nor new. This appropriation of the stage by the Gothic is a tribute to its resilience and its inexpungability. Refusing to stay confined within the margins of prose narrative, it has taken up residence where we would least expect—front and center stage.

# Notes

**Preface**

1. All three playwrights whom I interviewed—Peter Barnes, Stephen Poliakoff, and David Halliwell—when asked to define the term "Gothic," responded referring in some way to standard
   Gothic apparatus. Poliakoff and Barnes immediately alluded to the Gothic novel as such.
   Barnes and Halliwell expressed impatience with the notion of labelling with regard to their
   work, though Barnes did remark that, if pressed for a label, he would suggest "baroque" rather
   than Gothic. Halliwell explicitly rejected the designation "Gothic" for his work. I believe it is
   fair to conclude that their rejection of the term is attributable to understandable but fundamental
   misconceptions about the nature of the Gothic. (Stephen Poliakoff, personal interview, 22
   August 1985. Peter Barnes, personal interview, 21 August 1985. David Halliwell, personal
   interview, 20 August 1985.)

**Chapter 1**

1. See Day pp. 59–60 on this distinction.

2. Wilt writes, "No, as a social impulse it is not revolution that the Gothic celebrates, not even
   reform, but riot" (1980, 46).

3. For an alternative view, see Napier, p. 90, n. 61. She regards Jephson's Manfred as a "believ-
   able" as opposed to a "cardboard" figure. Jephson has succeeded whereas Walpole has failed.
   Mary Diane Neufeld, in her unpublished dissertation "The Adaptation of the Gothic Novel to
   the English Stage, 1765–1826," finds Jephson's Count "complex" and "interesting."

4. Thorp 1928, 476. This view has been recently qualified by Robert Reno who holds that, while
   contemporary critics inveighed against onstage ghosts (even those of Shakespeare), popular
   audiences loved them. See Robert P. Reno's "James Boadin's *Fountainville Forest*" and
   Matthew G. Lewis's "*The Castle Spectre:* Challenges of the Supernatural Ghost on the Late
   Eighteenth-Century Stage," *Eighteenth-Century Life* 9.1 (1984): 95–106.

5. Day's discussion of the 1937 film *King Kong* throws an interesting sidelight onto this encounter
   of beauty and beast. Day claims that in *Kong* the beast is first enthralled by the maiden and
   subsequently "dwarfed by modern technology" (152). Like Campton's monster, Kong, since
   he cannot be housebroken, must be exterminated. Day regards the film as Gothic, but, at least
   insofar as the beauty-beast conflict is concerned, it obeys the dictates of melodrama, even going
   so far as to invoke the ritualistic, concluding moral tag: "'Twas beauty killed the beast." Of

course, if one regards Anne as a *femme fatale* (thus herself a countercultural force) the melodramatic formula no longer applies.

6. See Stuart Curran's *Shelley's Cenci: Scorpions Ringed with Fire* (1970). The treatment of taboo subject matter—incest in this case—was in itself sufficient to guarantee rejection by the theatrical establishment.

7. The adaptation of Buchner's *Danton's Death* by Howard Brenton (1982) and the adaptation of Wedekind's *Pandora's Box* and *Earth Spirit* by Peter Barnes (which appeared as *Lulu* in 1971) suggests some affinity of Expressionism and the NeoGothic.

8. Deak 1974, 43. Deak maintains that the Grand Guignol was essentially of a conservative bent: "[T]he horrors of the Grand Guignol were well within the accepted norms of society" (43). Nonetheless, the very fact that the physical edifice which housed the Grand Guignol had once been a convent chapel is one of those marvelous quirks of theatrical history that have a resonance all their own.

## Chapter 2

1. For a discussion of the parodic relationship of *Jane Eyre* and *The Turn of the Screw*, see Alice Hall Petry, "Jamesian Parody, *Jane Eyre* and *The Turn of the Screw*," *Modern Language Studies* 13.4 (1983): 61–78.

2. 1987, 9. It is for this reason that Napier would probably not classify *Vathek* as a Gothic novel.

3. As Jerrold Hogle suggests, "[N]ew fabrications try and fill in the blanks in the old ones. Herein lies the engine behind the Gothic penchant for stories-within-stories." See his "The Restless Labyrinth: Cryptonymy in the Gothic novel," *Arizona Quarterly* 36 (1980): 340.

4. As Helene Keyssar observes, *Rosencrantz and Guildenstern* even has its own tennis match of "verbal volleying" with Ros and Guil keeping score in tennis jargon. See her "The Strategy of *Rosencrantz and Guildenstern Are Dead*," *Educational Theatre Journal* 27 (1975): 85–97.

5. Weiss, "Author's Note on the Historical Background to the Play," 109.

6. Peter Brook, introduction, *Marat-Sade*, vi.

7. 33. Emphasis mine.

8. 53. The ellipsis is Pinter's.

## Chapter 3

1. See Gay Clifford's "*Caleb William* and *Frankenstein:* First Person Narrators and 'Things as They Are,'" *Genre* 10 (1977): 601–17. Clifford observes that a "theatrical impulse is present in the novel's opening sentence" (606). I would add that a concern with human theatricality contributes substantially to the novel's overall shaping vision.

2. See Jacqueline Millar page 371 in this context.

3. A few readers *have* noticed the cosmic nature of injustice in *Caleb*. See, for example, Rudolf F. Storch's "Metaphors of Private Guilt and Social Rebellion in Godwin's *Caleb Williams*," *English Literary History* 34 (1967): 188–207 and Eric Rothstein's "Allusion and Analogy in the Romance of *Caleb Williams*," *University of Toronto Quarterly* 37 (1967): 18–30.

4. Edmund Burke, *Letter to a Noble Lord, The Works and Correspondence of the Right Honorable Edmund Burke*, new edition (London, 1852) 5:216. Quoted in Sterrenburg 154.

5. See Sandra Gilbert and Susan Gubar, *The Madwoman in the Attic* (Princeton: Princeton University Press, 1979), especially p. 291 for a feminist perspective on starvation and rebellion in nineteenth-century literature.

6. 74. Barnes chose to outfit his creature in Victorian garb because "Jack the Ripper was a Victorian figure." The underlying inspiration of the Gothic is especially clear in this scene—underneath the placid, polite surface of Victorian society, "monsters roamed." (Peter Barnes, letter to the author, 4 August 1986.)

7. This dual identity of the actor as demonic servant lies behind the characterization of *The Turn of the Screw*'s Quint: small wonder that one "so dreadfully below" should look "like an actor."

8. Weiss, "Author's Note" 105.

9. 19. Bracketed ellipses are Brenton's.

10. This intermeshing of dramatic realities deprives the audience of any stable point of reference. In this fashion, Caute achieves the ambiguity and troubling irresolution so central to the Gothic.

## Chapter 4

1. See Scarry 1985, 145 on mutilation of the domestic.

2. This new awareness of the stage as a Gothic place surfaces in Anne Rice's *Interview with the Vampire* (1976). In this novel a "performance" is given at the Théâtre des Vampires, the acting troupe for which is a community of vampires. Thus the actor's "languid, white hand . . . was not painted white. It was a vampire hand" (220). The play, which the human audience accepts as titillating make-believe, consists of the onstage murder of a real, human victim, conscripted from the Paris slums. Thus Rice's novel exploits the stage as a Gothic place: the victim, blinded by the spotlight, is "lost" on the stage (demoralized, then destroyed) while the offstage audience ignores her pleas for help since it is convinced that what it is witnessing is merely a "masterful illusion" (221).

3. Poliakoff, *Strawberry Fields* 8. Bracketed ellipses are Poliakoff's.

4. In the 1979 Royal Court revival, it was found necessary to install "a fan under the mound to keep Billie Whitelaw (the actress portraying Winnie) cool under the fierce intensity of the lighting" provided "primarily by aircraft lights." See James Knowlson, ed. *Happy Days: Samuel Beckett's Production Notebook*, 1985, 21–22.

5. Stoker [1897] 1965, 42. "Who's responsible," asks Davies, "for giving me bad dreams?" (66). *Wuthering Heights*'s Lockwood regrets his "doze in such a den" (Brontë, [1874] 1972, 41).

6. See Scarry 1985, 304–5: "Sometimes in a technological and automated society, the mimesis of sentient awareness may become so elaborate that the object may become frightening. . . . Civilization restructures the naturally existing external environment to be laden with humane awareness. . . ." In the Gothic world, however, this awareness is experienced as actual and inhuman.

7. Some productions of the play have sought to make plain the identity of the bathhouse as a torture chamber. A German production at Weisbaden, for example, in outfitting the room with pipes and ropes, made more overt the parallel to the Nazi death-camps. See E. M. Fleissner's "Revolution in Theatre: *Danton's Death* and *Marat-Sade*," *The Massachusetts Review* 7 (1966). The set of the Peter Brook production was described by one reviewer as "booby-trapped

with sunken pits." See Alan Brien's review of *Marat-Sade,* by Peter Weiss, *Sunday Telegraph* 23 August 1964.

8. *Marat-Sade* 33. Bathtubs and shower stalls are environments that enforce vulnerability. The slippery surface, the blurred vision, the body's nakedness together create a sense of defenselessness. Hence the thriller often selects the shower as the site for murder. The famous shower scene of Hitchcock's *Psycho* manages to combine the purgative and the sinister.

9. In his *Discipline and Punish,* Michel Foucault records the curious fact that real public executions—one could say the mirror image of staged executions—"did not, in fact, frighten the people" (63). The makeover of the execution into an intensely theatrical spectacle (via ritual, costuming, etc.) may have moved it out of the realm of common life and into the magical sphere of stage life. Hence the spectacle of the condemned elicited neither terror nor pity—his death had passed into the category of the unreal.

## Chapter 5

1. See Stoker ([1847] 1965, 294) and P. B. Shelley ([1886] 1970, 35).

2. Twentieth-century horror movies consistently image this ineffectuality of walls as a barrier against the onslaught of the monstrous—a running motif is the trampled-down door, the smashed window, the fist through the wall.

3. Craft 1984, 117. The smashing of a pane of window glass is often in the Gothic a signal of the eruption of the demonic, as for example in *Wuthering Heights* and *Dracula*. The governess apprehends Quint's "white face of damnation" pressed against the windowpane in just these terms.

4. The governess refers to herself as a "screen," adding that she will "fence about" the children so as to "absolutely save" them (James [1898] 1966, 26–28).

5. Stephen King, whose Gothics rigidly conform to prescribed formulas, exploits the runaway boiler in his *The Shining* (1977).

6. According to Ronald Knowles, the play "was originally conceived as a radio play" (1985, 141).

7. Leonard Pronko, *Avant-Garde: The Experimental Theater in France* (Berkeley: University of California Press, 1962), 92. Quoted in Witt, 1972, 315.

8. [1954] 1958, 2: 157. Although Amédée claims that his illness renders him incapable of writing, Ionesco's play itself affirms that "tales narrate trouble." Weiss's *Marat-Sade* seems to suggest that tale-telling causes trouble—that is, that writing makes one sick. Thus Simonne Evrard and Madeleine seem to be inverse images of one another.

9. Ionesco's stage directions indicate that "the whole set trembles as if the body were "dragging the whole house with it" (211–12). This effect seems to underscore the theatricality of this landscape—the flimsiness of stage backdrops and flats is a long-established theatrical cliché.

10. Stoppard's *The Real Inspector Hound* toys with the same possibility. We have already seen how the perimeter characters can be swept into the central vortex of the play. However, it should be noted that the two critics do not belong to diegetic space—they are residents of the mimetic zone from the outset.

11. Octave Mirbeau, *Gens de théâtre* (Paris: n.p., 1924), 110–17. Quoted in Barish (1981, 341).

12. I refer here to the usual distancing provided by the twentieth-century proscenium stage. An *extreme* physical overdistancing (as was common in the cavernous theatres of the Romantic stage) can have the effect of increasing physical distancing.

13. Quoted in "Subversion at Lunchtime," Rosalind Asquith (Craig 1980, 145).

14. "The Public-going Theatre" (Craig 1980, 64).

15. (1969, 171). Quoted in Parham (1977, 245).

# Bibliography

Almansi, Guido. "Harold Pinter's Idiom of Lies." In *Contemporary English Drama,* edited by C. W. E. Bigsby. Stratford-upon-Avon Studies, no. 19. London: E. Arnold, 1981.

Alpaugh, David. "Negative Definition in Samuel Beckett's *Happy Days.*" *Twentieth-Century Literature* 11 (1966): 202–10.

Anderson, Howard. Introduction to *The Monk,* by Matthew Gregory Lewis. New York: Oxford, 1973.

Ansorge, Peter. *Disrupting the Spectacle: Five Years of Experimental and Fringe Theatre in Britain.* London: Pitman, 1975.

Artaud, Antonin. *The Theater and Its Double.* New York: Grove Press, 1958.

Asquith, Rosalind. "Subversion at Lunchtime." In *Dreams and Deconstructions: Alternative Theatre in Britain,* edited by Sandy Craig. Ambergate: Amber Lane Press, 1980.

Athayde, Roberto. *Miss Margarida's Way.* New York: Avon, 1979.

Auerbach, Doris. *Sam Shepard, Arthur Kopit and the Off Broadway Theater.* Boston: Twayne, 1982.

Auerbach, Nina. "Magi and Maidens: The Romance of the Victorian Freud." *Critical Inquiry* 8, no. 2 (1981): 281–300.

Bachelard, Gaston. *The Poetics of Space.* Translated by Maria Jolas. New York: Orion Press, 1964.

Baillie, Joanna. *Orra: A Tragedy.* Vol. 3 of *A Series of Plays in Which It Is Attempted to Delineate the Stronger Passions of the Mind.* London, 1812.

Barish, Jonas. *The Antitheatrical Prejudice.* Berkeley and Los Angeles: University of California Press, 1981.

Barnes, Peter. *Peter Barnes: Collected Plays.* London: Heinemann, 1981.

———. *Red Noses.* London: Faber & Faber, 1985.

———. Letter to author. 4 August 1986.

Baron-Wilson, Mrs. Cornwall. *The Life and Correspondence of M. G. Lewis.* 2 Vols. London, 1839.

Beckett, Samuel. *Happy Days.* New York: Grove Press, 1961.

Beckford, William. *Vathek.* In *Three Gothic Novels,* edited by Peter Fairclough. Harmondsworth, England: Penguin Books, 1968.

Ben Chaim, Daphna. *Distance in the Theatre: The Aesthetics of Audience Response.* Ann Arbor: UMI Research Press, 1984.

Bensky, Lawrence. "Harold Pinter: An Interview with Lawrence Bensky." In *Theatre At Work: Playwrights in the Modern British Theatre,* edited by Charles Marowitz and Simon Trussler. London: Methuen, 1967.

Bentley, Eric. "Melodrama." In *Tragedy: Vision and Form,* edited by Robert W. Corrigan. San Francisco: Chandler, 1965.

Berkoff, Stephen. East, Agamemnon, *and* The Fall of the House of Usher. London: Calder, 1977.

Bermel, Albert. "Off and Off-Off." In *Theatre Byways,* edited by Joseph Aurbach. New Orleans: Polyanthos, 1978.

Blau, Herbert. "The American Dream in American Gothic: The Plays of Sam Shepard and Adrienne Kennedy." *Modern Drama* 27 (1984): 520–39.

Boaden, James. *The Life of Mrs. Jordan.* 2 Vols. London, 1831.

——— . *The Secret Tribunal.* In *The Plays of James Boaden,* edited by Steven Cohan. Eighteenth-Century English Drama, no. 5. New York: Garland, 1980.

Bond, Edward. A-A-America *and* Stone. 1976. London: Eyre Methuen, 1981.

Booth, Michael R. [1969] *Prefaces to English Nineteenth-Century Theatre.* Manchester: Manchester University Press, 1980.

——— , Richard Southern, Frederick and Lisa-Lone Marker, and Robertson Davies. *The Revels History of Drama in English.* 8 Vols. London: Methuen, 1975.

——— . *Victorian Spectacular Theatre 1850–1910.* Boston: Routledge & Kegan Paul, 1981.

Bradby, David. *Modern French Drama 1940–1980.* Cambridge: Cambridge University Press, 1984.

Braunmuller, A. R. "Harold Pinter: The Metamporphosis of Memory." In *Essays on Contemporary British Drama,* edited by Hedwig Bock and Albert Wertheim. Munich: M. Hueber, 1981.

Brenton, Howard. *The Churchill Play: As It Will Be Performed in the Winter of 1984 by the Internees of Churchill Camp Somewhere in England.* London: Methuen, 1974.

——— . *Christie in Love.* In *Plays for a Poor Theatre.* London: Methuen, 1980.

——— . "Writing for Democratic Laughter." *Drama: The Quarterly Theatre Review* 157, no. 3 (1985): 9–11.

Brien, Alan. Review of *Marat-Sade,* by Peter Weiss. *Sunday Telegraph* 23 August 1964.

Brontë, Charlotte. *Jane Eyre.* Edited by Richard J. Dunn. The Norton Critical Edition. New York: W. W. Norton, 1971.

Brontë, Emily. *Wuthering Heights.* Edited by William M. Sale. 2nd ed. The Norton Critical Edition. New York: W. W. Norton, 1972.

Brook, Peter. Introduction to *The Persecution and Assassination of Jean-Paul Marat as Performed by the Inmates of the Asylum of Charenton under the Direction of the Marquis de Sade,* by Peter Weiss. New York: Atheneum, 1981.

Brooks, Peter. "'Godlike Science/Unhallowed Arts': Language, Science and Monstrosity." In *The Endurance of* Frankenstein: *Essays on Mary Shelley's Novel,* edited by George Levine and U. C. Knoepflmacher. Berkley and Los Angeles: University of California Press, 1979.

——— . *The Melodramatic Imagination: Balzac, Henry James, Melodrama and the Mode of Excess.* New Haven: Yale University Press, 1976.

Brown, Charles Brockden. *Wieland, or The Transformation.* Garden City: Anchor-Doubleday, 1973.

Brustein, Robert. *Theatre as Revolution: Notes on the New Radical Style.* New York: Liveright, 1971.

Burke, Edmund. *Letters to a Noble Lord, The Works and Correspondence of the Right Honorable Edmund Burke.* London, 1852.

Burns, Elizabeth. *Theatricality: A Study of Convention in the Theatre and in Social Life.* New York: Harper, 1972.

Butler, Marilyn. "Godwin, Burke and *Caleb Williams.*" *Essays in Criticism* 32, no. 3 (1982): 237–57.

Byczkowska-Page, Ewa. *The Structure of Time and Space in Harold Pinter's Drama 1957–1975.* Wroclaw, Poland: Wydawn. Uniw. Wroclawskiego, 1983.

Calcraft, John William [John William Cole]. *The Bride of Lamermoor.* French's Standard Drama, no. 179. New York: Samuel French, n.d.

Campbell, Ian. "Hogg's *Confessions* and *The Heart of Darkness.*" *Studies in Scottish Literature* 15 (1980): 187–201.

Campton, David. Frankenstein: *A Gothic Thriller in Three Acts.* London: J. Garnet Miller, 1973.

Carpenter, Charles A. "The Absurdity of Dread: Pinter's *The Dumbwaiter." Modern Drama* 16 (1973): 279–85.

Caute, David. *The Demonstration.* London: André Deutsch, 1970.

Clifford, Gay. *"Caleb Williams* and *Frankenstein:* First-Person Narrators and 'Things As They Are.'" *Genre* 10 (1977): 601–617.

Cohan, Steven. Introduction to *The Plays of James Boaden.* Eighteenth-Century English Drama, no. 5. New York: Garland, 1980.

Cohn, Ruby. "Marat/Sade: An Education in Theatre." *Educational Theatre Journal* 19, no. 4 (1967): 478–85.

Coleman, John. *Fifty Years of an Actor's Life.* Vol. 1. N.p.: 1904.

Colman, George the Younger. *The Iron Chest.* In *The Plays of George Colman,* edited by Peter A. Tasch. 2 Vols. Eighteenth-Century English Drama, no. 11. New York: Garland, 1981.

Coult, Tony. *The Plays of Edward Bond.* London: Methuen, 1977.

Craft, Christopher. "'Kiss Me with Those Red Lips': Gender and Inversion in Bram Stoker's *Dracula." Representations* 8 (1984): 107–33.

Curran, Stuart. *Shelley's* Cenci: *Scorpions Ringed with Fire.* Princeton: Princeton University Press, 1970.

Day, William Patrick. *In the Circles of Fear and Desire: A Study of the Gothic Fantasy.* Chicago: University of Chicago Press, 1985.

Deák, Frantisek. "Théâtre du Grand Guignol." *The Drama Review* 18, no. 1 (1974): 34–43.

Deane, Hamilton and John Balderstone. *Dracula.* New York: Samuel French, 1927.

DePorte, Michael. "The Consolations of Fiction: Mystery in *Caleb Williams." Papers on Language and Literature* 20, no. 2 (1984): 154–64.

Dieckman, Suzanne. "Levels of Commitment: An Approach to the Role of Weiss's Marat," *Educational Theatre Journal* 30 (1978): 54–62.

Donohue, Joseph. *Theatre in the Age of Kean.* Totowa: Rowman & Littlefield, 1975.

Dukore, Bernard. *Harold Pinter.* New York: Grove Press, 1982.

––––––. *The Theatre of Peter Barnes.* London: Heinemann, 1981.

Dumas, D. Gilbert. "Things as They Were: The Original Ending of *Caleb Williams." Studies in English Literature* 6 (1966): 575–97.

Eden, Richard. "Stage: 'Margarida' Explores Power." Review of *Miss Margarida's Way* by Roberto Athayde. *Time* 10 Oct. 1977: C16.

Edwards, Gavin and Kelvin Everest. "William Godwin's *Caleb Williams:* Truth and 'Things as They Are.'" In *1789: Reading, Writing, Revolution: Proceedings of the Essex Conference on the Sociology of Literature,* edited by Francis Barker and J. Bernstein. Colchester: University of Essex, 1981.

Egan, Robert. "A Thin Beam of Light: The Purpose of Playing in *Rosencrantz and Guildenstern Are Dead." Theatre Journal* 31 (1979): 59–69.

Elam, Keir. *The Semiotics of Theatre and Drama.* London: Methuen, 1980.

Eliot, George. *Daniel Deronda.* Edited by Barbara Hardy. Harmondsworth, England: Penguin, 1967.

Esslin, Martin. *The Peopled Wound: The Work of Harold Pinter.* New York: Anchor, 1970.

Evans, Bertrand. *The Gothic Drama from Walpole to Shelley.* California Studies in English, no. 18. Berkeley: University of California Publications, 1947.

Farish, Gillian. "Into the Looking-Glass Bowl: An Instant of Grateful Terror." *University of Windsor Review* 10 (1975): 14–29.

Findlater, Richard. *Banned! A Review of Theatrical Censorship in Britain.* London: MacGibbon & Kee, 1976.

Fitz-ball, Edward. [1829]. *The Devil's Elixir*. In *The Hour of One: Six Gothic Melodramas*, edited by Stephen Wischhusen. London: Gordon Fraser, 1975.

Fleissner, E. M. "Revolution As Theater: *Danton's Death* and *Marat-Sade*." *The Massachusetts Review* 7 (1966): 542–56.

Foucault, Michel. *Discipline and Punish*. Translated by Allan Sheridan. New York: Pantheon, 1977.

Franks, Frederick S. "The Aqua-Gothic Voyage of 'A Descent into the Maelström.'" *American Transcendental Quarterly* 29 (1976): 86–92.

Frye, Northrop. *Backgrounds to Victorian Literature*. San Francisco: Chandler, 1967.

"Gambit Discussion: New Gothics, Realists and Phantasists." *Gambit* 8 no. 29 (1976): 5–29.

Gilbert, Sandra and Susan Gubar. *The Madwoman in the Attic*. Princeton: Princeton University Press, 1979.

Gillen, Francis. " 'Nowhere to Go': Society and the Individual in Harold Pinter's *The Hothouse*." *Twentieth-Century Literature* 29, no. 1 (1983): 86–96.

Godwin, William. *Caleb Williams*. Edited by David McCracken. New York: Norton, 1977.

Gordon, Jan. "The Imaginary Portrait: Fin-de-Siècle Icon." *University of Wisconsin Review* 7, no. 1 (1970): 81–104.

———. "Narrative Enclosure as Textual Ruin." *Dickens Studies Annual* 11 (1983): 209–38.

Graham, Kenneth. "The Gothic Unity of Godwin's *Caleb Williams*." *Papers on Language and Literature* 16 (1980): 47–59.

Gray, Simon. Review of *K. D. Dufford Hears K. D. Dufford Ask K. D. Dufford How K. D. Dufford'll Make K. D. Dufford*, by David Halliwell. *New Statesman* 26 Sept. 1969: 440.

Grillo, John. "An Excess of Nightmare." *Gambit* 23 (1973): 18–24.

Halliwell, David. *K. D. Dufford Hears K. D. Dufford Ask K. D. Dufford How K. D. Dufford'll Make K. D. Dufford*. London: Faber, 1970.

Handke, Peter. *Kaspar and Other Plays*. Translated by Michael Roloff. New York: Farrar, 1969.

Harpham, Geoffrey G. *On the Grotesque: Strategies of Contradiction in Art and Literature*. Princeton: Princeton University Press, 1982.

Harwood, Ronald. *The Dresser*. New York: Grove Press, 1981.

Hawkes, Terrence. "Opening Closure." *Modern Drama* 34 (1981): 353–56.

Hayman, Ronald. *Theatre and Anti-Theatre: New Movements since Beckett*. New York: Oxford University Press, 1979.

Hennelly, Mark. *"Melmoth the Wanderer* and Gothic Existentialism." *Studies in English Literature*. 21, no. 4 (1981): 665–79.

Hill, Linda. "Obscurantism and Verbal Resistance in Handke's *Kaspar*." *The Germanic Review* 52 (1977): 304–15.

Hogg, James. *The Private Memoirs and Confessions of a Justified Sinner*. New York: Norton, 1970.

Hogle, Jerrold. "The Restless Labyrinth: Cryptonomy in the Gothic Novel." *Arizona Quarterly* 36 (1980): 330–58.

Holcroft, Thomas. [1802]. *A Tale of Mystery*. In *The Hour of One*. See Fitz-ball.

Huet, Marie-Hélène. *Rehearsing the Revolution: The Staging of Marat's Death 1793–1797*. Translated by Robert Hurley. Berkeley and Los Angeles: University of California Press, Quantum Books, 1982.

Hunter, Jim. *Tom Stoppard's Plays: A Study of His Life and Works*. New York: Grove Press, 1982.

Ionesco, Eugene. *Amédée, The New Tenant, Victims of Duty*. In *Three Plays*. Translated by Donald Watson. London: John Calder, 1958.

Issacharoff, Michael. "Space and Reference in Drama." *Poetics Today* 2, no. 3 (1981): 211–24.

Itzin, Catherine. *Stages in the Revolution: Political Theatre in Britain since 1968*. London: Methuen, 1980.

Jackson, Rosemary. *Fantasy: The Literature of Subversion*. London: Methuen, 1981.

———. "The Silenced Text: Shades of Gothic in Victorian Fiction." *Minnesota Review* n.s. 13 (1979): 98–112.

James, Henry. *The Turn of the Screw*. Edited by Robert Kimbrough. The Norton Critical Edition. New York: W. W. Norton, 1966.

James, Louis. "Was Jerrold's Black-eyed Susan More Popular Than Wordsworth's Lucy?" In *Performance and Politics in Popular Drama,* edited by David Bradby, Louis James and Bernard Sharratt. Cambridge: Cambridge University Press, 1980.

Kalem, T. E. "Ms Himmler." Review of *Miss Margarida's Way,* by Roberto Athayde. *Time* 10 Oct. 1977: 108.

Keech, James M. "The Survival of the Gothic Response." *Studies in the Novel* 6 (1974): 130–44.

Kerensky, Oleg. *The New British Drama*. London: Hamish Hamilton, 1977.

Kernodle, George R. *Invitation to the Theater*. New York: Harcourt, 1967.

Keysar-Franke, Helene. "The Strategy of *Rosencrantz and Guildenstern Are Dead*." *Educational Theater Journal* 27 (1975): 85–97.

Kiely, Robert. *The Romantic Novel in England*. Cambridge: Harvard University Press, 1972.

Kierkegaard, Søren. *Crisis in the Life of an Actress and Other Essays on Drama*. Translated by Stephen Crites. London: Collins, 1967.

King, Stephen. *The Shining*. New York: Signet, 1977.

Kitchin, Laurence. "Compressionism—What Is It?" *Plays and Players* August 1963: 12–13.

Knowles, Ronald. "*The Hothouse* and the Epiphany of Harold Pinter." *Journal of Beckett Studies* 10 (1985): 134–44.

Knowlson, James, ed. Happy Days: *Samuel Beckett's Production Notebook*. New York: Grove Press, 1985.

———. "Ionesco." In *Forces in Modern French Drama,* edited by John Fletcher. New York: Ungar, 1972.

Knowlson, James and John Pilling. *Frescoes of the Skull: The Later Prose and Drama of Samuel Beckett*. London: John Calder, 1979.

Kowsar, Mohammad. "Analytics of Schizophrenia: A Deleuze-Guattarian Consideration of *Danton's Death* and Weiss's *Marat/Sade*." *Modern Drama* 27 (1984): 361–81.

Kramer, Dale. *Charles Robert Maturin*. Boston: Twayne, 1973.

Kyle, Linda Davis. "The Grotesque in *Amédée*." *Modern Drama* 19 (1976): 282–91.

Lavalley, Albert J. "The Stage and Film Children of *Frankenstein*: A Survey." In *The Endurance of Frankenstein. See* Brooks.

LeTellier, Robert Ignatius. *An Intensifying Vision of Evil: The Gothic Novel 1762–1820 as a Self-Contained Literary Cycle*. Salzburg Studies in English Literature, vol. 33, no. 2. Salzburg: Institut für Anglistik und Amerikanistik Universität Salzburg, 1980.

Lewis, Leopold. *The Bells*. In *Hiss the Villain: Six Melodramas,* edited by Michael R. Booth. London: Eyre and Spottswoode, 1964.

Lewis, Matthew Gregory. *The Monk*. New York: Grove Press, 1952.

———. *One O'Clock! Or the Knight and the Wood Demon*. Edited by William Oxberry. Oxberry's English Drama no. 19. London, 1824.

Lewis, Paul. "Mysterious Laughter: Humor and Fear in Gothic Fiction." *Genre* 14 (1981): 309–27.

Liu, Alan. "Toward a Theory of Common Sense: Beckford's *Vathek* and Johnson's *Rasselas*." *Texas Studies in Language and Literature* 26 (1984): 183–217.

Maturin, Charles Robert. *Melmoth the Wanderer*. Lincoln: University of Nebraska Press, Bison Books, 1961.

Meisel, Martin. *Realizations: Narrative, Pictorial, and Theatrical Arts in the Nineteenth Century*. Princeton: Princeton University Press, 1983.

Miller, Jacqueline. "The Imperfect Tale: Articulation, Rhetoric, and Self in *Caleb Williams*." *Criticism* 20 (1978): 366–82.

Miller, Leslie. "Peter Weiss, Marat and Sade: Comments on an Author's Commentary." *Symposium* 25 (1971): 39–58.

Milner, H. M. [1826]. *Frankenstein; or, The Man and the Monster.* In *The Hour of One. See* Fitz-ball.

Morris, David B. "Gothic Sublimity." *New Literary History* 16 (1985): 299–319.

Morse, David. *Romanticism: A Structural Analysis.* Totowa: Barnes & Noble, 1982.

Mottram, Ron. *Inner Landscapes: The Theater of Sam Shepard.* Columbia: University of Missouri Press, 1984.

Napier, Elizabeth R. *The Failure of Gothic: Problems of Disjunction in an Eighteenth-Century Literary Form.* Oxford: Oxford University Press, 1987.

Neufeld, Mary Diana. "The Adaptation of the Gothic Novel to the English Stage, 1765–1826." Ph.D. diss., Cornell University, 1978.

Newman, Beth. "Narratives of Seduction and the Seduction of Narrative: The Frame Structure of *Frankenstein.*" *ELH* 53, no. 1 (1986): 141–63.

Oates, Joyce Carol. *"The Picture of Dorian Gray:* Wilde's Parable of the Fall." *Critical Inquiry* 7 (1980): 419–28.

Parham, Sidney F. *"Marat/Sade:* The Politics of Experience or the Experience of Politics." *Modern Drama* 20 (1977): 235–50.

Patraka, Vivian M. and Mark Siegel. *Sam Shepard.* Western Writers Series no. 69. Boise: Boise State University Press, 1985.

Paulson, Ronald. *Representations of Revolution 1789–1820.* New Haven: Yale, 1983.

Peacock, Keith. "The Fascination of Fascism: The Plays of Stephen Poliakoff." *Modern Drama* 16 (1983): 494–505.

Perlette, John. "Theater at the Limit: *Rosencrantz and Guildenstern Are Dead.*" *Modern Drama* 18 (1985): 659–69.

Petry, Alice Hall. "Jamesian Parody, *Jane Eyre* and *The Turn of the Screw.*" *Modern Language Studies* 13, no. 4 (1983): 61–78.

Pickering, Jerry V. *Readers Theater.* Belmont: Dickenson Publishing, 1975.

Pinter, Harold. The Caretaker *and* The Dumbwaiter: *Two Plays by Harold Pinter.* New York: Grove Press, 1961.

————. *The Homecoming.* New York: Grove Press, 1967.

————. *The Hothouse.* New York: Grove Press, 1980.

Planché J. R. [1820]. *The Vampire.* In *The Hour of One. See* Fitz-ball.

Poe, Edgar Allan. *Great Short Works of Edgar Allan Poe,* edited by G. R. Thompson. New York: Harper, Perrenial Books, 1970.

Poliakoff, Stephen. Hitting Town *and* City Sugar. London: Methuen, 1975.

————. *A Shout across the River.* London: Methuen, 1979.

————. *Strawberry Fields.* London: Methuen, 1977.

Polidori, John. "The Vampire." In *Three Gothic Novels,* edited by E. F. Bleiler. New York: Dover Publications, 1966.

Praz, Mario. Introduction to *Three Gothic Novels,* edited by Peter Fairclough. *See* Beckford.

Punter, David. *The Literature of Terror.* New York: Longmans, 1980.

Quigley, Austin E. *"The Dumbwaiter:* Undermining the Tacit Dimension." *Modern Drama* 21 (1978): 1–11.

Radcliffe, Ann. *The Italian,* edited by Frederick Garber. New York: Oxford, 1968.

Reinert, Otto, ed. *Classics through Modern Drama: An Introductory Anthology.* Boston: Little, Brown, 1970.

Reno, Robert P. "James Boaden's *Fountainville Forest* and Matthew G. Lewis's *The Castle Spectre:* Challenges of the Supernatural Ghost on the Late Eighteenth-Century Stage." *Eighteenth-Century Life* 9, no. 1 (1984): 95–106.

Rice, Anne. *Interview with the Vampire*. New York: Knopf, 1976.

Richter, David. "The Gothic Response: Recent Studies." *Dickens Studies Annual* 11 (1983): 279–311.

Ricouer, Paul. *The Symbolism of Evil*. Translated by Emerson Buchanan. Boston: Beacon, 1969.

Roberts, David. "*Marat-Sade*, or the Birth of Postmodernism from the Spirit of the Avantgarde." *New German Critique* 38 (1986): 112–30.

Roberts, Patrick. *The Psychology of Tragic Drama*. London: Routledge & Kegan Paul, 1975.

Roddy, Joseph. "*Marat/Sade* Stuns Playgoers with Sanity from the Asylum." *Look* 22 Feb. 1966: 107–10.

Rosen, Carol. *Plays of Impasse: Contemporary Drama Set in Confining Institutions*. Princeton: Princeton University Press, 1983.

Rosenberg, James L. "Melodrama." In *Tragedy: Vision and Form. See* Bentley.

Rothstein, Eric. "Allusion and Analogy in the Romance of *Caleb Williams*." *University of Toronto Quarterly* 37 (1967): 18–30.

Rudin, Seymour. "The Urban Gothic: From Transylvania to the South Bronx." *Extrapolation* 25 (1984): 115–26.

Sandy, Stephen. *The Raveling of the Novel: Studies in Gothic Fiction from Walpole to Scott*. New York: Arno, 1980.

Scarry, Elaine. *The Body in Pain: The Making and Unmaking of the World*. New York: Oxford, 1985.

Schechner, Richard, ed. "*Marat/Sade* Forum." *Tulane Drama Review* 10 (1966): 214–37.

Schleifer, Ronald. "The Trap of the Imagination: The Gothic Tradition, Fiction and 'The Turn of the Screw.'" *Criticism* 22 (1980): 297–319.

Schlueter, June. "'Goats and Monkeys' and the 'Idiocy of Language': Handke's *Kaspar* and Shakespeare's *Othello*." *Modern Drama* 23 (1980): 25–32.

Seed, David. "The Narrative Method of *Dracula*." *Nineteenth-Century Fiction* 40 (1985): 61–75.

Shelley, Mary. *Frankenstein*. In *Three Gothic Novels*, edited by Peter Fairclough. *See* Beckford.

Shelley, Percy Bysshe. *The Cenci: A Tragedy in Five Acts*. New York: Phaeton Press, 1970.

Shepard, Sam. *Buried Child*. In *Sam Shepard: Seven Plays*. New York: Bantam, 1981.

Shewey, Don. *Sam Shepard*. New York: Dell, 1985.

Siebers, Tobin. "Hesitation, History, and Reading: Henry James's *The Turn of the Screw*." *Texas Studies in Language and Literature* 25, no. 4 (1983): 558–73.

Smith, James L. *Melodrama*. The Critical Idiom no. 28. London: Methuen, 1973.

Solomon, Stanley. "Subverting Propriety as a Pattern of Irony in Three Eighteenth-Century Novels: *The Castle of Otranto, Vathek,* and *Fanny Hill*." *Erasmus Review* 1 (1971): 107–16.

Sontag, Susan. *Illness as Metaphor*. New York: Farrar, 1977.

Spurling, John. "Stephen Poliakoff." In *Contemporary Dramatists*, edited by James Vinson. 3rd ed. New York: St. Martin's Press, 1985.

Stamm, Rudolf. "*The Hothouse*: Harold Pinter's Tribute to Anger." *English Studies* 62 (1981): 290–98.

States, Bert O. *Great Reckonings in Little Rooms: On the Phenomenology of Theatre*. Berkeley and Los Angeles: University of California Press, 1985.

Sterrenburg, Lee. "Mary Shelley's Monster: Politics and Psyche in *Frankenstein*." In *The Endurance of* Frankenstein. *See* Brooks.

Stevenson, Robert Louis, Mary Shelley, and Bram Stoker. *Dr. Jekyll and Mr. Hyde, Frankenstein, Dracula*. New York: Signet, 1978.

Stoker, Bram. *Dracula*. New York: Signet, 1965.

Stoppard, Tom. *The Real Inspector Hound* and *After Magritte*. New York: Grove Press, 1968.

—————. *Rosencrantz and Guildenstern Are Dead*. New York: Grove Press, 1967.

Storch, Rudolf F. "Metaphors of Private Guilt and Social Rebellion in Godwin's *Caleb Williams*." *ELH* 34 (1967): 188–207.

Strindberg, August. "The Author's Preface" to *A Dream Play*. In *A Treasury of the Theater from Henrik Ibsen to Robert Lowell*. 4th ed. Edited by John Gassner and Bernard Dukore. New York: Simon, 1970.

Summers, Montague. *The Gothic Quest*. New York: Russell & Russell, 1964.

Tasch, Peter A., ed. Introduction to *The Plays of George Colman*. Eighteenth-Century English Drama no. 11. Vol. 1. New York: Garland Publishing, 1981.

Thorp, Willard. "The Stage Adventure of Some Gothic Novels." *PMLA* 43 (1928): 476–86.

Thorslev, Peter. *Romantic Contraries: Freedom vs Destiny*. New Haven: Yale, 1984.

Todd, Janet. "Posture and Imposture: The Gothic Manservant in Ann Radcliffe's *The Italian*." *Women and Literature* n.s. 2 (1982): 25–38.

Todorov, Tzvetan. *The Fantastic: A Structural Approach to a Literary Genre*. Translated by Richard Howard. Ithaca: Cornell University Press, 1975.

Trewin, J. C. *Peter Brook: A Biography*. London: Macdonald, 1971.

Ubersfeld, Ann. "The Pleasure of the Spectator." Translated by Pierre Bouillaguet and Charles Jose. *Modern Drama* 25 (1982): 127–39.

Wall, Geoffrey. "Different from Writing: *Dracula* in 1897." *Literature and History* 10, no.1 (1984): 15–23.

Ware, Malcolm. "The Telescope Reversed: Ann Radcliffe and Natural Scenery." In *A Provision of Human Nature: Essays on Fielding and Others in Honor of Miriam Austin Locke*, edited by Donald Kay. University: University of Alabama Press, 1977.

Webling, Peggy. "Frankenstein, A Play in a Prologue and Three Acts (Based upon Mrs. Shelley's Well-Known Book)," 1927. Lord Chamberlain Collection, Department of Manuscripts, British Library, London.

Weiss, Peter. *The Persecution and Assassination of Jean-Paul Marat as Performed by the Inmates of the Asylum of Charenton under the Direction of the Marquis de Sade*. New York: Atheneum, 1981.

Weiss, Samuel A. "Peter Weiss's *Marat/Sade*." *Drama Survey* 5 (1966): 123–30.

Wellworth, George. "Beyond Realism: Ionesco's Theory of the Drama." In *The Dream and the Play: Ionesco's Theatrical Quest*, edited by Moshe Lazar. Malibu: Undena Publications, 1982.

West, Benjamin. *Melmoth the Wanderer: A Melo-Dramatic Romance*. Baltimore, 1831.

Whitaker, Thomas R. *Fields of Play in Modern Drama*. Princeton: Princeton University Press, 1977.

Wilde, Oscar. *The Picture of Dorian Gray*. Harmondsworth, England: Penguin, 1949.

Wilt, Judith. *Ghosts of the Gothic: Austen, Eliot, & Lawrence*. Princeton: Princeton University Press, 1980.

Witt, Mary Ann. "Eugene Ionesco and the Dialectic of Space." *Modern Language Quarterly* 33 (1972): 312–26.

Worth, Katherine. *Revolutions in Modern English Drama*. London: G. Bell, 1972.

Zinman, Toby Silverman. "Sam Shepard and Super-Realism." *Modern Drama* 29 (1986): 423–30.

Zweig, Paul. *The Adventurer*. New York: Basic Books, 1974.

# Index